GRIMM FAIRY TALES CREATED BY
JOE BRUSHA AND RALPH TEDESCO

Grimm Fairy Tales presents:

QUEST

AGE OF DARKNESS

zenescope
WWW.ZENESCOPE.COM
FACEBOOK.COM/ZENESCOPE

QUEST

STORY
JOE BRUSHA
RALPH TEDESCO
RAVEN GREGORY
PAT SHAND

WRITER
PAT SHAND

ART DIRECTOR
ANTHONY SPAY

TRADE DESIGN
CHRISTOPHER COTE
STEPHEN SCHAFFER

EDITOR
RALPH TEDESCO

ASSISTANT EDITOR
NICOLE GLADE

This volume reprints the comic
series Grimm Fairy Tales Presents:
Quest #1-5 published by Zenescope
Entertainment.

First Edition, April 2014
ISBN: 978-1-939683-55-7

WWW.ZENESCOPE.COM
FACEBOOK.COM/ZENESCOPE

ZENESCOPE ENTERTAINMENT, INC.
Joe Brusha • President & Chief Creative Officer
Ralph Tedesco • Editor-in-Chief
Jennifer Bermel • Director of Licensing & Business Development
Raven Gregory • Executive Editor
Anthony Spay • Art Director
Christopher Cote • Senior Designer & Production Manager
Dave Franchini • Direct Market Sales & Customer Service

Grimm Fairy Tales presents

QUEST

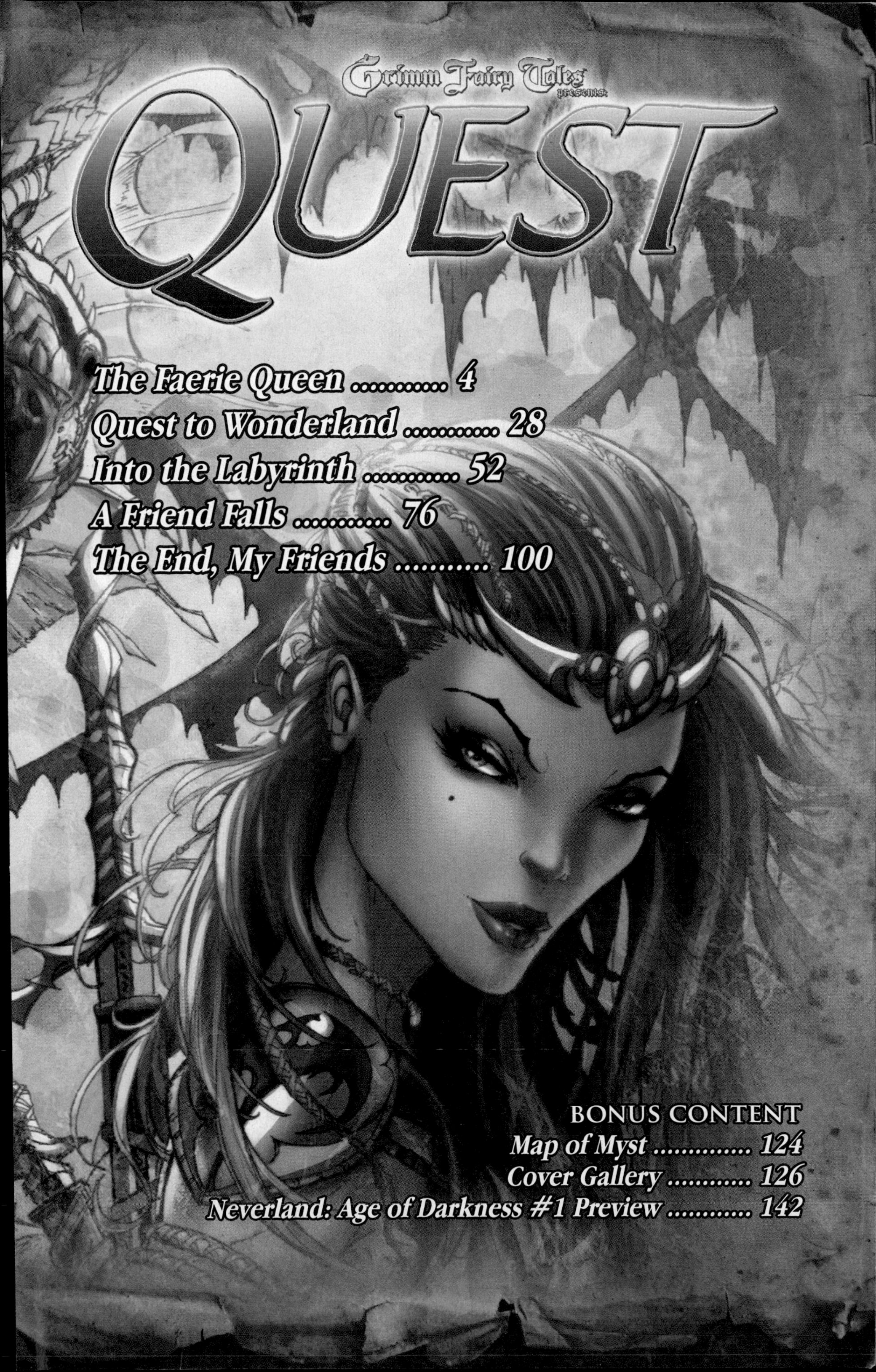

BONUS CONTENT

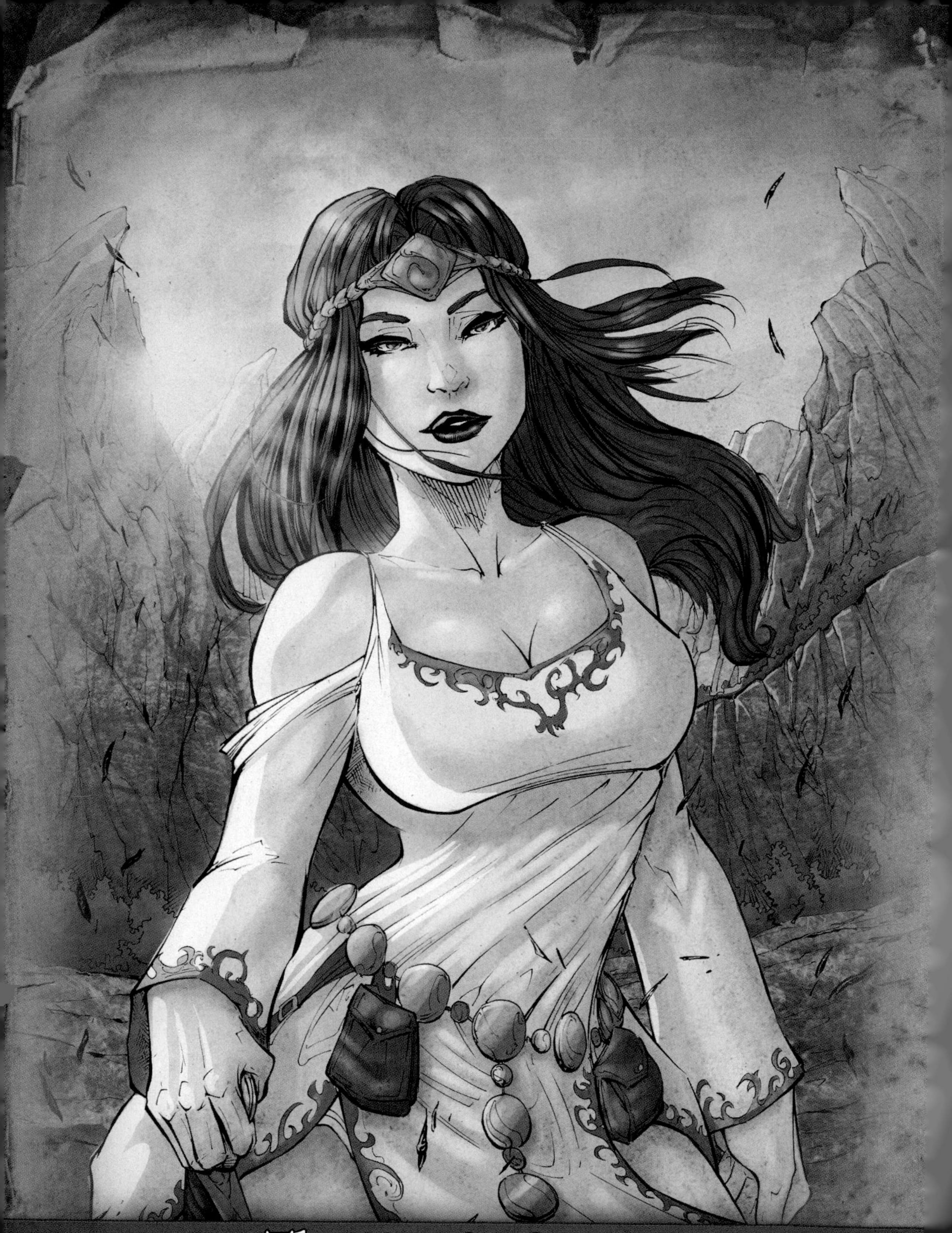

The Faerie Queen

WRITER PAT SHAND
ARTWORK SERGIO OSUNA & DAVID T. CABRERA
COLORS FRANCESCA ZAMBON
LETTERS JIM CAMPBELL

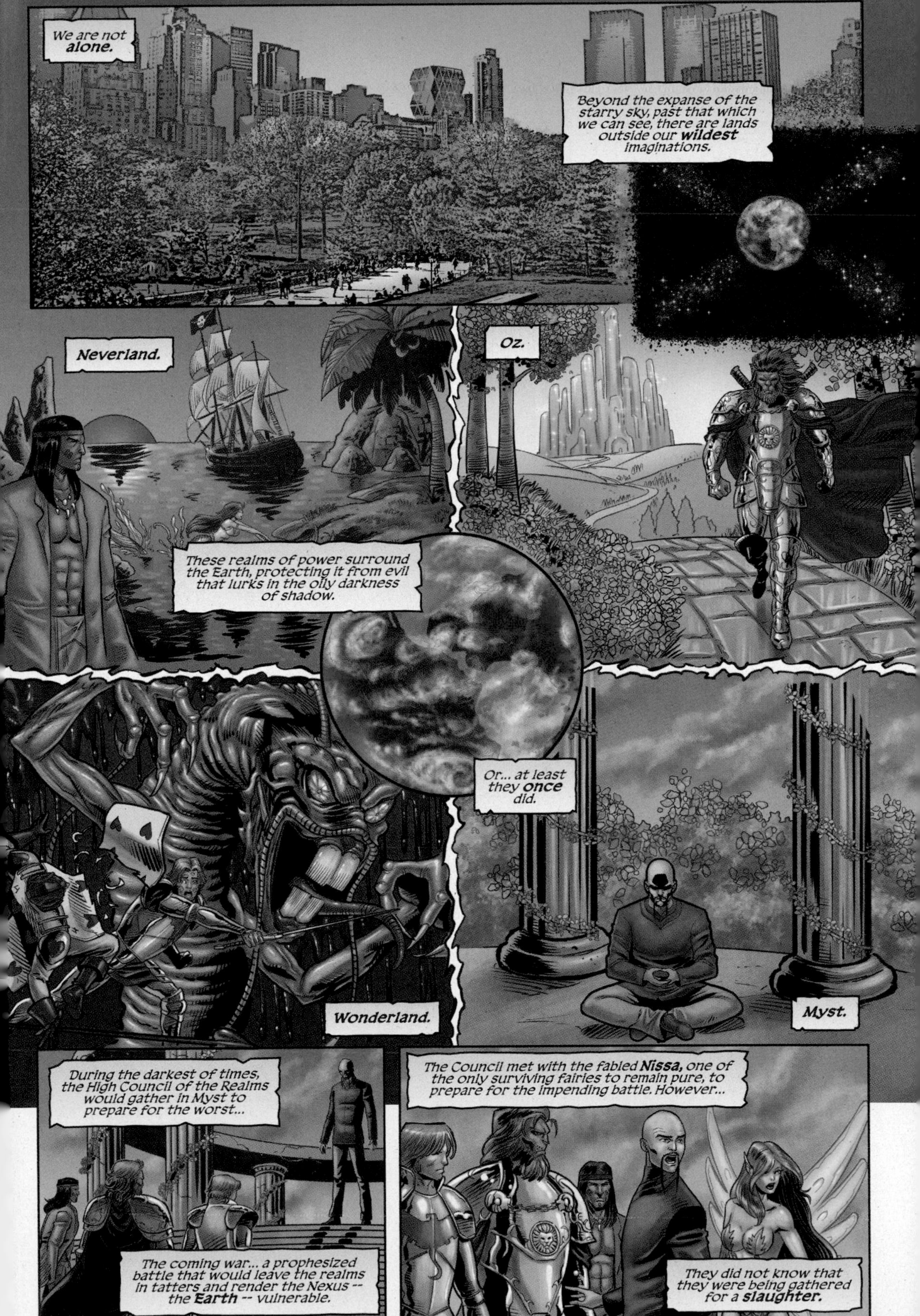

We are not alone.
Beyond the expanse of the starry sky, past that which we can see, there are lands outside our wildest imaginations.
Neverland.
Oz.
These realms of power surround the Earth, protecting it from evil that lurks in the oily darkness of shadow.
Or... at least they once did.
Wonderland.
Myst.
During the darkest of times, the High Council of the Realms would gather in Myst to prepare for the worst...
The coming war... a prophesized battle that would leave the realms in tatters and render the Nexus -- the Earth -- vulnerable.
The Council met with the fabled Nissa, one of the only surviving fairies to remain pure, to prepare for the impending battle. However...
They did not know that they were being gathered for a slaughter.

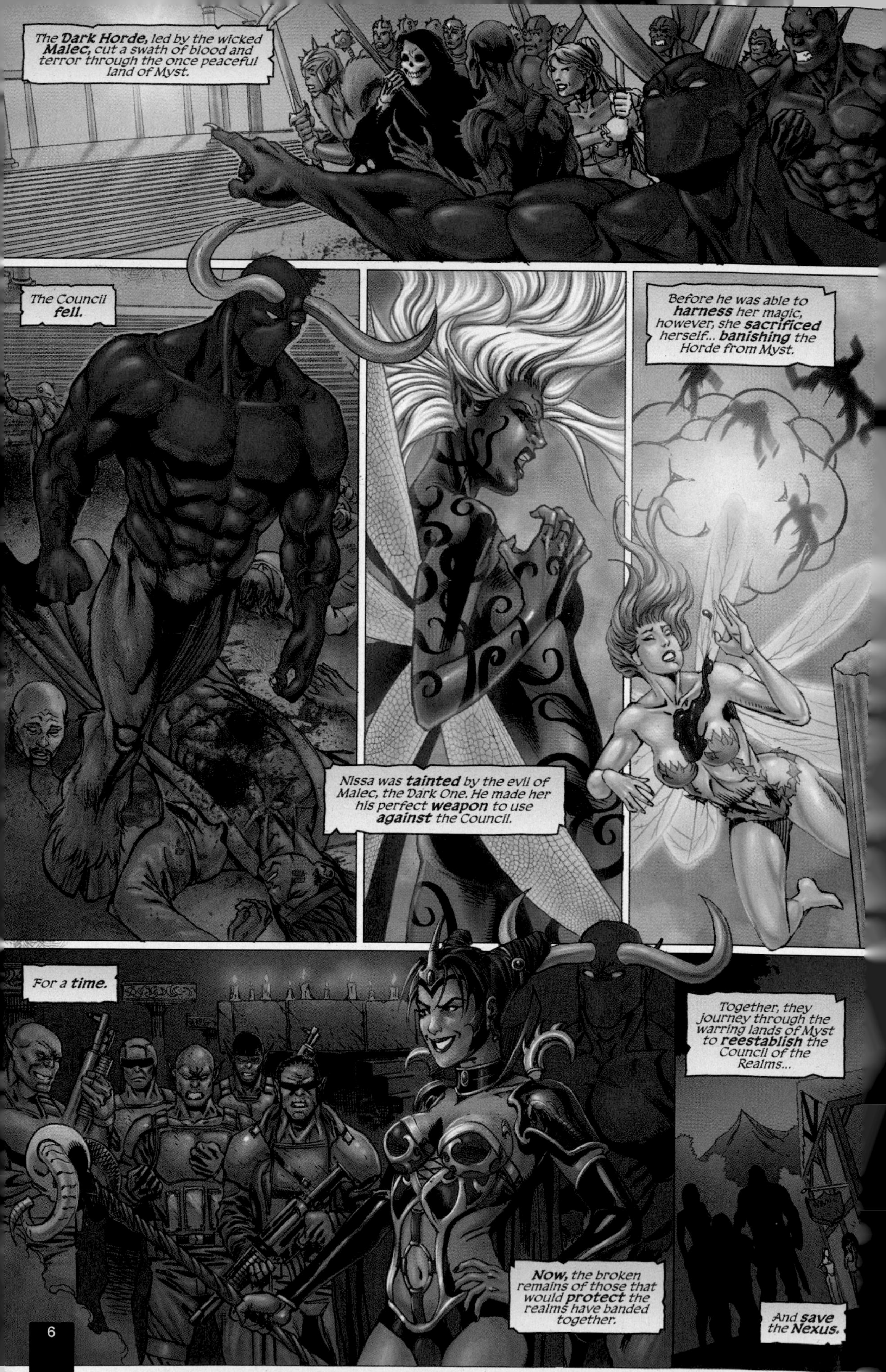
The Dark Horde, led by the wicked Malec, cut a swath of blood and terror through the once peaceful land of Myst.
The Council fell.
Nissa was tainted by the evil of Malec, the Dark One. He made her his perfect weapon to use against the Council.
Before he was able to harness her magic, however, she sacrificed herself... banishing the Horde from Myst.
For a time.
Now, the broken remains of those that would protect the realms have banded together.
Together, they journey through the warring lands of Myst to reestablish the Council of the Realms...
And save the Nexus.

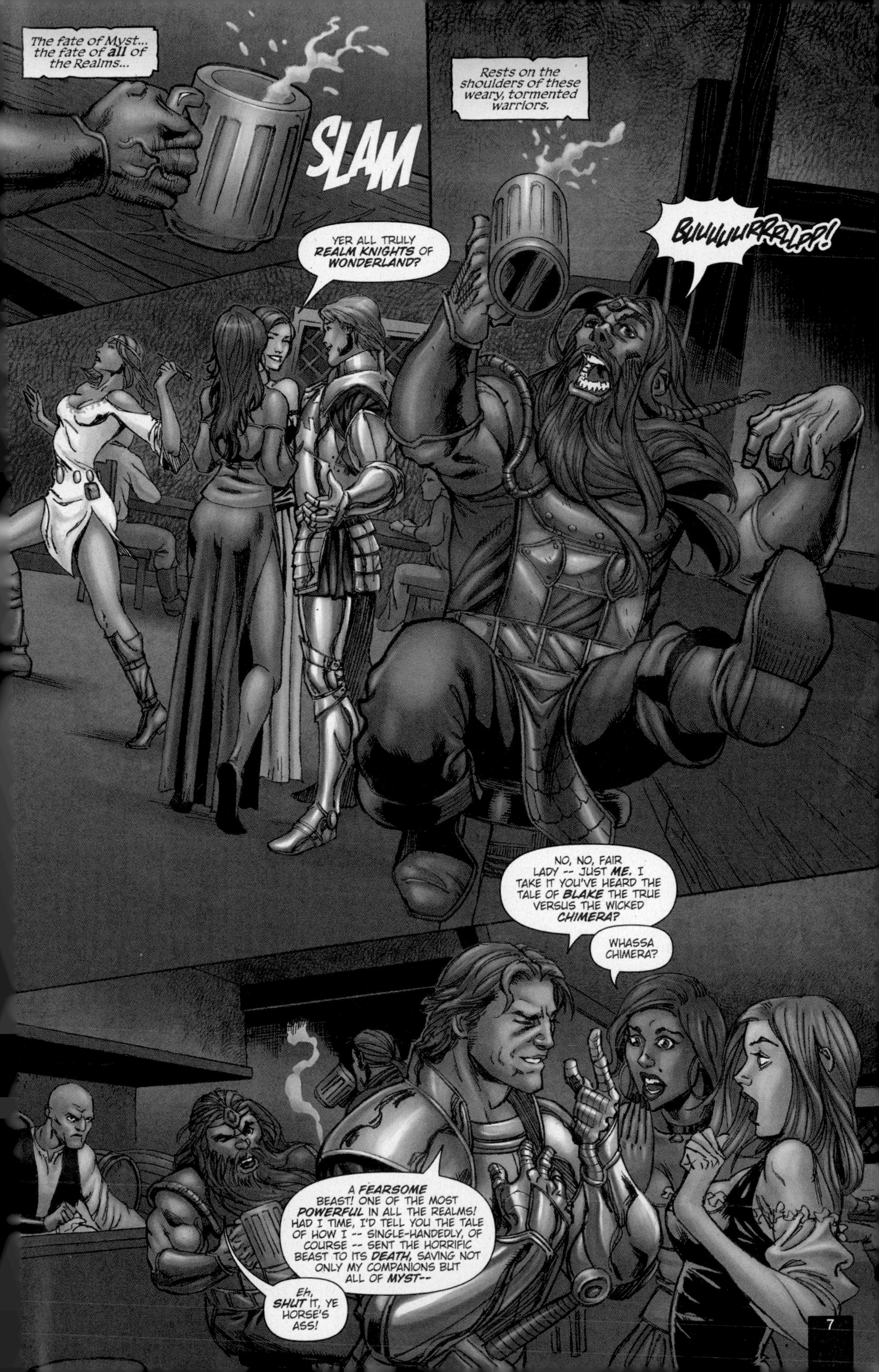
The fate of Myst... the fate of **all** of the Realms...
SLAM
Rests on the shoulders of these weary, tormented warriors.
BUUUUURRRRLLP!
YER ALL TRULY **REALM KNIGHTS** OF **WONDERLAND**?
NO, NO, FAIR LADY -- JUST **ME.** I TAKE IT YOU'VE HEARD THE TALE OF **BLAKE** THE TRUE VERSUS THE WICKED **CHIMERA**?
WHASSA CHIMERA?
A **FEARSOME** BEAST! ONE OF THE MOST **POWERFUL** IN ALL THE REALMS! HAD I TIME, I'D TELL YOU THE TALE OF HOW I -- SINGLE-HANDEDLY, OF COURSE -- SENT THE HORRIFIC BEAST TO ITS **DEATH**, SAVING NOT ONLY MY COMPANIONS BUT ALL OF **MYST**--
Eh, **SHUT** IT, YE HORSE'S ASS!

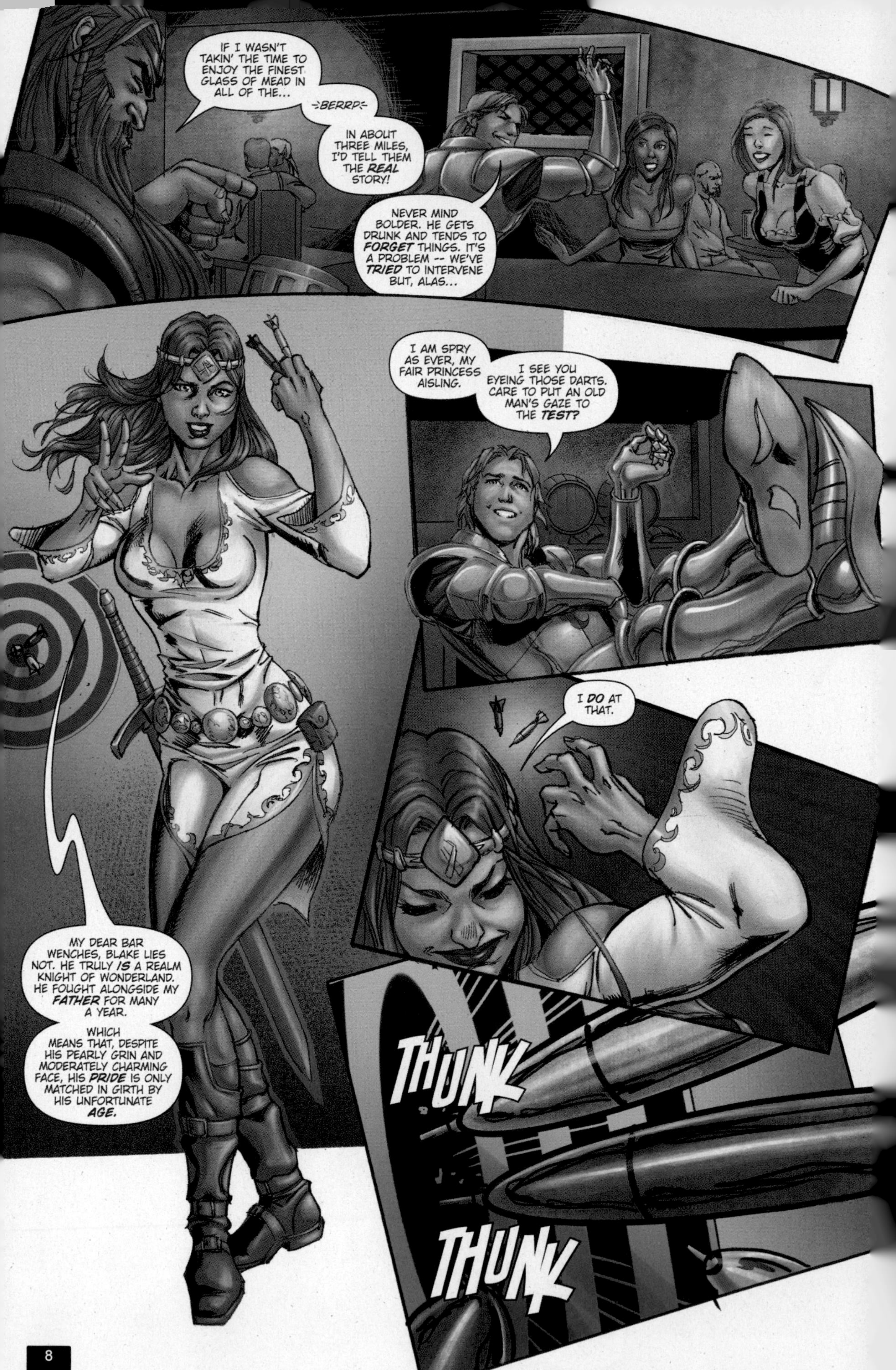

IF I WASN'T TAKIN' THE TIME TO ENJOY THE FINEST GLASS OF MEAD IN ALL OF THE...
=BERRP=
IN ABOUT THREE MILES, I'D TELL THEM THE REAL STORY!
NEVER MIND BOLDER. HE GETS DRUNK AND TENDS TO FORGET THINGS. IT'S A PROBLEM -- WE'VE TRIED TO INTERVENE BUT, ALAS...
MY DEAR BAR WENCHES, BLAKE LIES NOT. HE TRULY IS A REALM KNIGHT OF WONDERLAND. HE FOUGHT ALONGSIDE MY FATHER FOR MANY A YEAR.
WHICH MEANS THAT, DESPITE HIS PEARLY GRIN AND MODERATELY CHARMING FACE, HIS PRIDE IS ONLY MATCHED IN GIRTH BY HIS UNFORTUNATE AGE.
I AM SPRY AS EVER, MY FAIR PRINCESS AISLING.
I SEE YOU EYEING THOSE DARTS. CARE TO PUT AN OLD MAN'S GAZE TO THE TEST?
I DO AT THAT.
THUNK
THUNK

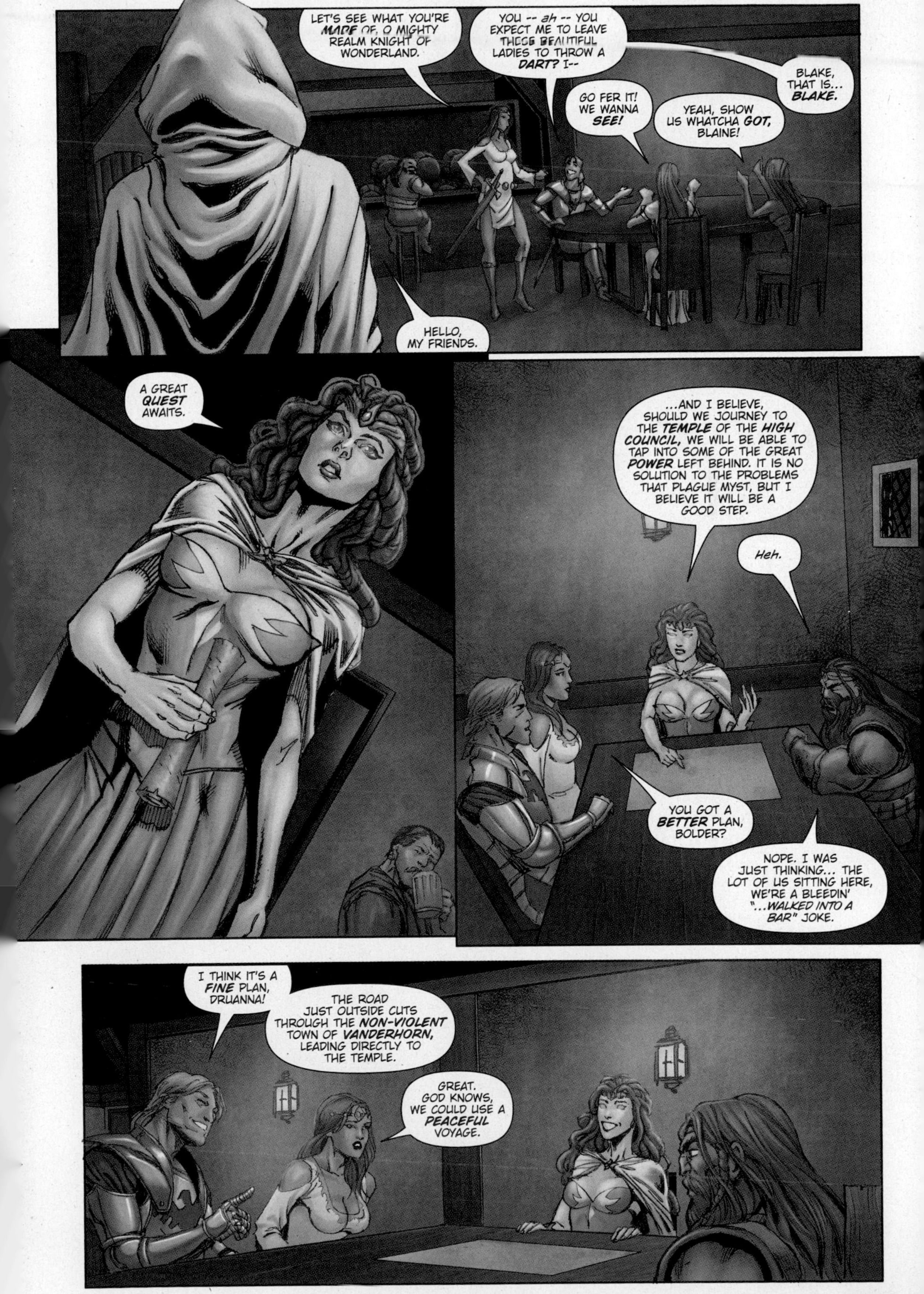
LET'S SEE WHAT YOU'RE MADE OF, O MIGHTY REALM KNIGHT OF WONDERLAND.
YOU -- ah -- YOU EXPECT ME TO LEAVE THESE BEAUTIFUL LADIES TO THROW A DART? I--
BLAKE, THAT IS... BLAKE.
GO FER IT! WE WANNA SEE!
YEAH, SHOW US WHATCHA GOT, BLAINE!
HELLO, MY FRIENDS.
A GREAT QUEST AWAITS.
...AND I BELIEVE, SHOULD WE JOURNEY TO THE TEMPLE OF THE HIGH COUNCIL, WE WILL BE ABLE TO TAP INTO SOME OF THE GREAT POWER LEFT BEHIND. IT IS NO SOLUTION TO THE PROBLEMS THAT PLAGUE MYST, BUT I BELIEVE IT WILL BE A GOOD STEP.
Heh.
YOU GOT A BETTER PLAN, BOLDER?
NOPE. I WAS JUST THINKING... THE LOT OF US SITTING HERE, WE'RE A BLEEDIN' "...WALKED INTO A BAR" JOKE.
I THINK IT'S A FINE PLAN, DRUANNA!
THE ROAD JUST OUTSIDE CUTS THROUGH THE NON-VIOLENT TOWN OF VANDERHORN, LEADING DIRECTLY TO THE TEMPLE.
GREAT. GOD KNOWS, WE COULD USE A PEACEFUL VOYAGE.

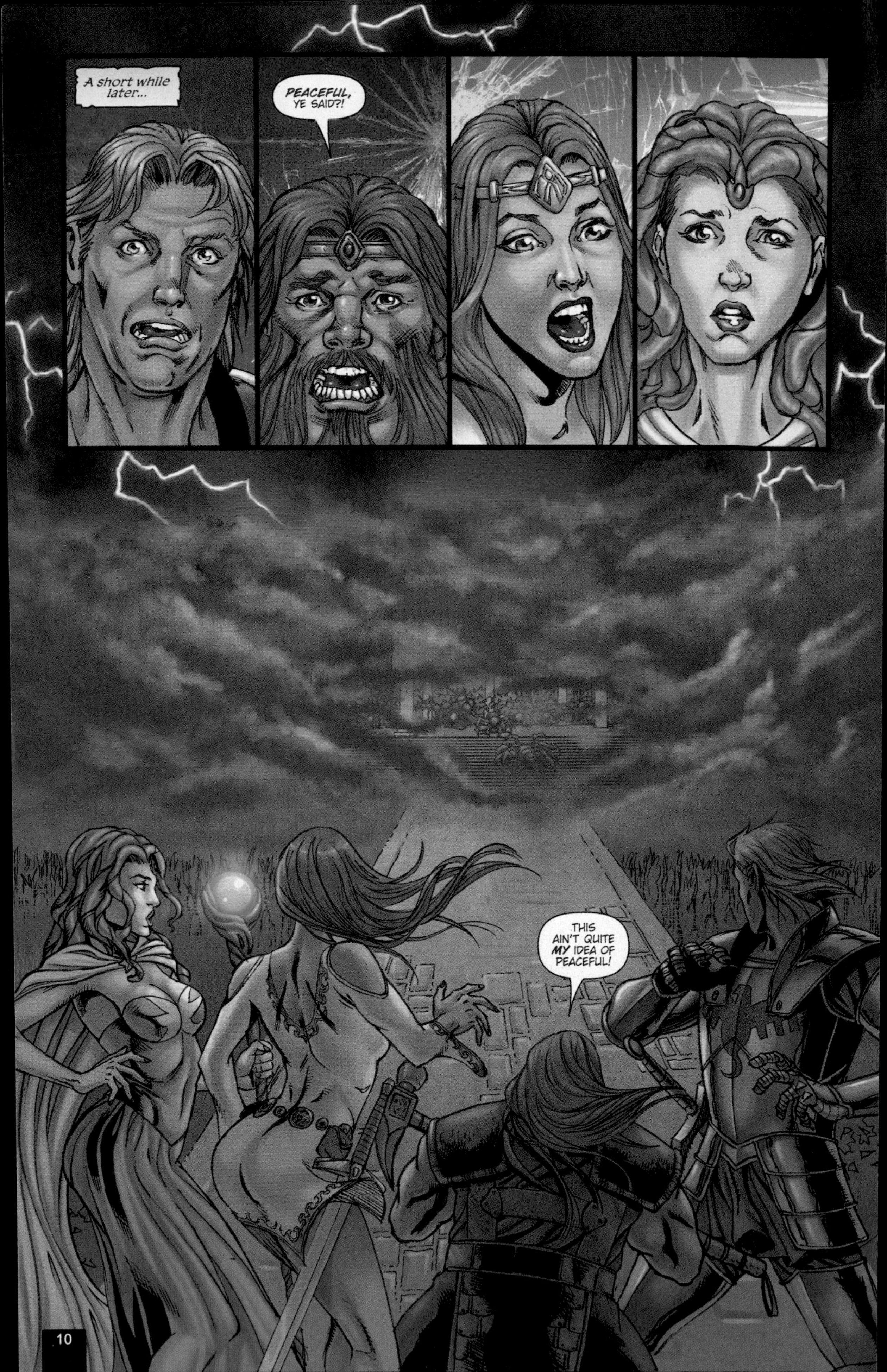
A short while later...
PEACEFUL, YE SAID?!
THIS AIN'T QUITE MY IDEA OF PEACEFUL!

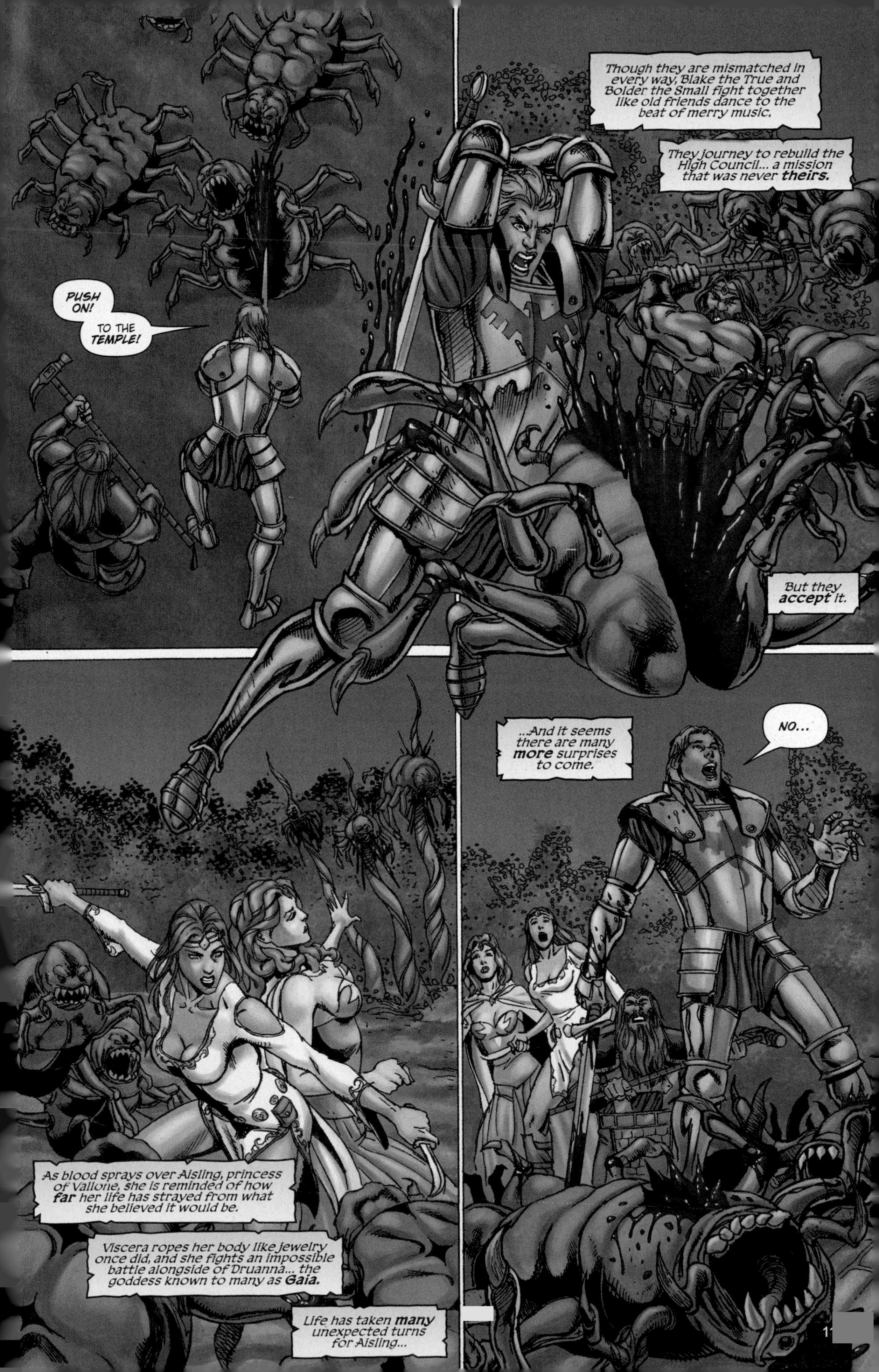

PUSH ON!
TO THE TEMPLE!
Though they are mismatched in every way, Blake the True and Bolder the Small fight together like old friends dance to the beat of merry music.
They journey to rebuild the High Council... a mission that was never theirs.
But they accept it.
As blood sprays over Aisling, princess of Vallone, she is reminded of how far her life has strayed from what she believed it would be.
Viscera ropes her body like jewelry once did, and she fights an impossible battle alongside of Druanna... the goddess known to many as Gaia.
Life has taken many unexpected turns for Aisling...
...And it seems there are many more surprises to come.
NO...

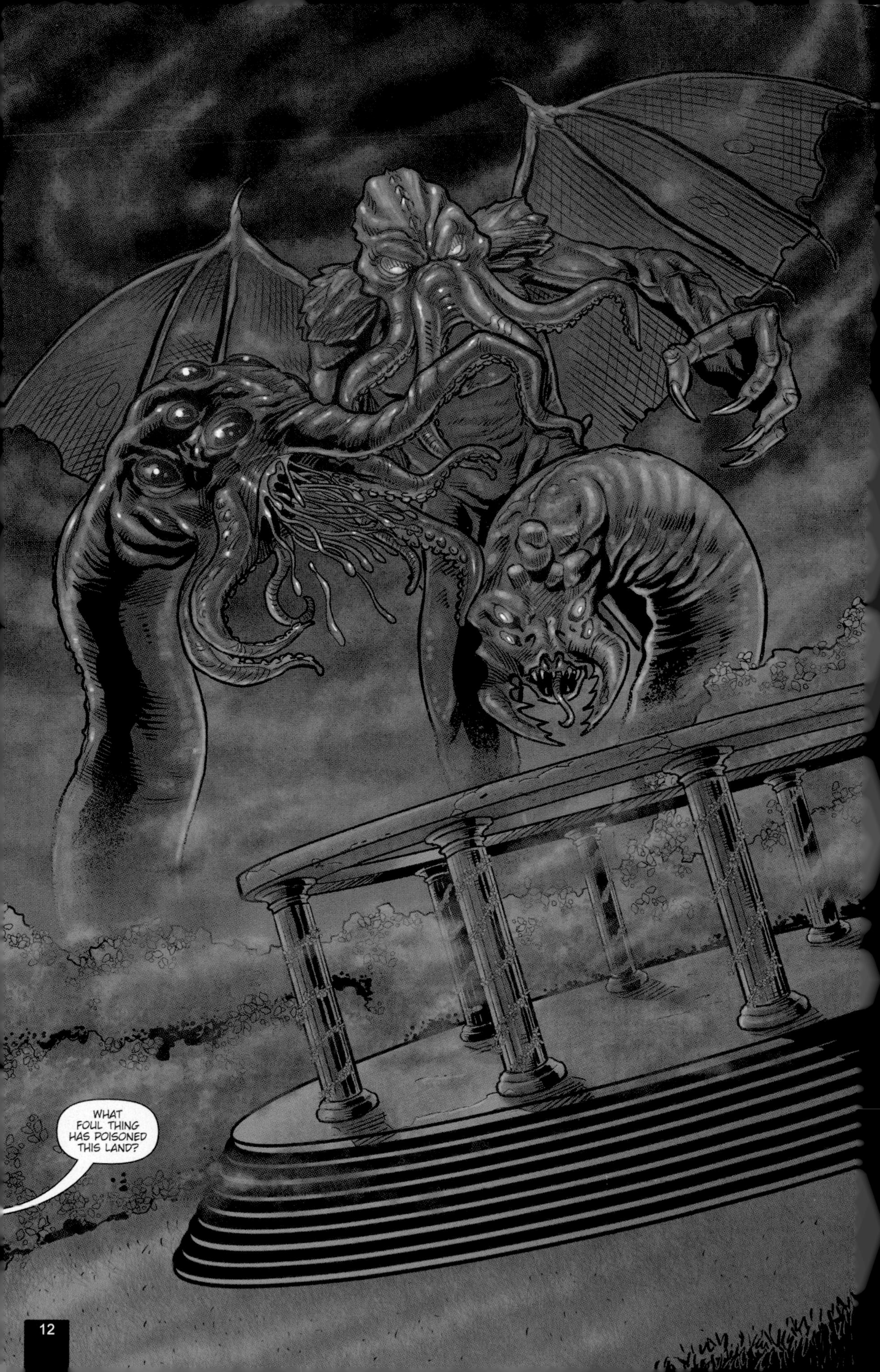
WHAT FOUL THING HAS POISONED THIS LAND?

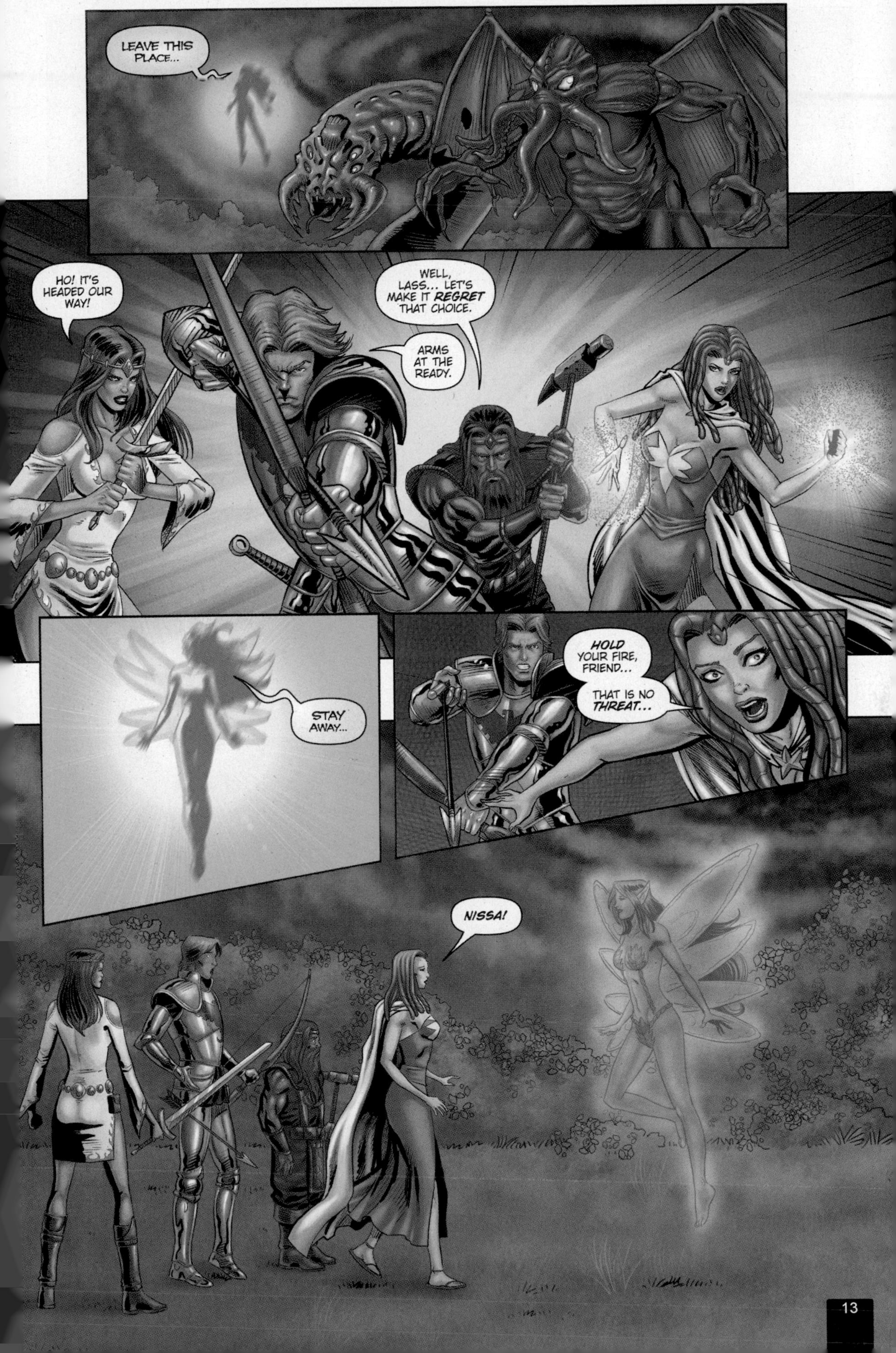
LEAVE THIS PLACE...
HO! IT'S HEADED OUR WAY!
WELL, LASS... LET'S MAKE IT REGRET THAT CHOICE.
ARMS AT THE READY.
STAY AWAY...
HOLD YOUR FIRE, FRIEND...
THAT IS NO THREAT...
NISSA!

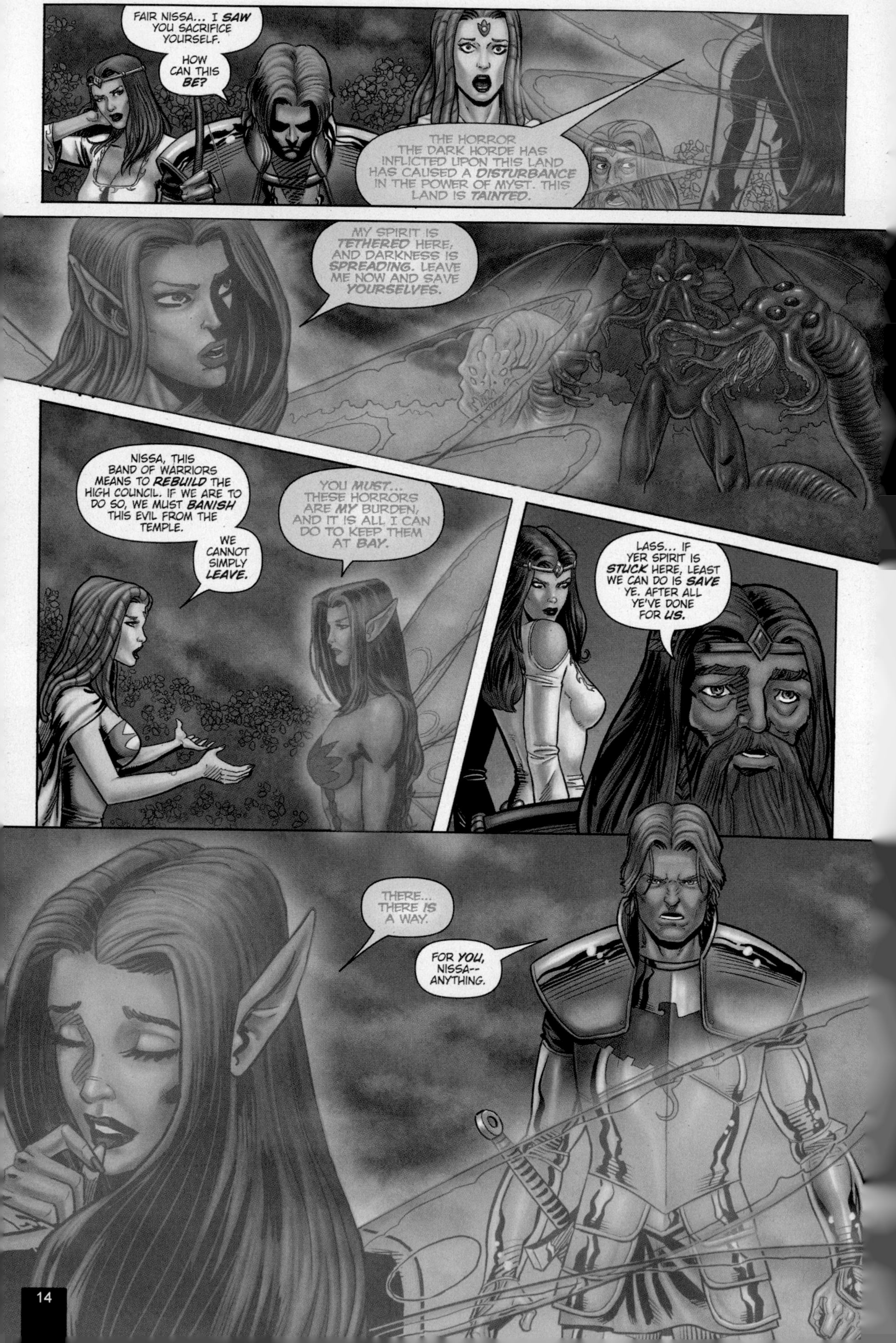
FAIR NISSA... I SAW YOU SACRIFICE YOURSELF.
HOW CAN THIS BE?
THE HORROR THE DARK HORDE HAS INFLICTED UPON THIS LAND HAS CAUSED A DISTURBANCE IN THE POWER OF MYST. THIS LAND IS TAINTED.
MY SPIRIT IS TETHERED HERE, AND DARKNESS IS SPREADING. LEAVE ME NOW AND SAVE YOURSELVES.
NISSA, THIS BAND OF WARRIORS MEANS TO REBUILD THE HIGH COUNCIL. IF WE ARE TO DO SO, WE MUST BANISH THIS EVIL FROM THE TEMPLE.
WE CANNOT SIMPLY LEAVE.
YOU MUST... THESE HORRORS ARE MY BURDEN, AND IT IS ALL I CAN DO TO KEEP THEM AT BAY.
LASS... IF YER SPIRIT IS STUCK HERE, LEAST WE CAN DO IS SAVE YE. AFTER ALL YE'VE DONE FOR US.
THERE... THERE IS A WAY.
FOR YOU, NISSA-- ANYTHING.

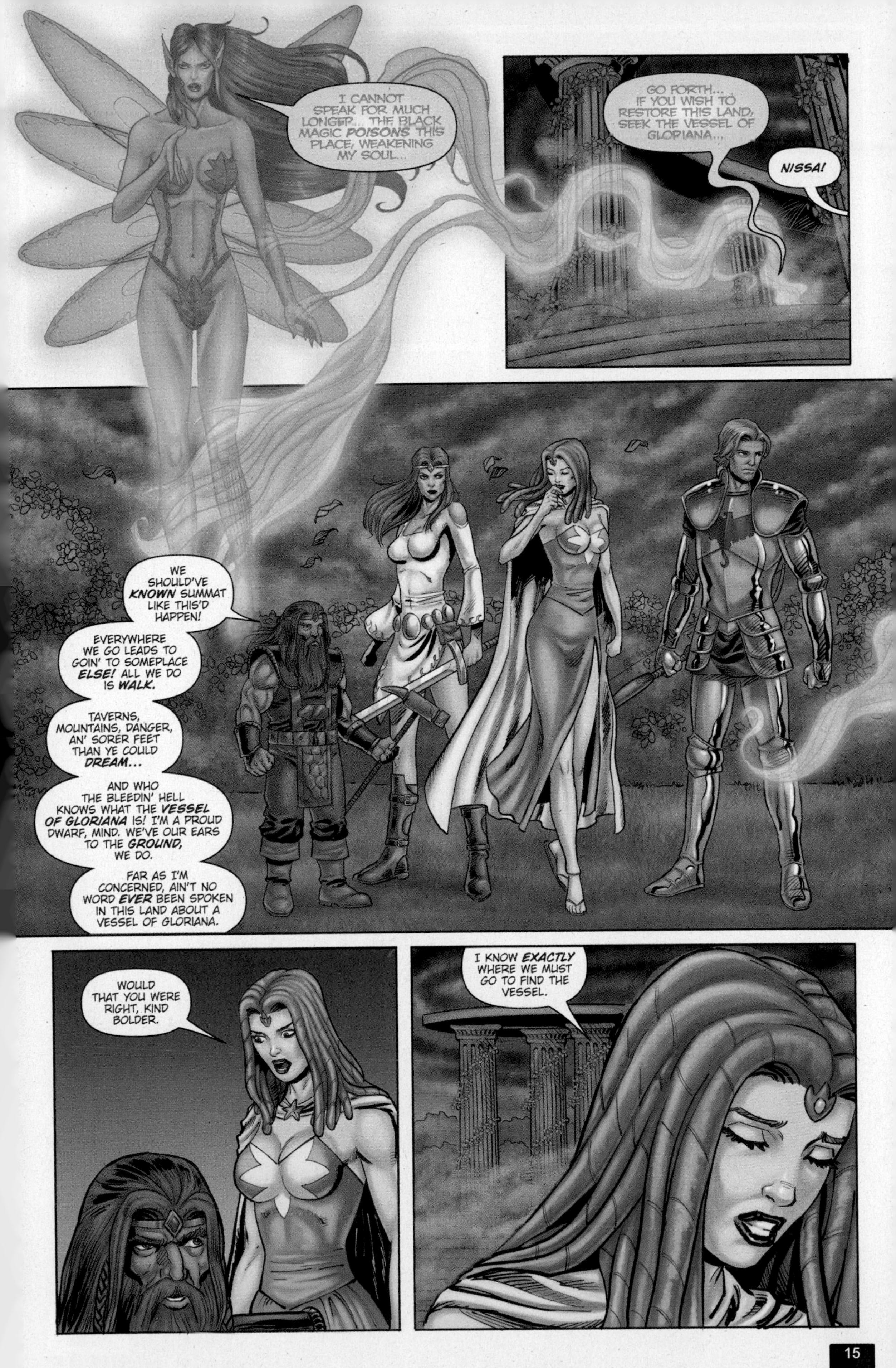
I CANNOT SPEAK FOR MUCH LONGER... THE BLACK MAGIC POISONS THIS PLACE, WEAKENING MY SOUL...
GO FORTH... IF YOU WISH TO RESTORE THIS LAND, SEEK THE VESSEL OF GLORIANA...
NISSA!
WE SHOULD'VE KNOWN SUMMAT LIKE THIS'D HAPPEN!
EVERYWHERE WE GO LEADS TO GOIN' TO SOMEPLACE ELSE! ALL WE DO IS WALK.
TAVERNS, MOUNTAINS, DANGER, AN' SORER FEET THAN YE COULD DREAM...
AND WHO THE BLEEDIN' HELL KNOWS WHAT THE VESSEL OF GLORIANA IS! I'M A PROUD DWARF, MIND. WE'VE OUR EARS TO THE GROUND, WE DO.
FAR AS I'M CONCERNED, AIN'T NO WORD EVER BEEN SPOKEN IN THIS LAND ABOUT A VESSEL OF GLORIANA.
WOULD THAT YOU WERE RIGHT, KIND BOLDER.
I KNOW EXACTLY WHERE WE MUST GO TO FIND THE VESSEL.

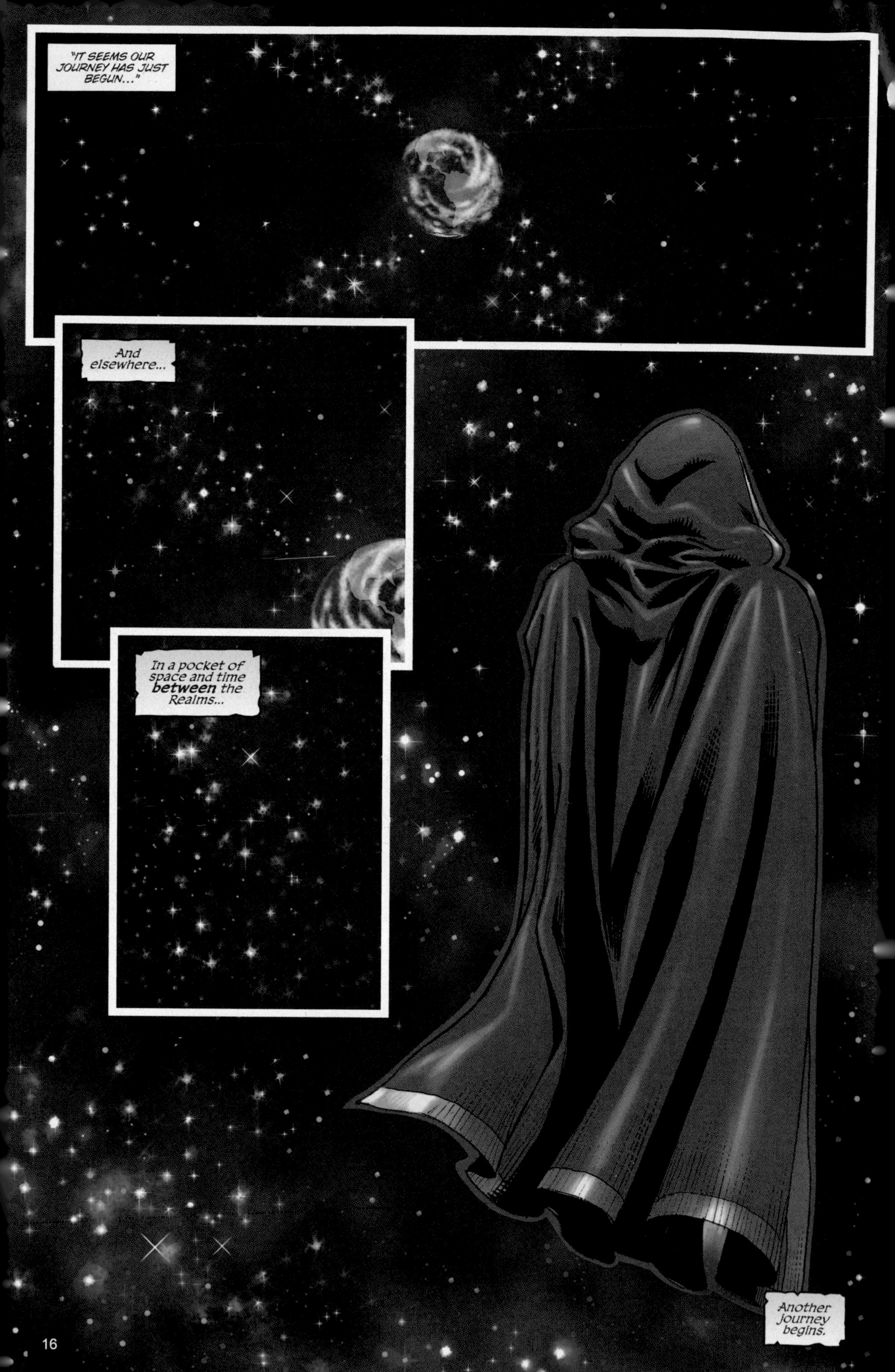
"IT SEEMS OUR JOURNEY HAS JUST BEGUN..."
And elsewhere...
In a pocket of space and time **between** the Realms...
Another journey begins.

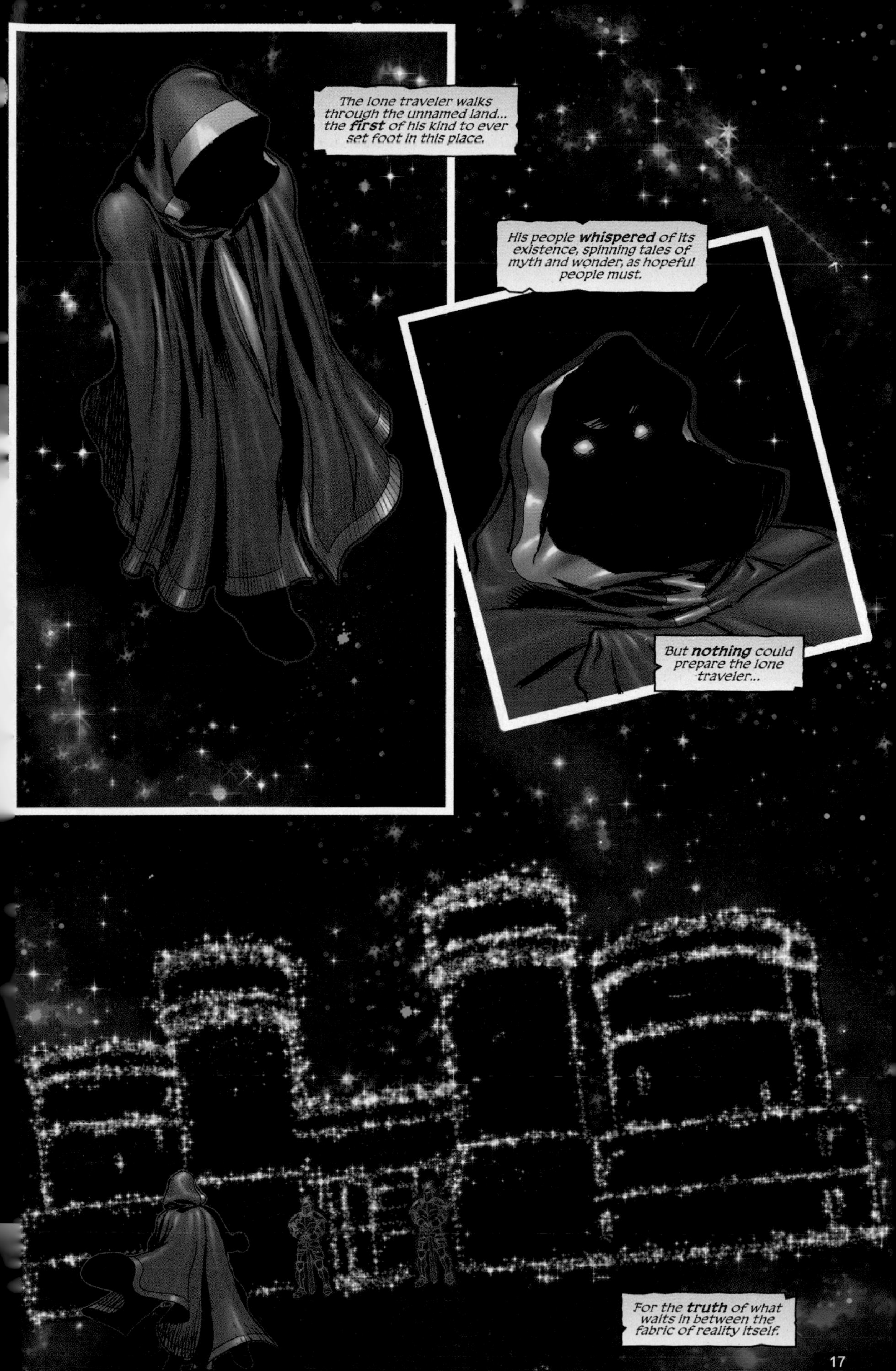

The lone traveler walks through the unnamed land... the first of his kind to ever set foot in this place.
His people whispered of its existence, spinning tales of myth and wonder, as hopeful people must.
But nothing could prepare the lone traveler...
For the truth of what waits in between the fabric of reality itself.

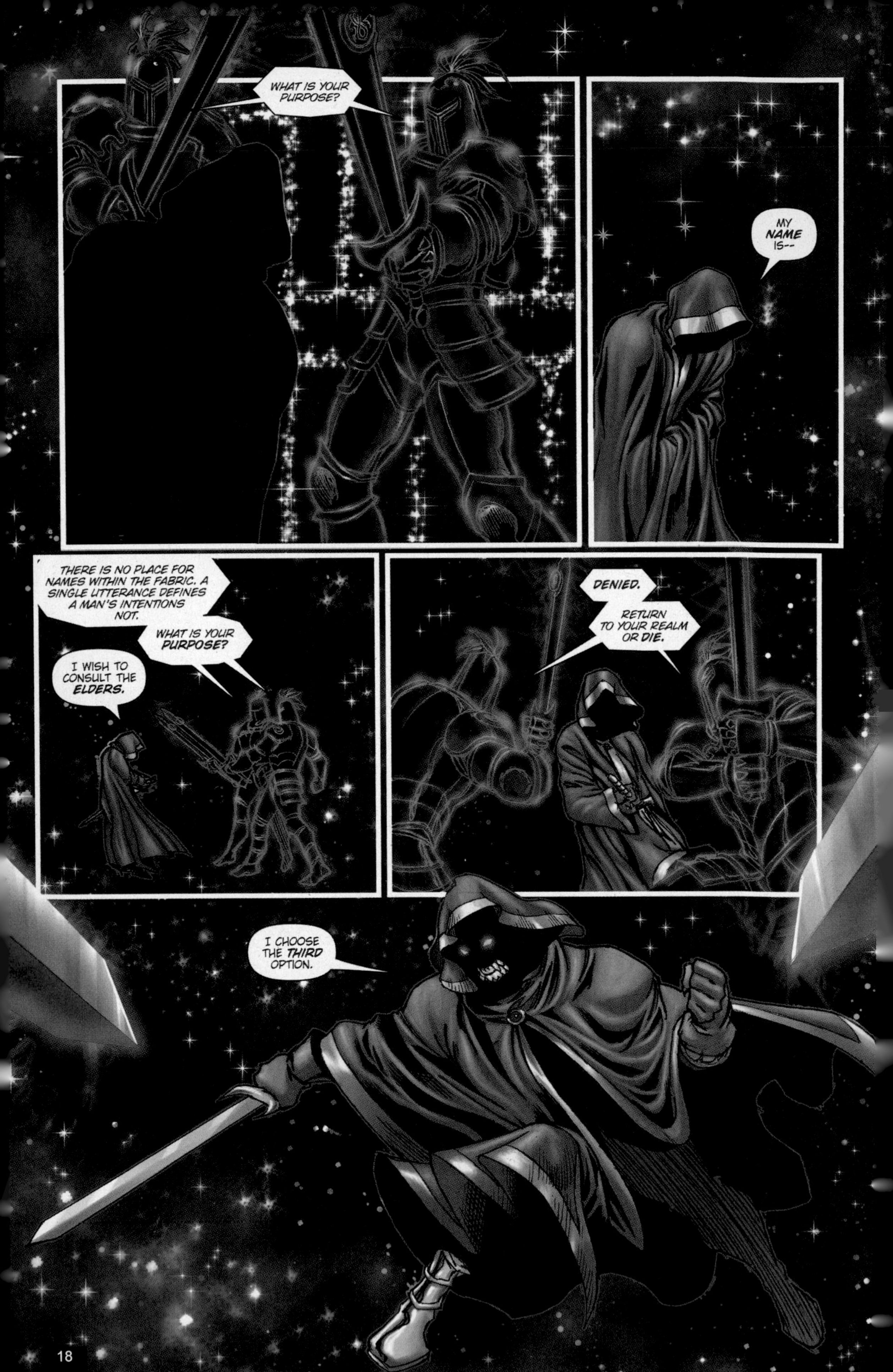
WHAT IS YOUR PURPOSE?
MY NAME IS--
THERE IS NO PLACE FOR NAMES WITHIN THE FABRIC. A SINGLE UTTERANCE DEFINES A MAN'S INTENTIONS NOT.
WHAT IS YOUR PURPOSE?
I WISH TO CONSULT THE ELDERS.
DENIED.
RETURN TO YOUR REALM OR DIE.
I CHOOSE THE THIRD OPTION.

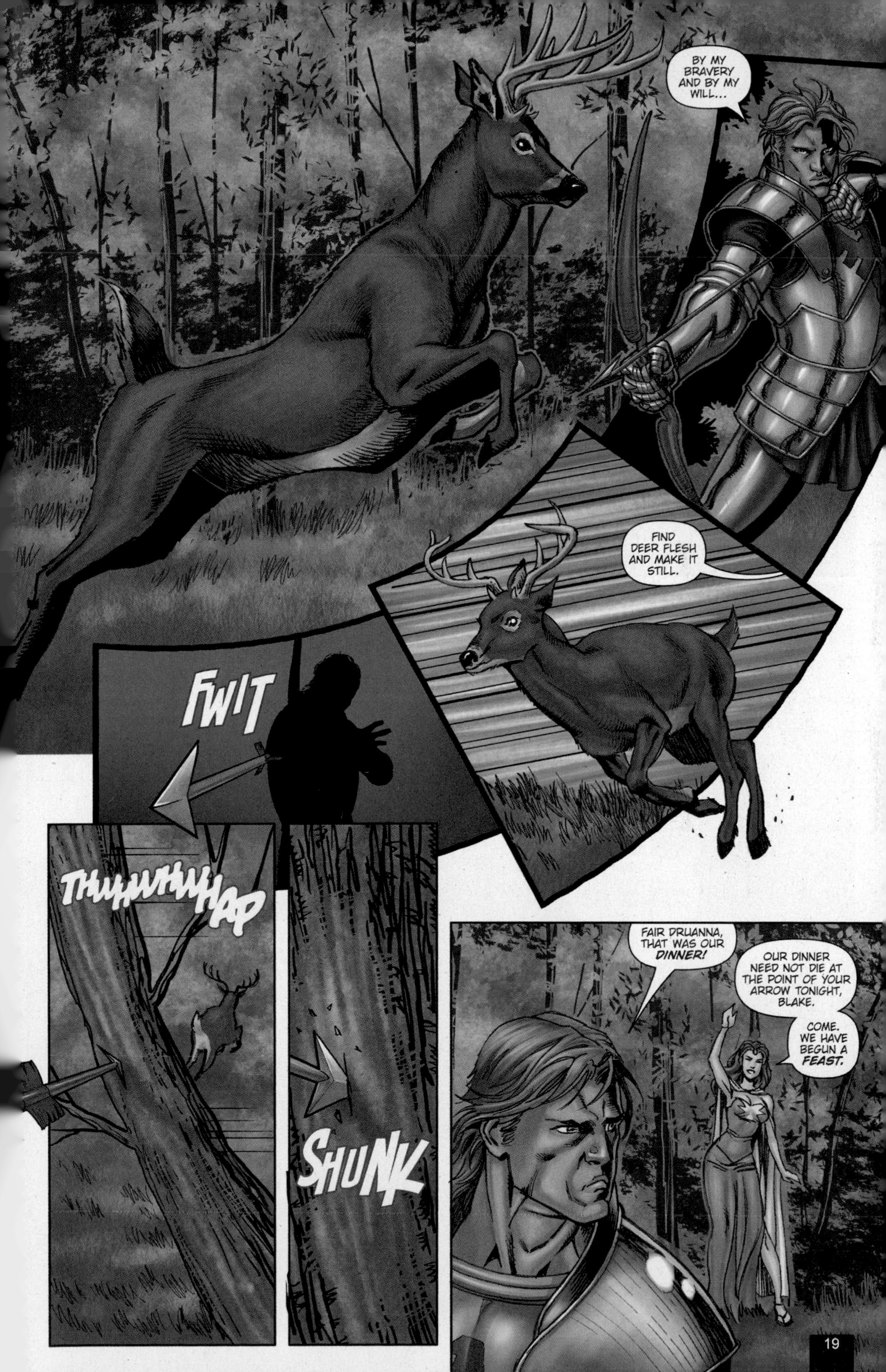
BY MY BRAVERY AND BY MY WILL...
FIND DEER FLESH AND MAKE IT STILL.
FWIT
THWWHHHAP
SHUNK
FAIR DRUANNA, THAT WAS OUR DINNER!
OUR DINNER NEED NOT DIE AT THE POINT OF YOUR ARROW TONIGHT, BLAKE.
COME. WE HAVE BEGUN A FEAST.

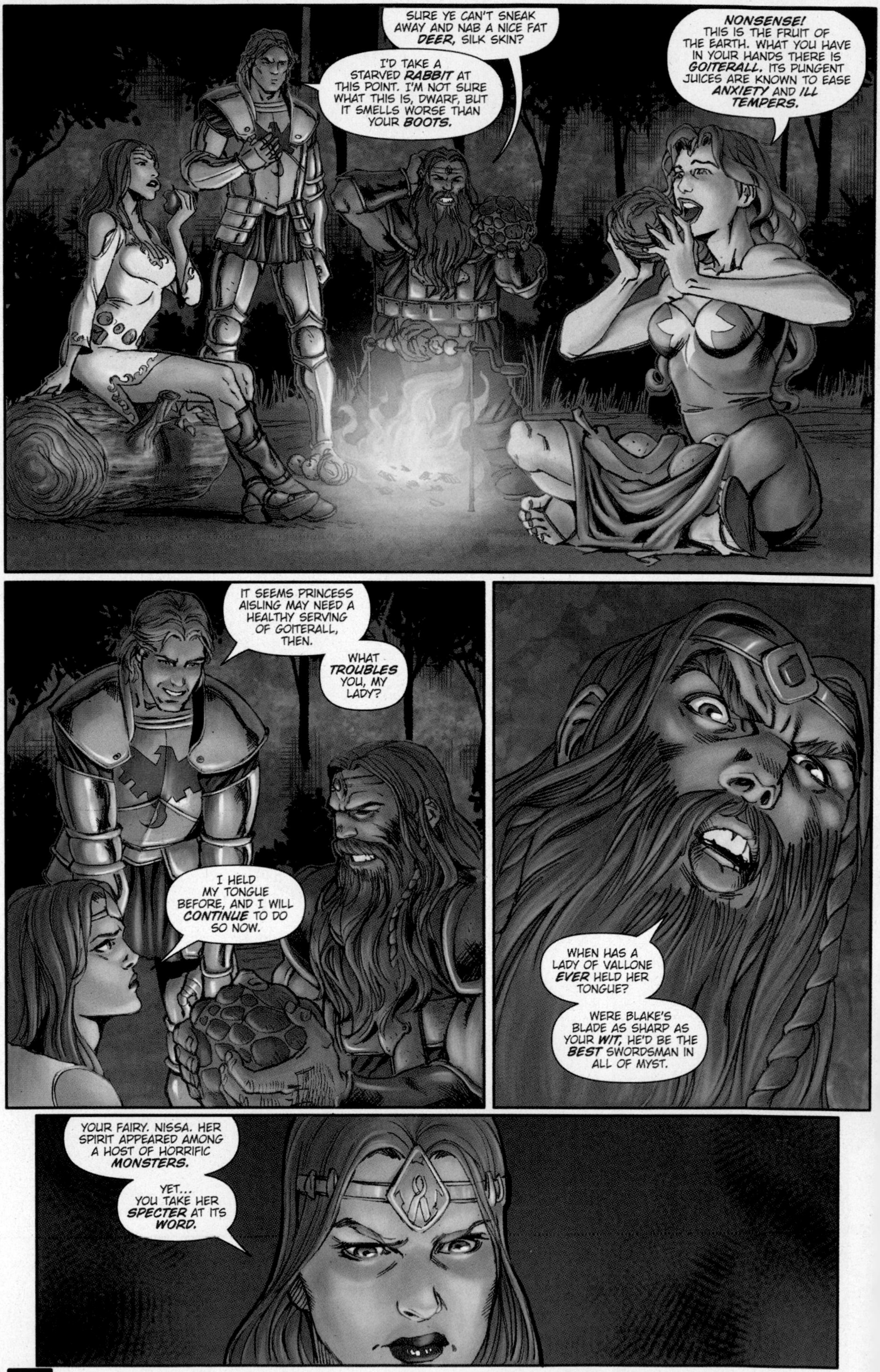
SURE YE CAN'T SNEAK AWAY AND NAB A NICE FAT DEER, SILK SKIN?
I'D TAKE A STARVED RABBIT AT THIS POINT. I'M NOT SURE WHAT THIS IS, DWARF, BUT IT SMELLS WORSE THAN YOUR BOOTS.
NONSENSE! THIS IS THE FRUIT OF THE EARTH. WHAT YOU HAVE IN YOUR HANDS THERE IS GOITERALL. ITS PUNGENT JUICES ARE KNOWN TO EASE ANXIETY AND ILL TEMPERS.
IT SEEMS PRINCESS AISLING MAY NEED A HEALTHY SERVING OF GOITERALL, THEN.
WHAT TROUBLES YOU, MY LADY?
I HELD MY TONGUE BEFORE, AND I WILL CONTINUE TO DO SO NOW.
WHEN HAS A LADY OF VALLONE EVER HELD HER TONGUE?
WERE BLAKE'S BLADE AS SHARP AS YOUR WIT, HE'D BE THE BEST SWORDSMAN IN ALL OF MYST.
YOUR FAIRY. NISSA. HER SPIRIT APPEARED AMONG A HOST OF HORRIFIC MONSTERS.
YET... YOU TAKE HER SPECTER AT ITS WORD.

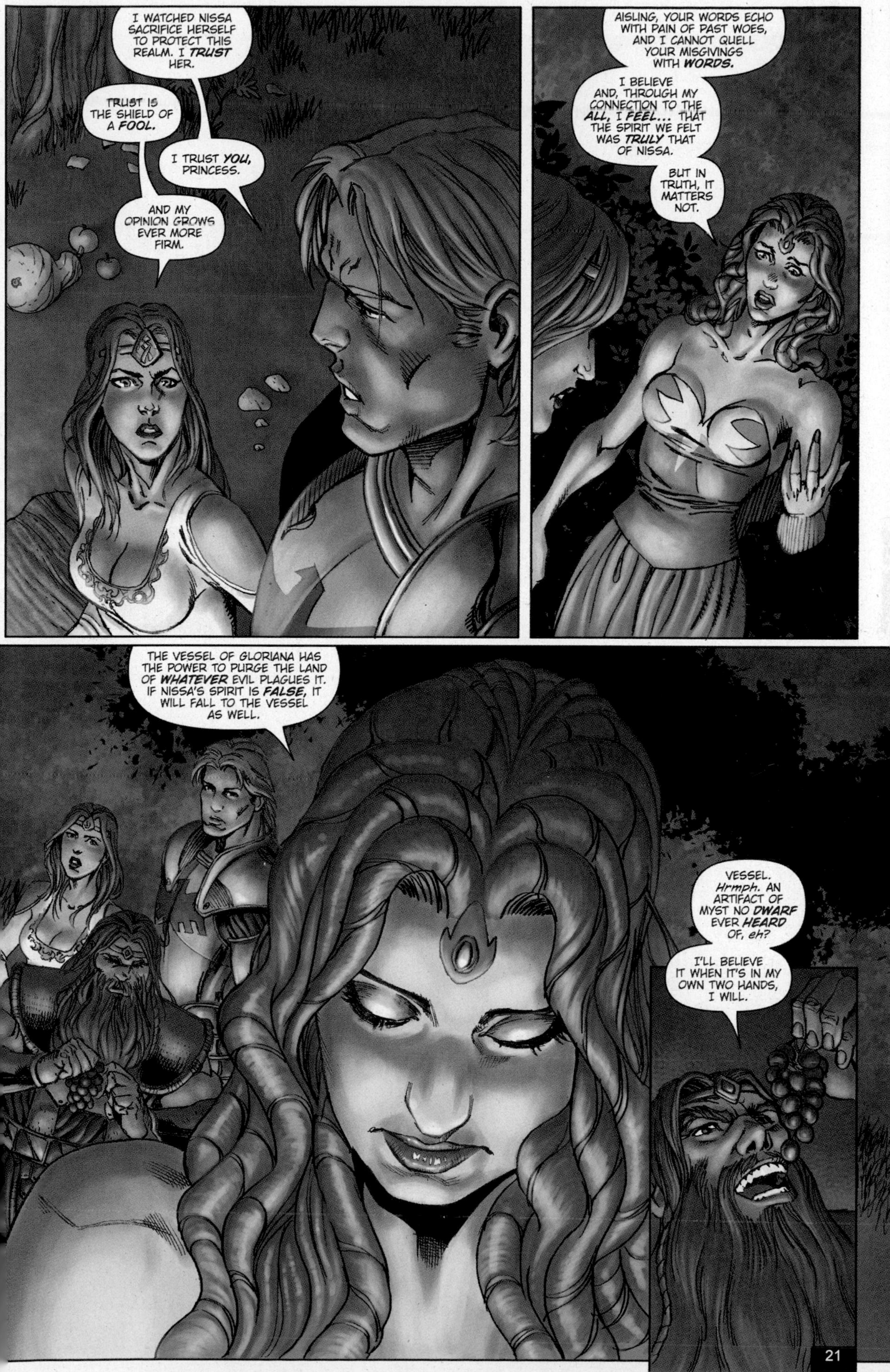
I WATCHED NISSA SACRIFICE HERSELF TO PROTECT THIS REALM. I TRUST HER.
TRUST IS THE SHIELD OF A FOOL.
I TRUST YOU, PRINCESS.
AND MY OPINION GROWS EVER MORE FIRM.
AISLING, YOUR WORDS ECHO WITH PAIN OF PAST WOES, AND I CANNOT QUELL YOUR MISGIVINGS WITH WORDS.
I BELIEVE AND, THROUGH MY CONNECTION TO THE ALL, I FEEL... THAT THE SPIRIT WE FELT WAS TRULY THAT OF NISSA.
BUT IN TRUTH, IT MATTERS NOT.
THE VESSEL OF GLORIANA HAS THE POWER TO PURGE THE LAND OF WHATEVER EVIL PLAGUES IT. IF NISSA'S SPIRIT IS FALSE, IT WILL FALL TO THE VESSEL AS WELL.
VESSEL. Hrmph. AN ARTIFACT OF MYST NO DWARF EVER HEARD OF, eh?
I'LL BELIEVE IT WHEN IT'S IN MY OWN TWO HANDS, I WILL.

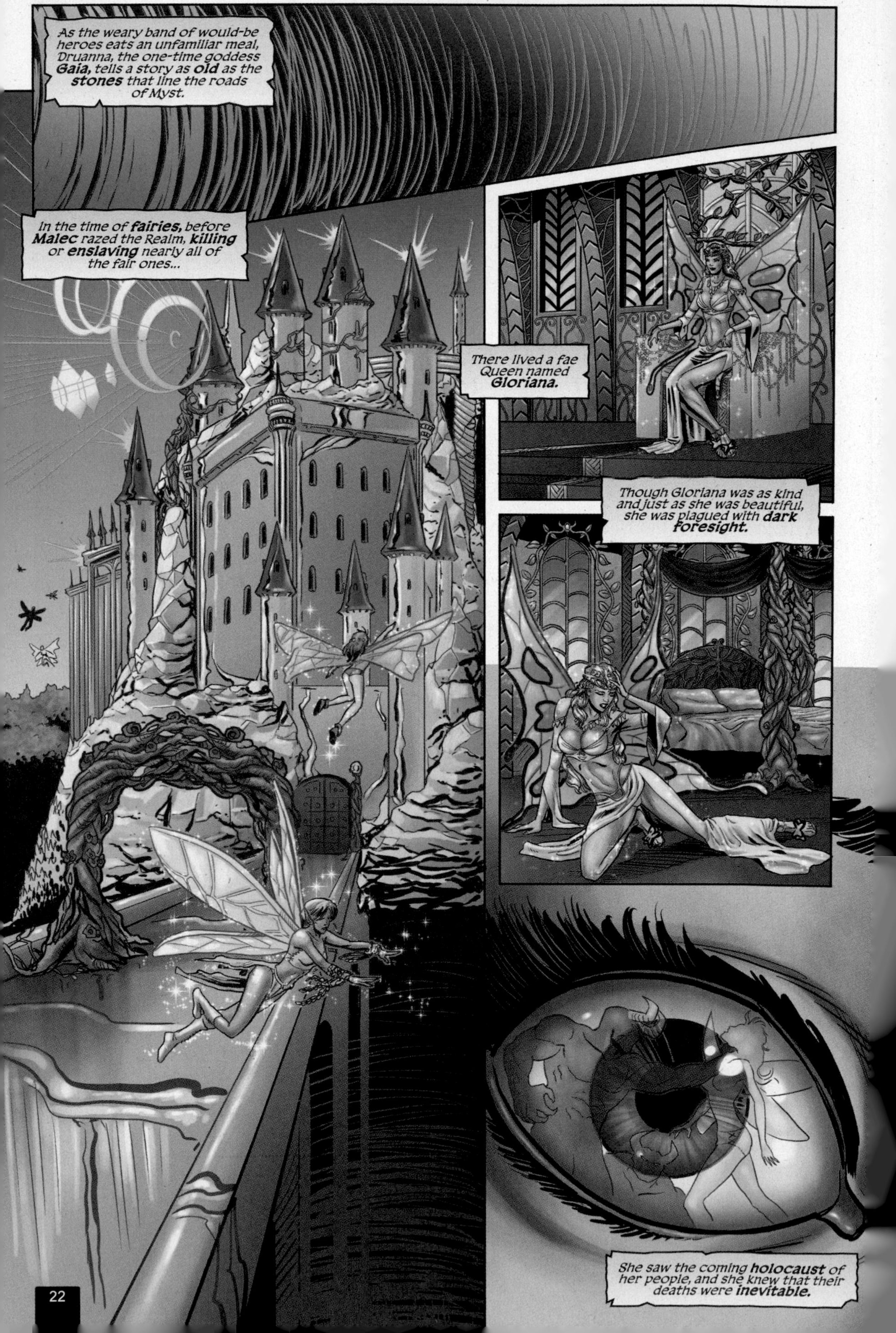

As the weary band of would-be heroes eats an unfamiliar meal, Druanna, the one-time goddess Gaia, tells a story as old as the stones that line the roads of Myst.
In the time of fairies, before Malec razed the Realm, killing or enslaving nearly all of the fair ones...
There lived a fae Queen named Gloriana.
Though Gloriana was as kind and just as she was beautiful, she was plagued with dark foresight.
She saw the coming holocaust of her people, and she knew that their deaths were inevitable.

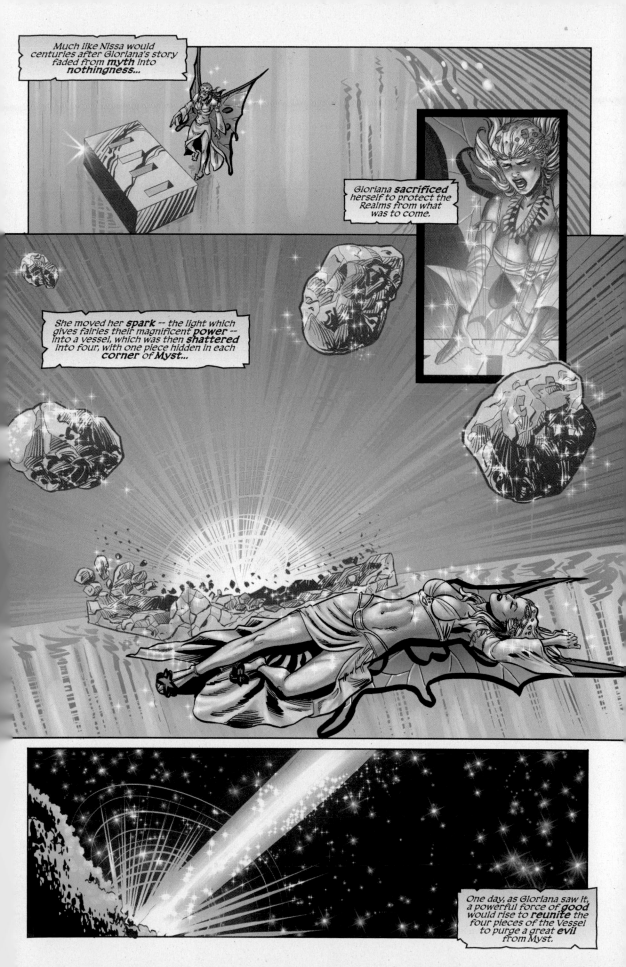

Much like Nissa would centuries after Gloriana's story faded from **myth** into **nothingness**...

Gloriana **sacrificed** herself to protect the Realms from what was to come.

She moved her **spark** -- the light which gives fairies their magnificent **power** -- into a vessel, which was then **shattered** into four, with one piece hidden in each **corner** of Myst...

One day, as Gloriana saw it, a powerful force of **good** would rise to **reunite** the four pieces of the Vessel to purge a great **evil** from Myst.

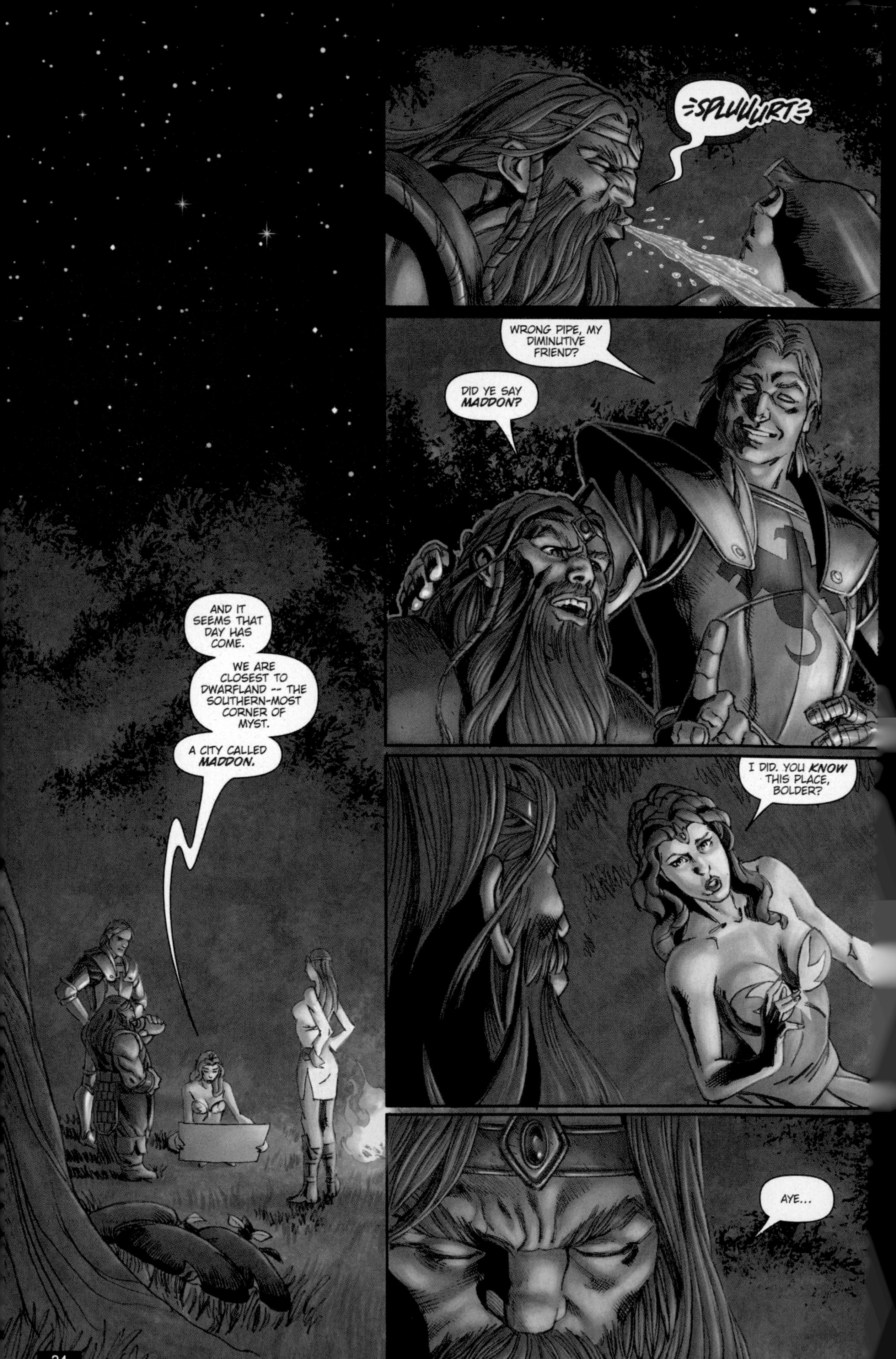
AND IT SEEMS THAT DAY HAS COME.
WE ARE CLOSEST TO DWARFLAND -- THE SOUTHERN-MOST CORNER OF MYST.
A CITY CALLED MADDON.
SPLUUURT
WRONG PIPE, MY DIMINUTIVE FRIEND?
DID YE SAY MADDON?
I DID. YOU KNOW THIS PLACE, BOLDER?
AYE...

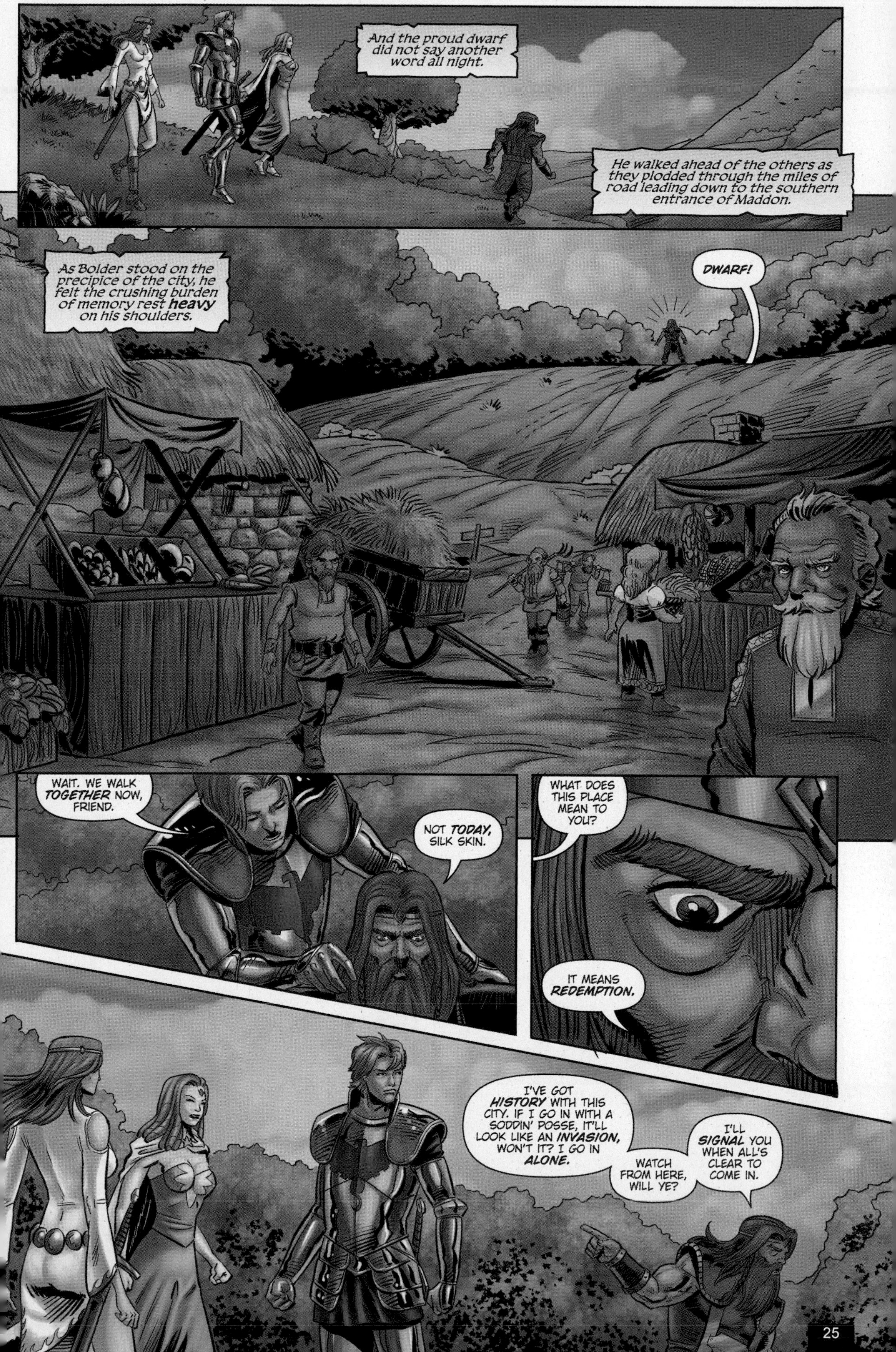
And the proud dwarf did not say another word all night.
He walked ahead of the others as they plodded through the miles of road leading down to the southern entrance of Maddon.
As Bolder stood on the precipice of the city, he felt the crushing burden of memory rest **heavy** on his shoulders.
DWARF!
WAIT. WE WALK ***TOGETHER*** NOW, FRIEND.
NOT ***TODAY,*** SILK SKIN.
WHAT DOES THIS PLACE MEAN TO YOU?
IT MEANS ***REDEMPTION.***
I'VE GOT ***HISTORY*** WITH THIS CITY. IF I GO IN WITH A SODDIN' POSSE, IT'LL LOOK LIKE AN ***INVASION,*** WON'T IT? I GO IN ***ALONE.***
WATCH FROM HERE, WILL YE?
I'LL ***SIGNAL*** YOU WHEN ALL'S CLEAR TO COME IN.

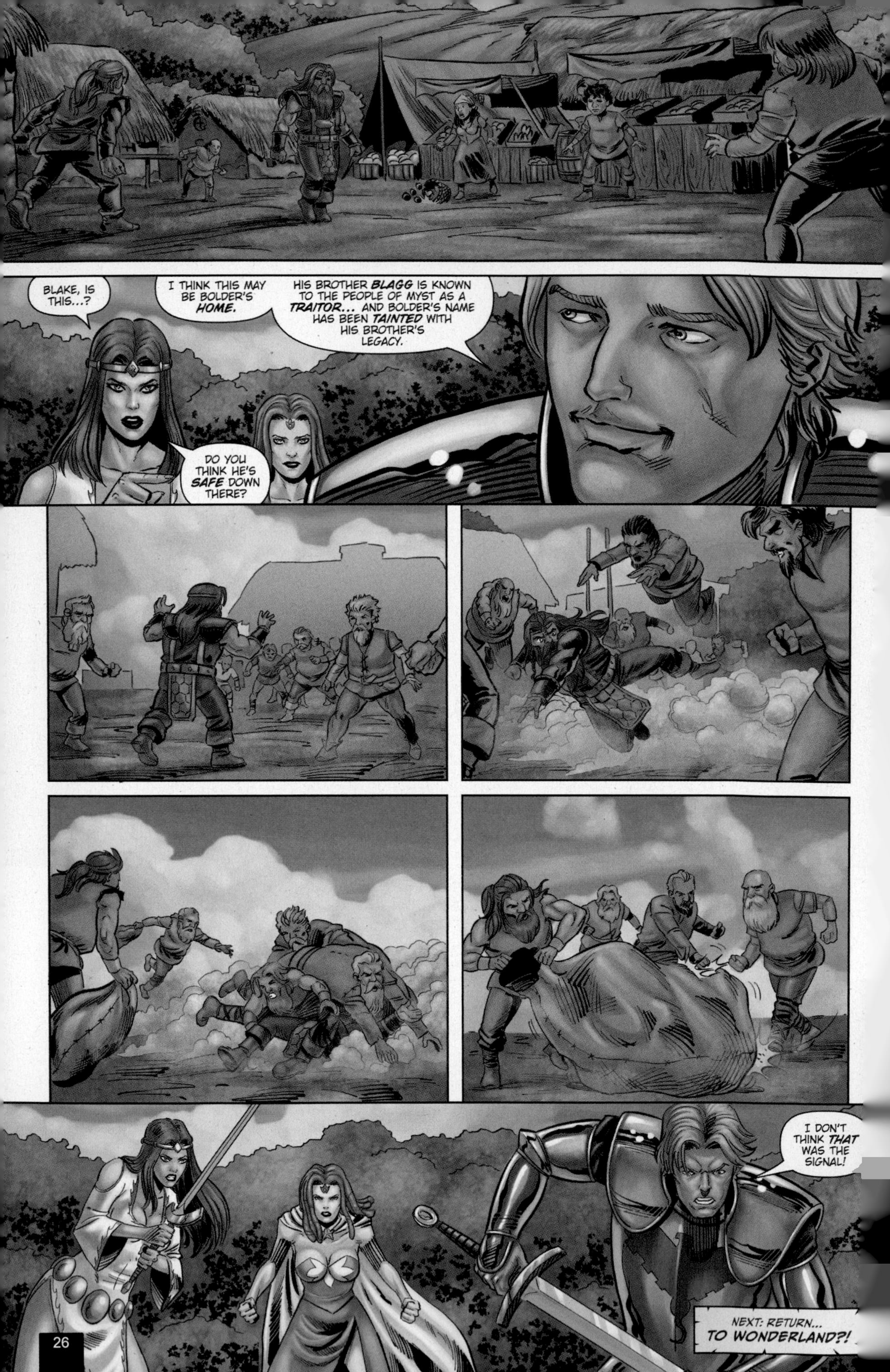
BLAKE, IS THIS...?
I THINK THIS MAY BE BOLDER'S HOME.
HIS BROTHER BLAGG IS KNOWN TO THE PEOPLE OF MYST AS A TRAITOR... AND BOLDER'S NAME HAS BEEN TAINTED WITH HIS BROTHER'S LEGACY.
DO YOU THINK HE'S SAFE DOWN THERE?
I DON'T THINK THAT WAS THE SIGNAL!
NEXT: RETURN... TO WONDERLAND?!

Grimm Fairy Tales presents:

QUEST

AGE OF DARKNESS

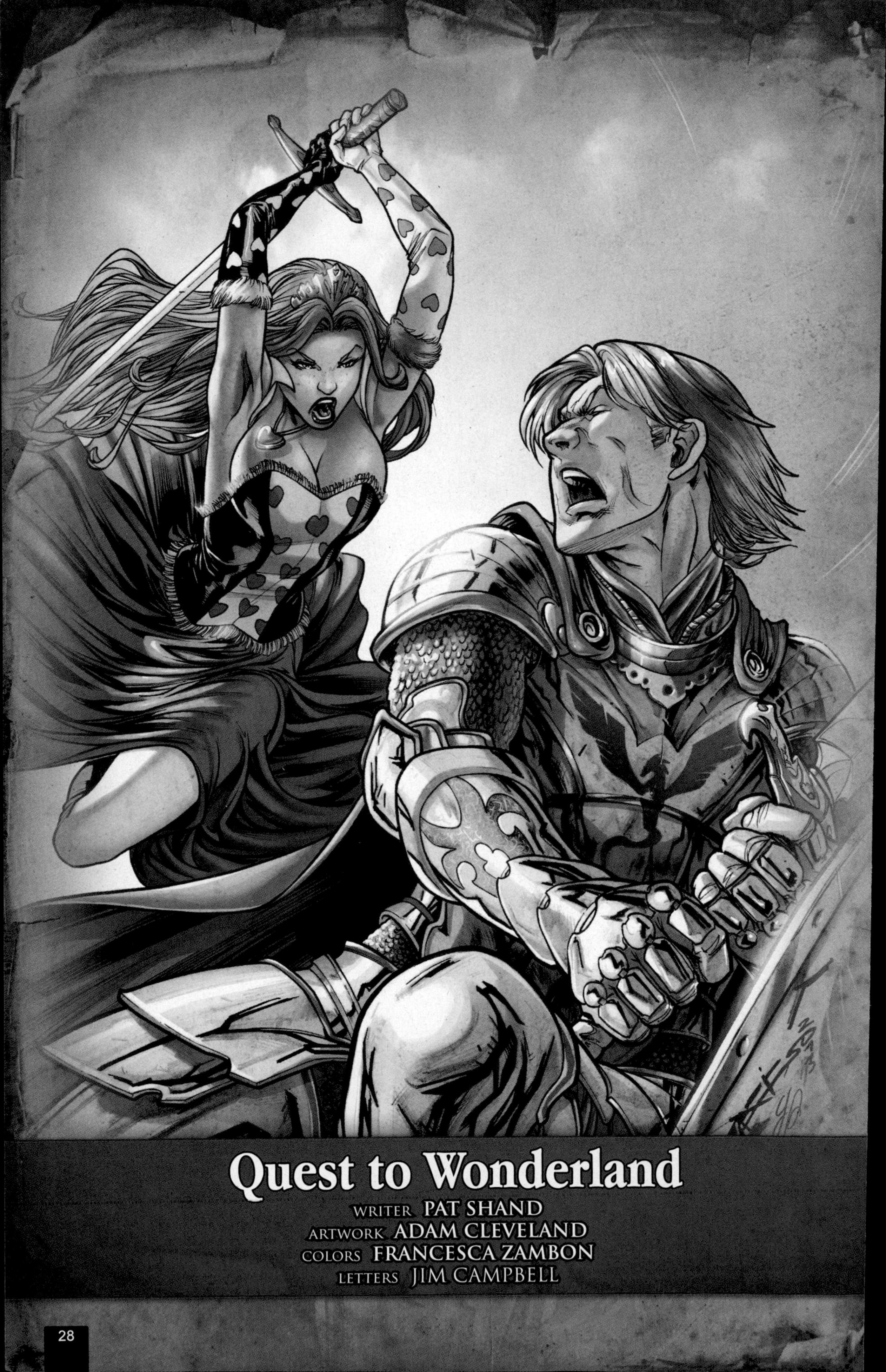

Quest to Wonderland

WRITER PAT SHAND
ARTWORK ADAM CLEVELAND
COLORS FRANCESCA ZAMBON
LETTERS JIM CAMPBELL

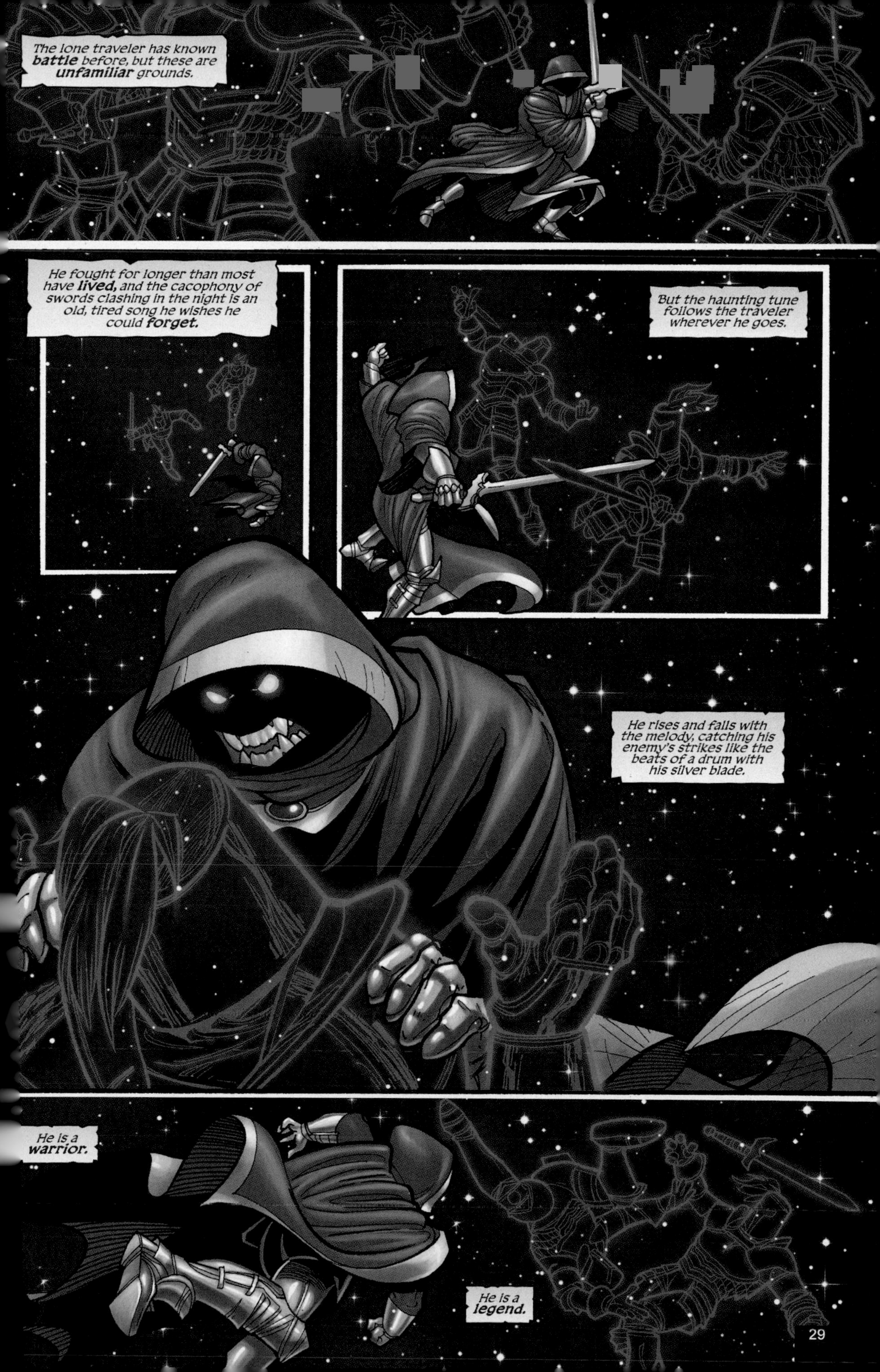
The lone traveler has known battle before, but these are unfamiliar grounds.
He fought for longer than most have lived, and the cacophony of swords clashing in the night is an old, tired song he wishes he could forget.
But the haunting tune follows the traveler wherever he goes.
He rises and falls with the melody, catching his enemy's strikes like the beats of a drum with his silver blade.
He is a warrior.
He is a legend.

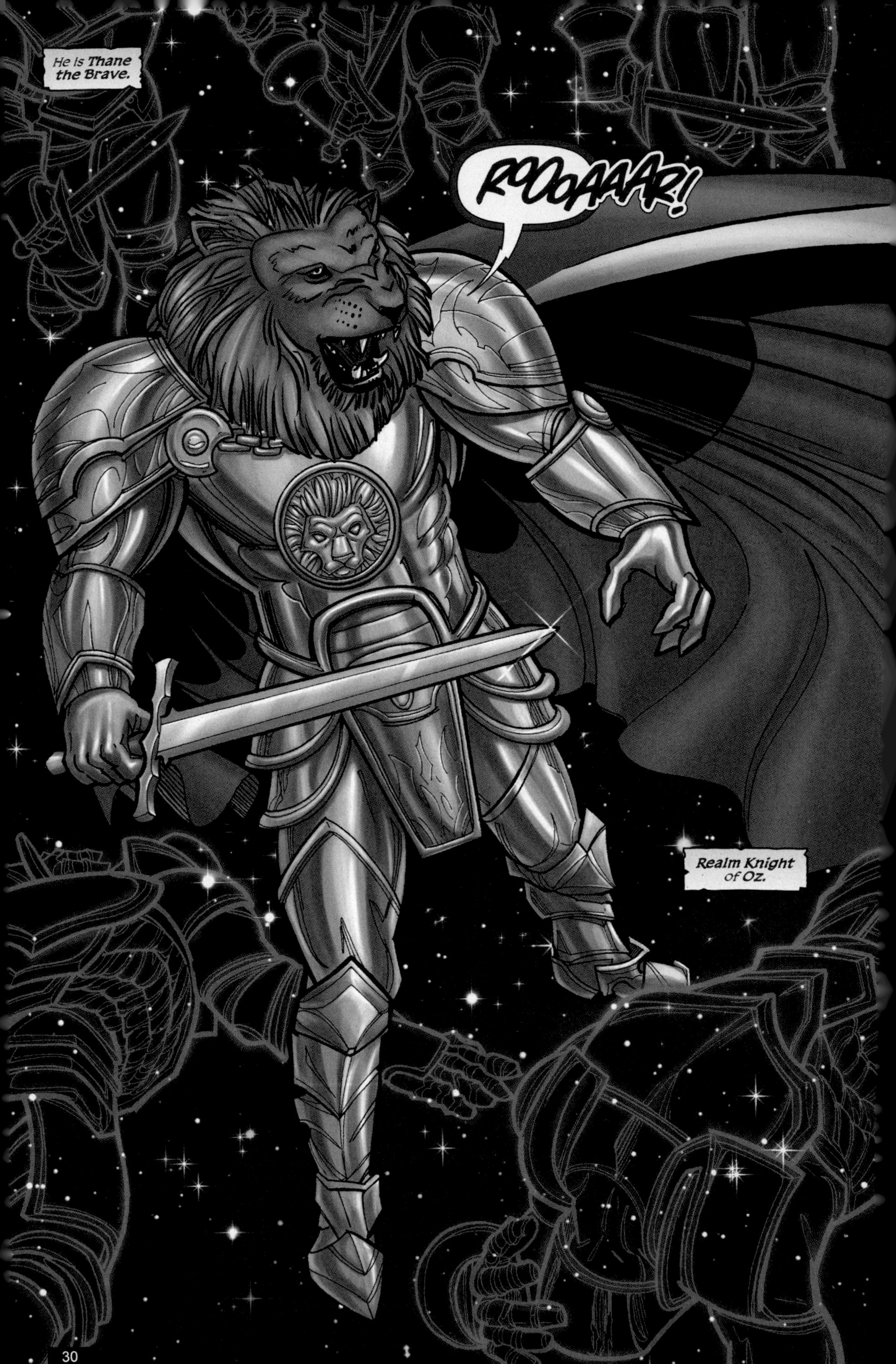
He is Thane the Brave.
ROOOAAAR!
Realm Knight of Oz.

YOU ARE PROTECTING THAT WHICH IS *SACRED*-- THIS I UNDERSTAND. IN THIS QUEST, WE ARE *KIN*.

I *REFUSE* TO SPILL THE BLOOD OF THOSE WHO FIGHT *WITH* AND *FOR* HONOR, BUT KNOW THIS -- I WILL BATTLE UNTIL MY *FINAL* BREATH.

YOU HAVE NO BUSINESS HERE. WE TAKE NO QUARREL WITH YOUR DEATH.

THE NIGHT CASTLE IS IMPENETRABLE TU--

YES, ELDERS.

THANE OF OZ. YOUR BATTLE IS *OVER*.

THOUGH I SUSPECT THE *WAR* HAS ONLY BEGUN... I THOUGHT *NAMES* WERE *USELESS* IN THIS LAND, ELDER?

THE NAME OF *THANE THE BRAVE* TRANSCENDS THE LIMITING HOLD OF WORDS. THANE RISEN INTO *LEGEND*

FACE THE ELDERS... AND FACE YOUR FINAL *FATE*.

31

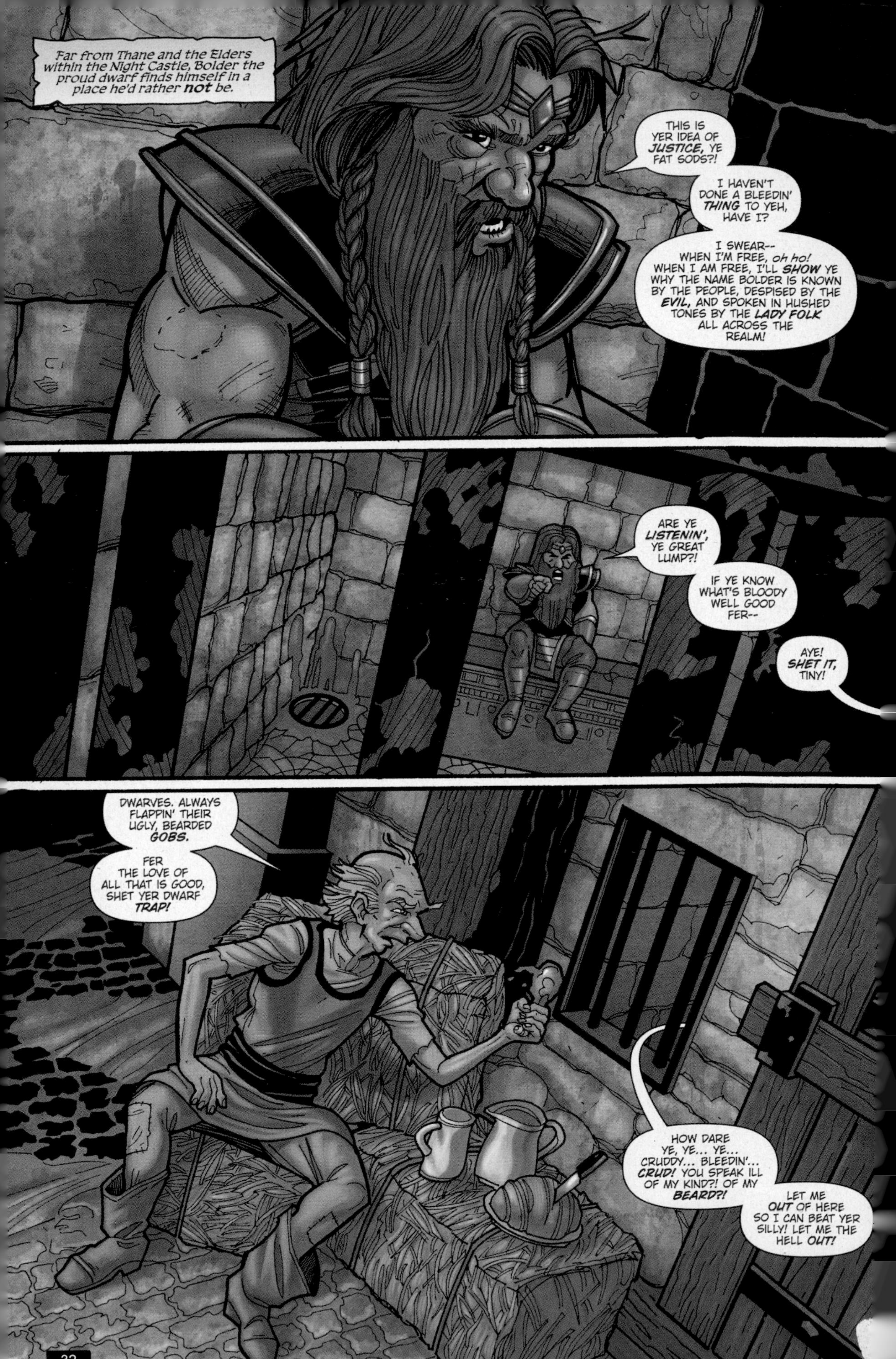
Far from Thane and the Elders within the Night Castle, Bolder the proud dwarf finds himself in a place he'd rather **not** be.
THIS IS YER IDEA OF **JUSTICE,** YE FAT SODS?!
I HAVEN'T DONE A BLEEDIN' **THING** TO YEH, HAVE I?
I SWEAR-- WHEN I'M FREE, *oh ho!* WHEN I AM FREE, I'LL **SHOW** YE WHY THE NAME BOLDER IS KNOWN BY THE PEOPLE, DESPISED BY THE **EVIL,** AND SPOKEN IN HUSHED TONES BY THE **LADY FOLK** ALL ACROSS THE REALM!
ARE YE **LISTENIN',** YE GREAT LUMP?!
IF YE KNOW WHAT'S BLOODY WELL GOOD FER--
AYE! **SHET IT,** TINY!
DWARVES. ALWAYS FLAPPIN' THEIR UGLY, BEARDED **GOBS.**
FER THE LOVE OF ALL THAT IS GOOD, SHET YER DWARF **TRAP!**
HOW DARE YE, YE... YE... CRUDDY... BLEEDIN'... **CRUD!** YOU SPEAK ILL OF MY KIND?! OF MY **BEARD?!**
LET ME **OUT** OF HERE SO I CAN BEAT YER SILLY! LET ME THE HELL **OUT!**

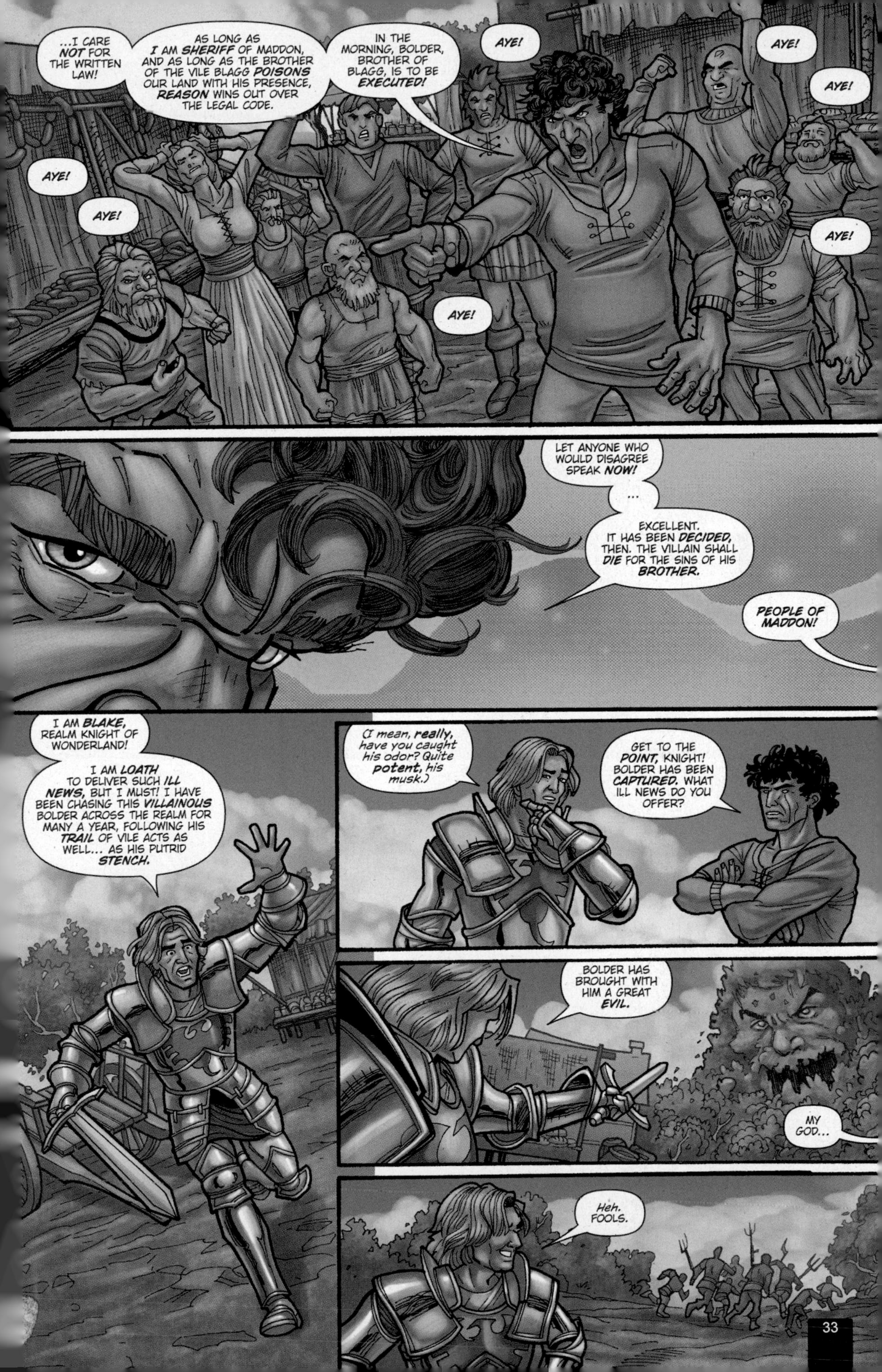
...I CARE NOT FOR THE WRITTEN LAW!
AS LONG AS I AM SHERIFF OF MADDON, AND AS LONG AS THE BROTHER OF THE VILE BLAGG POISONS OUR LAND WITH HIS PRESENCE, REASON WINS OUT OVER THE LEGAL CODE.
IN THE MORNING, BOLDER, BROTHER OF BLAGG, IS TO BE EXECUTED!
AYE!
AYE!
AYE!
AYE!
AYE!
AYE!
AYE!
LET ANYONE WHO WOULD DISAGREE SPEAK NOW!
...
EXCELLENT. IT HAS BEEN DECIDED, THEN. THE VILLAIN SHALL DIE FOR THE SINS OF HIS BROTHER.
PEOPLE OF MADDON!
I AM BLAKE, REALM KNIGHT OF WONDERLAND!
I AM LOATH TO DELIVER SUCH ILL NEWS, BUT I MUST! I HAVE BEEN CHASING THIS VILLAINOUS BOLDER ACROSS THE REALM FOR MANY A YEAR, FOLLOWING HIS TRAIL OF VILE ACTS AS WELL... AS HIS PUTRID STENCH.
(I mean, really, have you caught his odor? Quite potent, his musk.)
GET TO THE POINT, KNIGHT! BOLDER HAS BEEN CAPTURED. WHAT ILL NEWS DO YOU OFFER?
BOLDER HAS BROUGHT WITH HIM A GREAT EVIL.
MY GOD...
Heh. FOOLS.

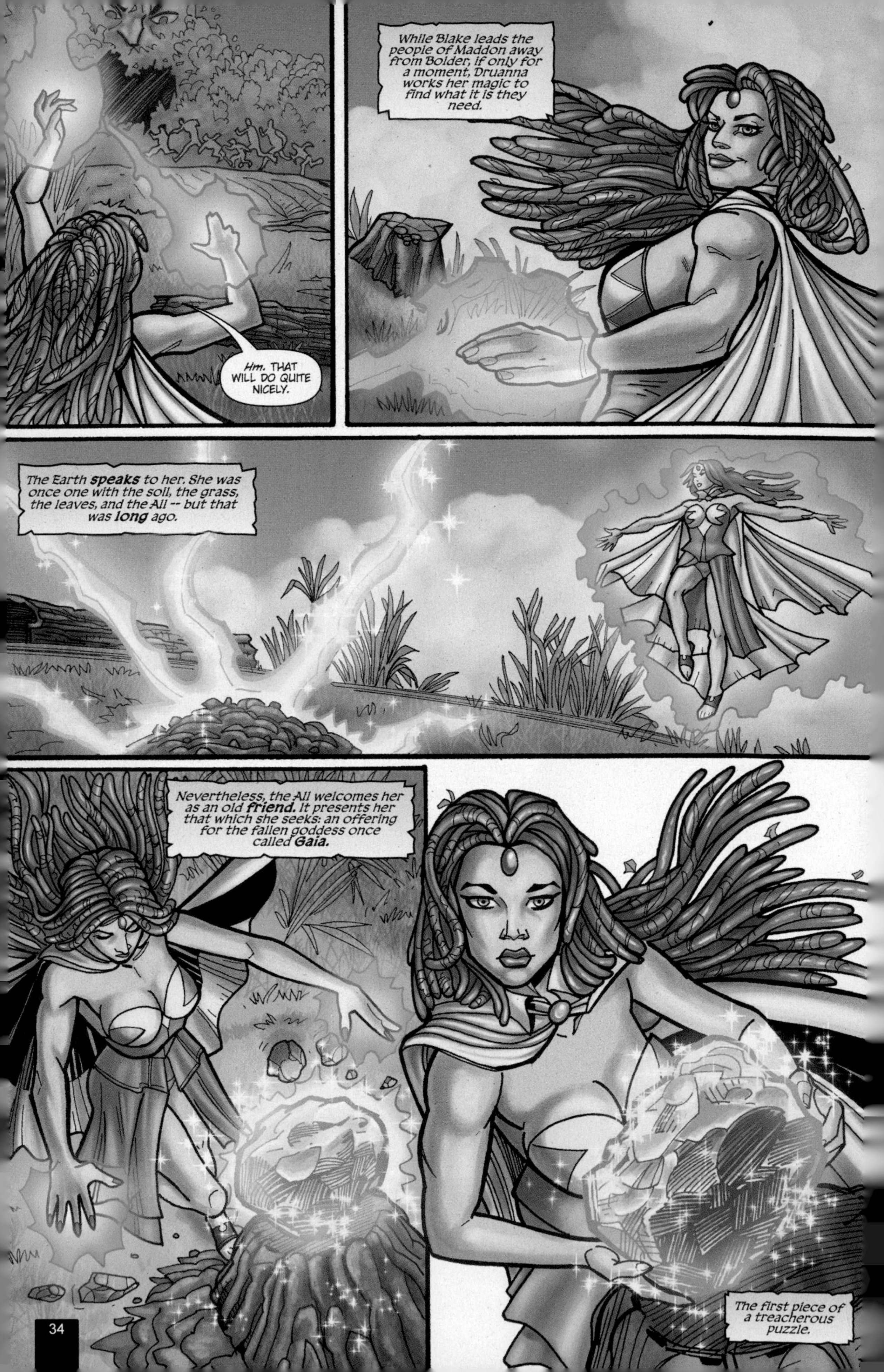

Hm. THAT WILL DO QUITE NICELY.
While Blake leads the people of Maddon away from Bolder, if only for a moment, Druanna works her magic to find what it is they need.
The Earth speaks to her. She was once one with the soil, the grass, the leaves, and the All -- but that was long ago.
Nevertheless, the All welcomes her as an old friend. It presents her that which she seeks: an offering for the fallen goddess once called Gaia.
The first piece of a treacherous puzzle.

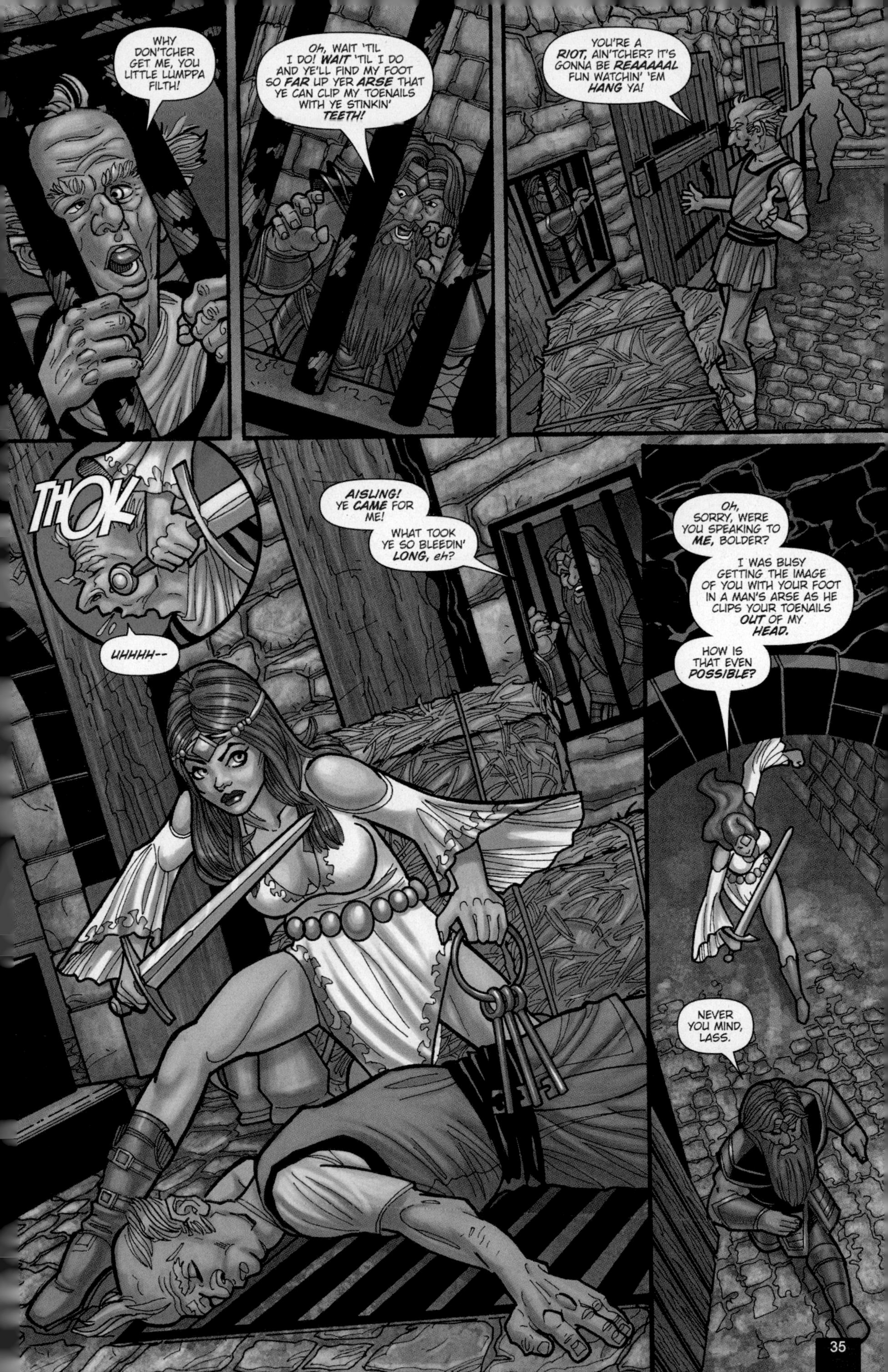
WHY DON'TCHER GET ME, YOU LITTLE LUMPPA FILTH!
Oh, WAIT 'TIL I DO! WAIT 'TIL I DO AND YE'LL FIND MY FOOT SO FAR UP YER ARSE THAT YE CAN CLIP MY TOENAILS WITH YE STINKIN' TEETH!
YOU'RE A RIOT, AIN'TCHER? IT'S GONNA BE REAAAAAL FUN WATCHIN' 'EM HANG YA!
THOK
UHHHH--
AISLING! YE CAME FOR ME!
WHAT TOOK YE SO BLEEDIN' LONG, eh?
Oh, SORRY, WERE YOU SPEAKING TO ME, BOLDER?
I WAS BUSY GETTING THE IMAGE OF YOU WITH YOUR FOOT IN A MAN'S ARSE AS HE CLIPS YOUR TOENAILS OUT OF MY HEAD.
HOW IS THAT EVEN POSSIBLE?
NEVER YOU MIND, LASS.

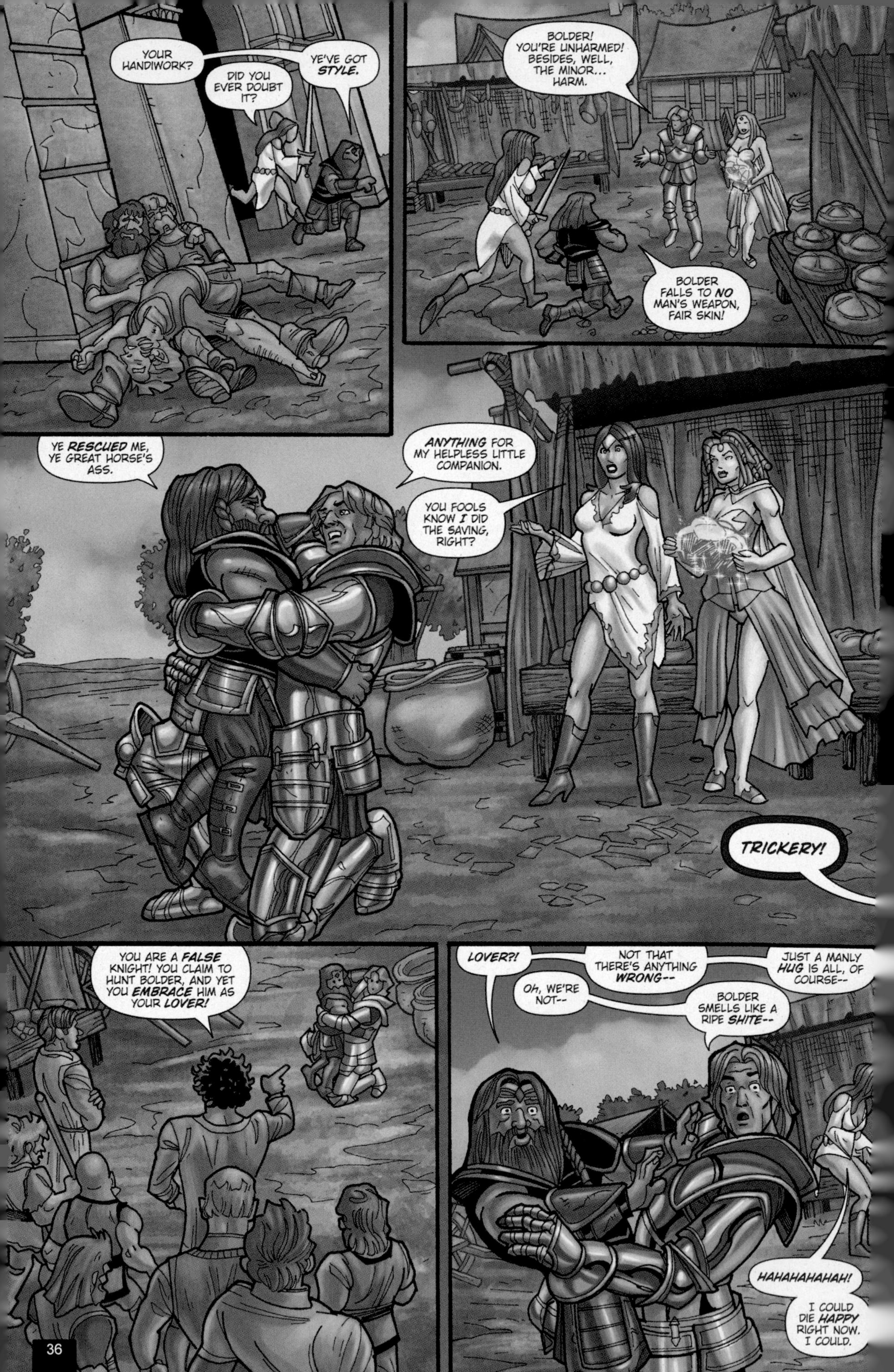
YOUR HANDIWORK?
DID YOU EVER DOUBT IT?
YE'VE GOT STYLE.
BOLDER! YOU'RE UNHARMED! BESIDES, WELL, THE MINOR... HARM.
BOLDER FALLS TO NO MAN'S WEAPON, FAIR SKIN!
YE RESCUED ME, YE GREAT HORSE'S ASS.
ANYTHING FOR MY HELPLESS LITTLE COMPANION.
YOU FOOLS KNOW I DID THE SAVING, RIGHT?
TRICKERY!
YOU ARE A FALSE KNIGHT! YOU CLAIM TO HUNT BOLDER, AND YET YOU EMBRACE HIM AS YOUR LOVER!
LOVER?!
NOT THAT THERE'S ANYTHING WRONG--
JUST A MANLY HUG IS ALL, OF COURSE--
Oh, WE'RE NOT--
BOLDER SMELLS LIKE A RIPE SHITE--
HAHAHAHAHAH!
I COULD DIE HAPPY RIGHT NOW. I COULD.

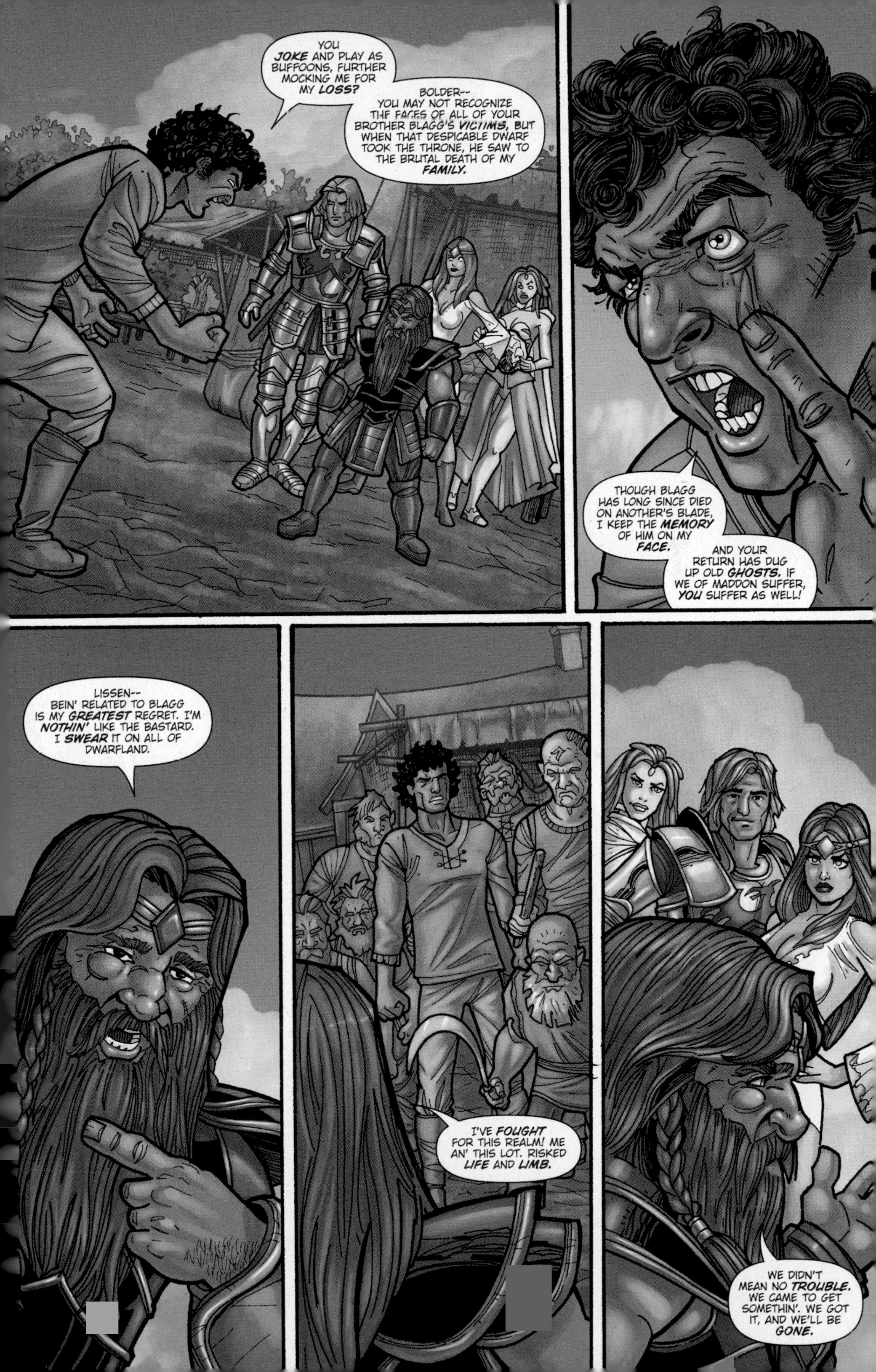
YOU JOKE AND PLAY AS BUFFOONS, FURTHER MOCKING ME FOR MY LOSS?
BOLDER-- YOU MAY NOT RECOGNIZE THE FACES OF ALL OF YOUR BROTHER BLAGG'S VICTIMS, BUT WHEN THAT DESPICABLE DWARF TOOK THE THRONE, HE SAW TO THE BRUTAL DEATH OF MY FAMILY.
THOUGH BLAGG HAS LONG SINCE DIED ON ANOTHER'S BLADE, I KEEP THE MEMORY OF HIM ON MY FACE.
AND YOUR RETURN HAS DUG UP OLD GHOSTS. IF WE OF MADDON SUFFER, YOU SUFFER AS WELL!
LISSEN-- BEIN' RELATED TO BLAGG IS MY GREATEST REGRET. I'M NOTHIN' LIKE THE BASTARD. I SWEAR IT ON ALL OF DWARFLAND.
I'VE FOUGHT FOR THIS REALM! ME AN' THIS LOT. RISKED LIFE AND LIMB.
WE DIDN'T MEAN NO TROUBLE. WE CAME TO GET SOMETHIN'. WE GOT IT, AND WE'LL BE GONE.

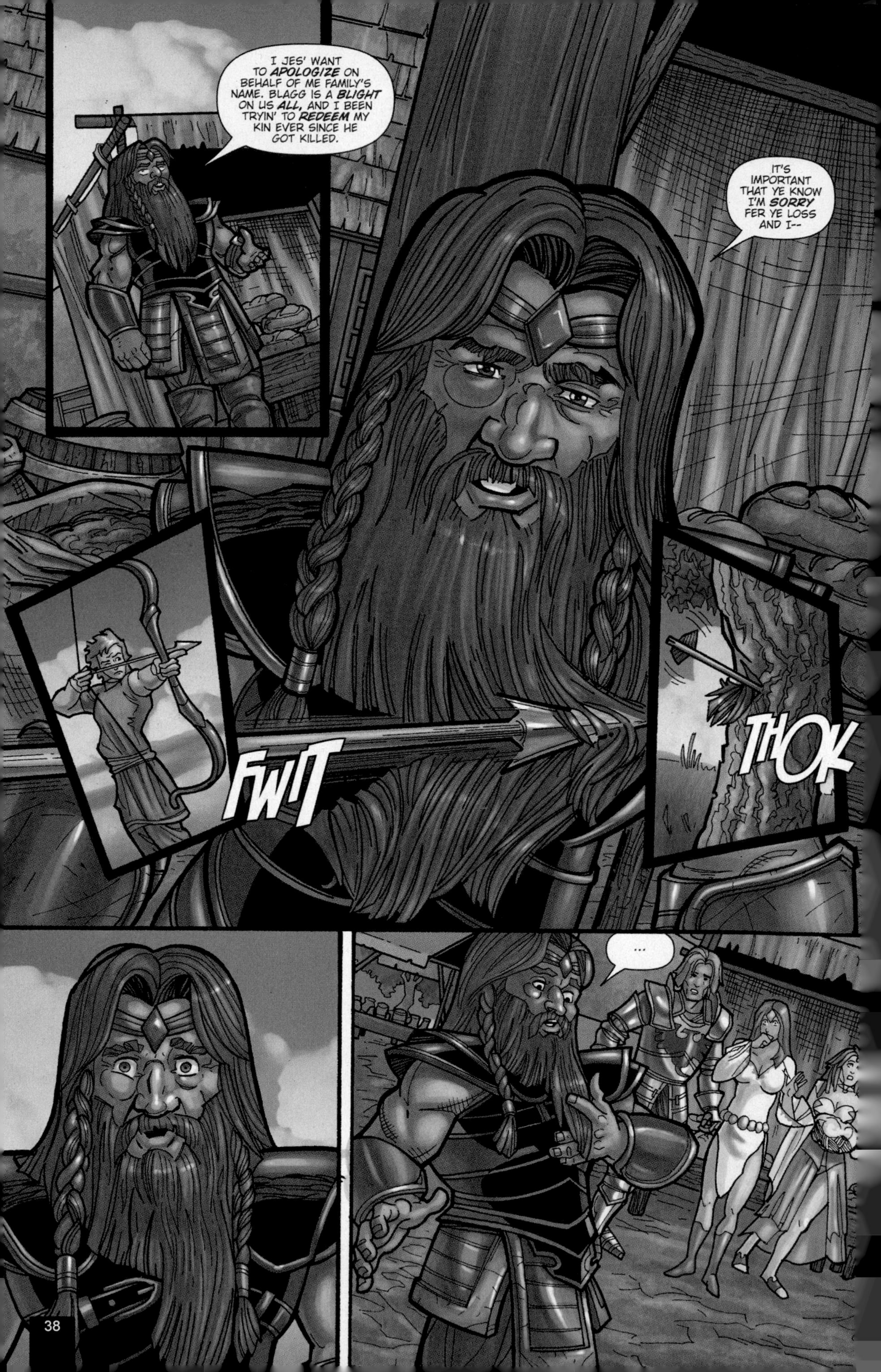
I JES' WANT TO APOLOGIZE ON BEHALF OF ME FAMILY'S NAME. BLAGG IS A BLIGHT ON US ALL, AND I BEEN TRYIN' TO REDEEM MY KIN EVER SINCE HE GOT KILLED.
IT'S IMPORTANT THAT YE KNOW I'M SORRY FER YE LOSS AND I--
FWIT
THOK
...

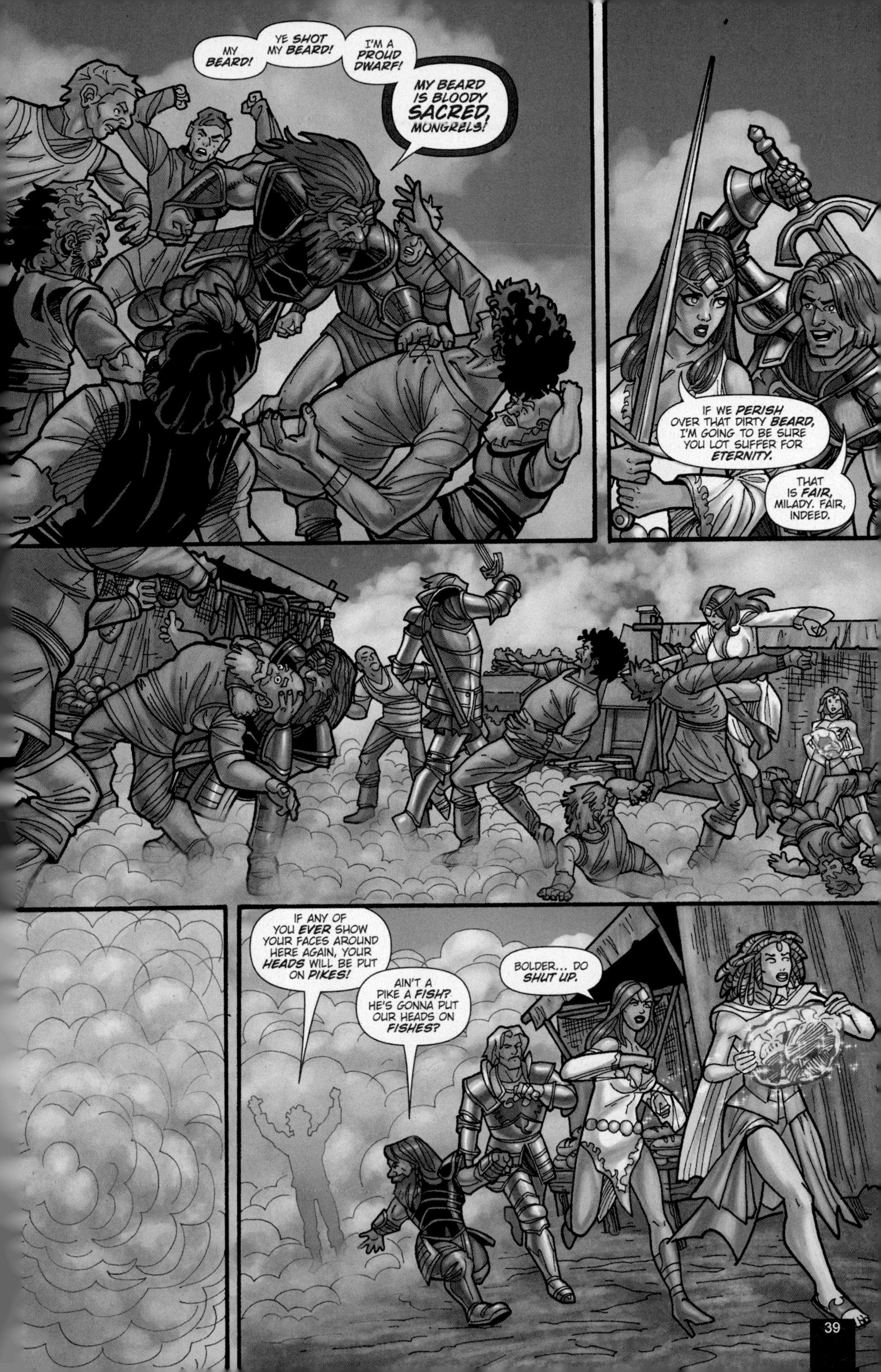
MY BEARD!
YE SHOT MY BEARD!
I'M A PROUD DWARF!
MY BEARD IS BLOODY SACRED, MONGRELS!
IF WE PERISH OVER THAT DIRTY BEARD, I'M GOING TO BE SURE YOU LOT SUFFER FOR ETERNITY.
THAT IS FAIR, MILADY. FAIR, INDEED.
IF ANY OF YOU EVER SHOW YOUR FACES AROUND HERE AGAIN, YOUR HEADS WILL BE PUT ON PIKES!
AIN'T A PIKE A FISH? HE'S GONNA PUT OUR HEADS ON FISHES?
BOLDER... DO SHUT UP.

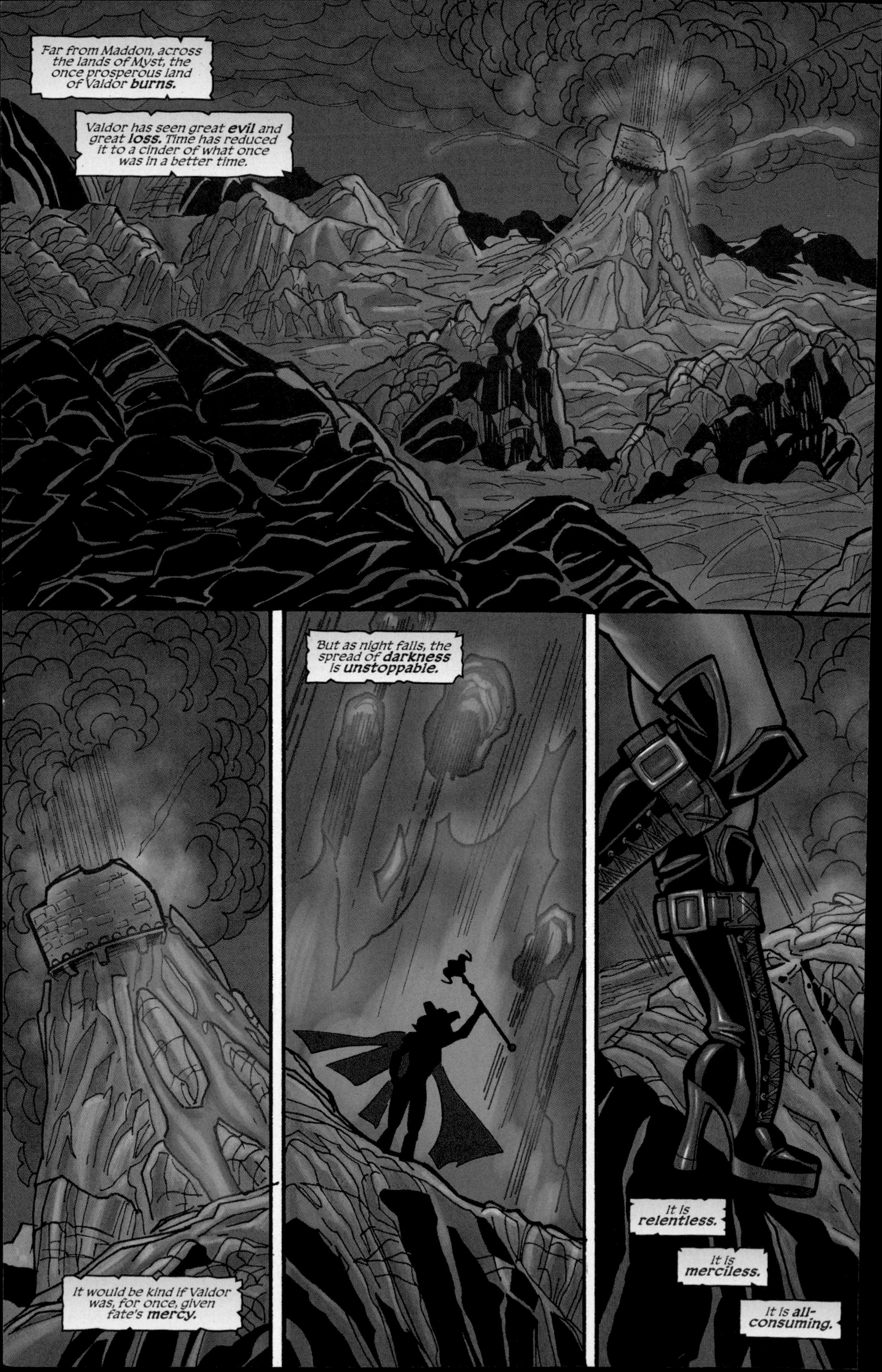
Far from Maddon, across the lands of Myst, the once prosperous land of Valdor **burns.**
Valdor has seen great **evil** and great **loss.** Time has reduced it to a cinder of what once was in a better time.
It would be kind if Valdor was, for once, given fate's **mercy.**
But as night falls, the spread of **darkness** is **unstoppable.**
It is **relentless.**
It is **merciless.**
It is **all-consuming.**

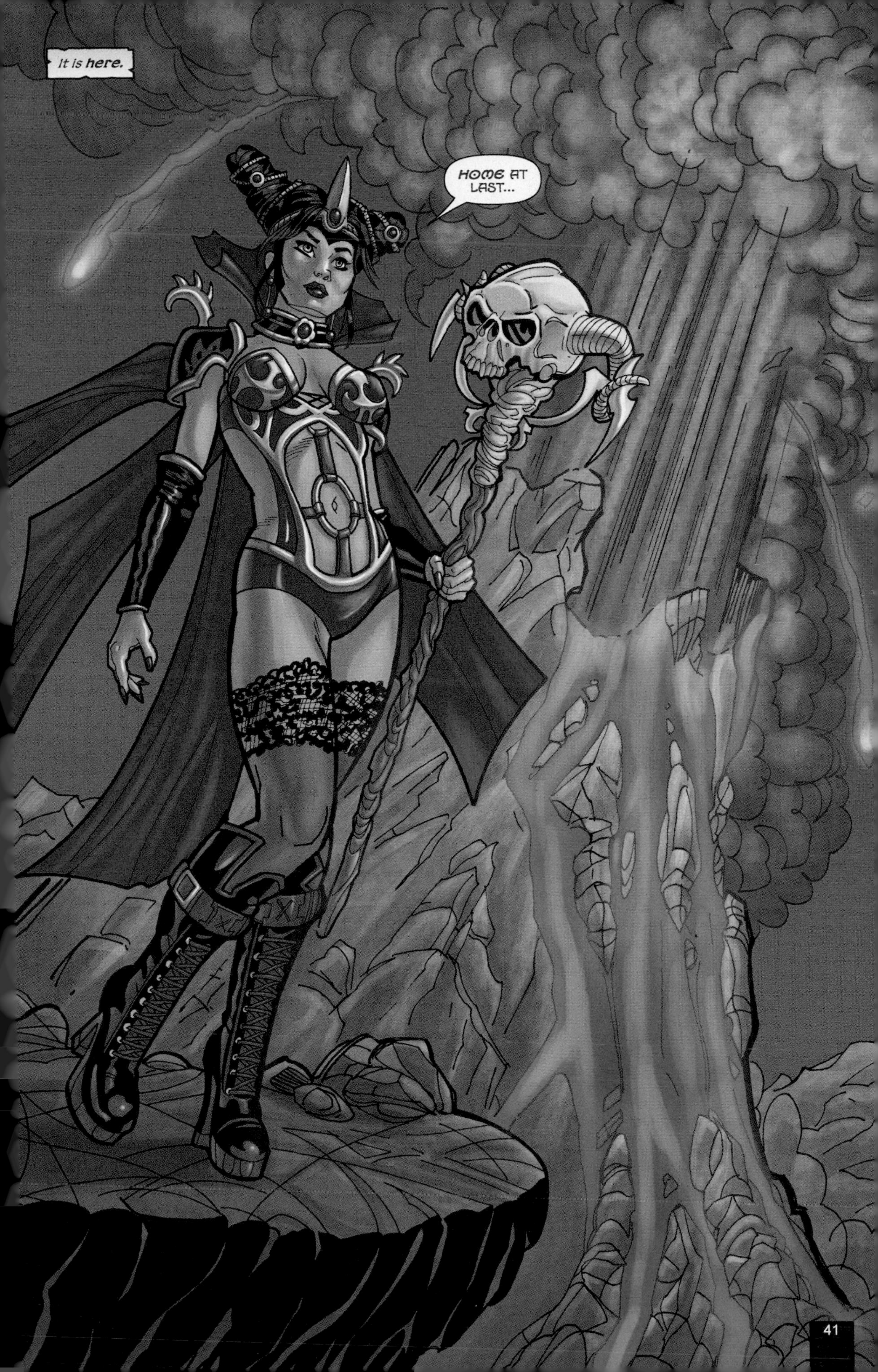
It is here.
HOME AT LAST...

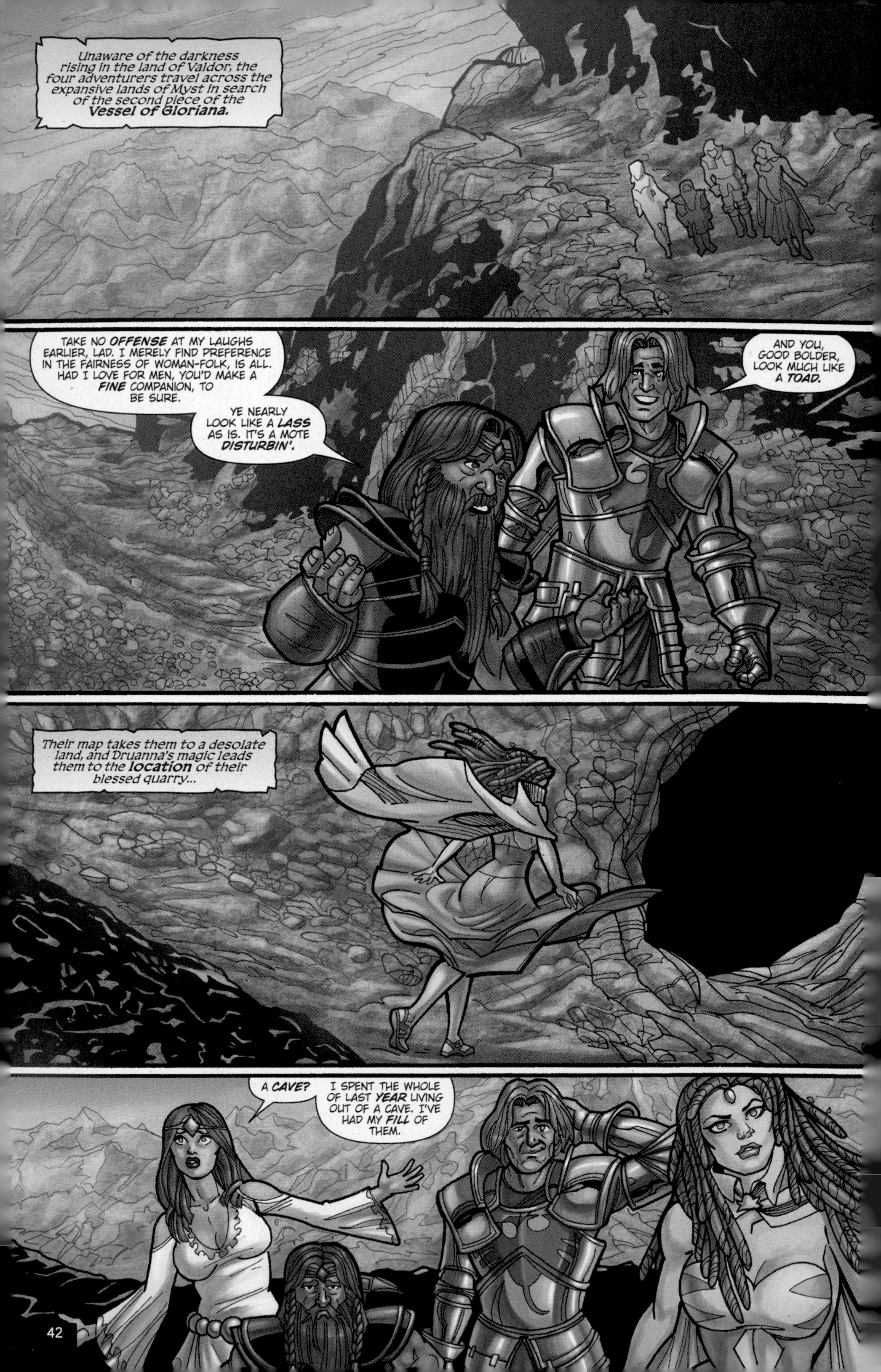
Unaware of the darkness rising in the land of Valdor, the four adventurers travel across the expansive lands of Myst in search of the second piece of the Vessel of Gloriana.
TAKE NO OFFENSE AT MY LAUGHS EARLIER, LAD. I MERELY FIND PREFERENCE IN THE FAIRNESS OF WOMAN-FOLK, IS ALL. HAD I LOVE FOR MEN, YOU'D MAKE A FINE COMPANION, TO BE SURE.
YE NEARLY LOOK LIKE A LASS AS IS. IT'S A MOTE DISTURBIN'.
AND YOU, GOOD BOLDER, LOOK MUCH LIKE A TOAD.
Their map takes them to a desolate land, and Druanna's magic leads them to the location of their blessed quarry...
A CAVE?
I SPENT THE WHOLE OF LAST YEAR LIVING OUT OF A CAVE. I'VE HAD MY FILL OF THEM.

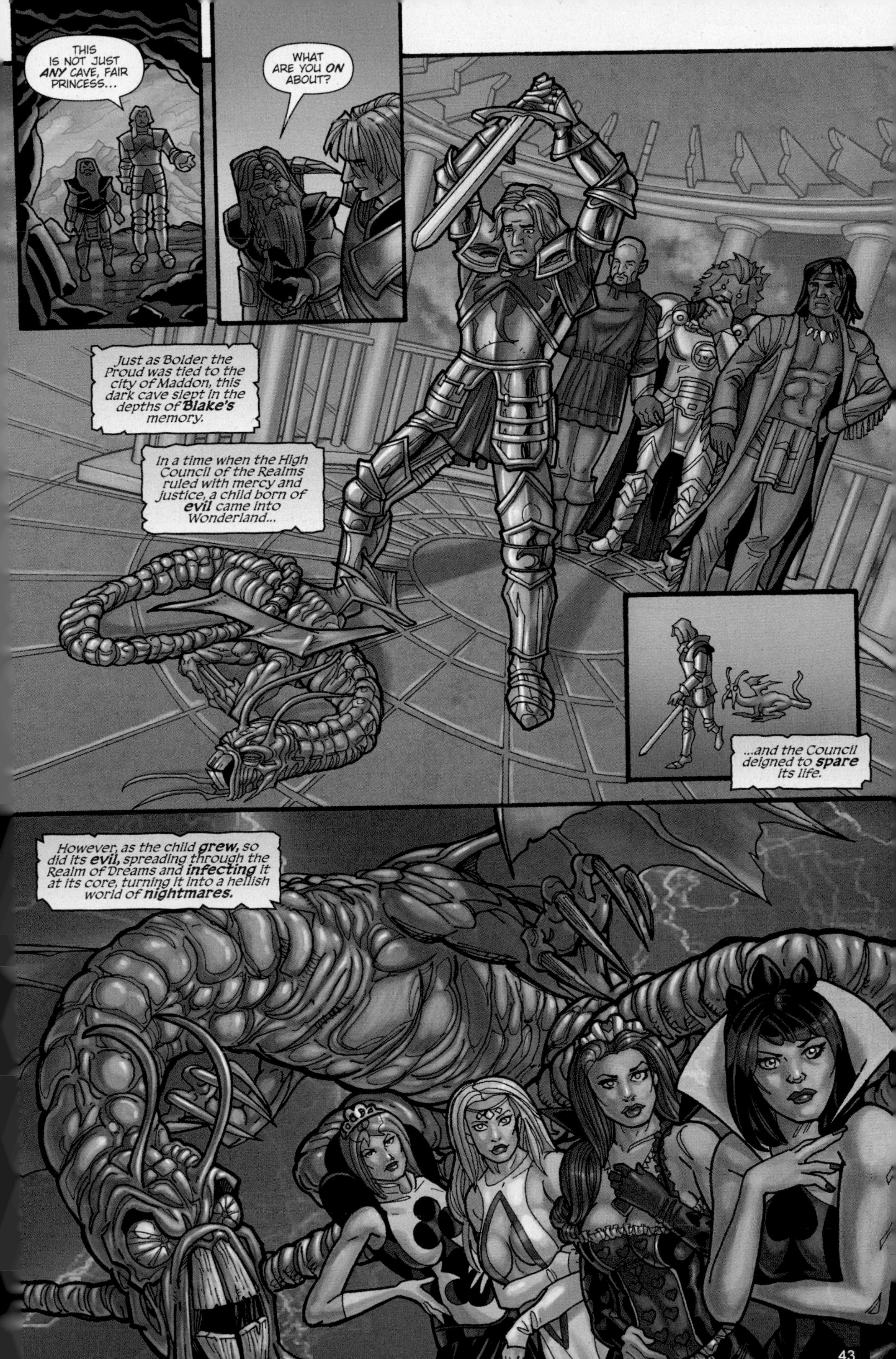
THIS IS NOT JUST ANY CAVE, FAIR PRINCESS...
WHAT ARE YOU ON ABOUT?
Just as Bolder the Proud was tied to the city of Maddon, this dark cave slept in the depths of Blake's memory.
In a time when the High Council of the Realms ruled with mercy and justice, a child born of evil came into Wonderland...
...and the Council deigned to spare its life.
However, as the child grew, so did its evil, spreading through the Realm of Dreams and infecting it at its core, turning it into a hellish world of nightmares.

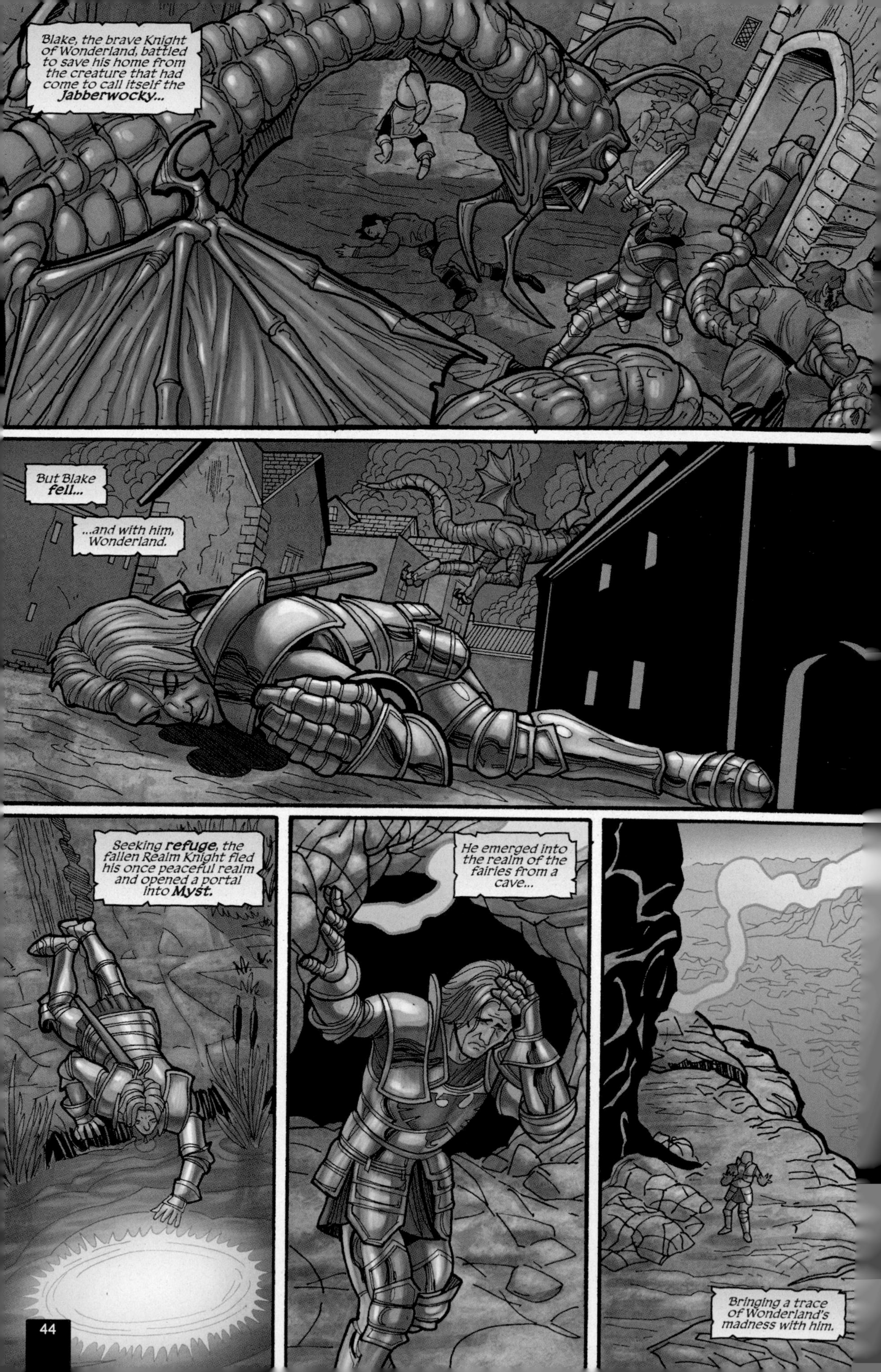
Blake, the brave Knight of Wonderland, battled to save his home from the creature that had come to call itself the Jabberwocky...
But Blake fell...
...and with him, Wonderland.
Seeking refuge, the fallen Realm Knight fled his once peaceful realm and opened a portal into Myst.
He emerged into the realm of the fairies from a cave...
Bringing a trace of Wonderland's madness with him.

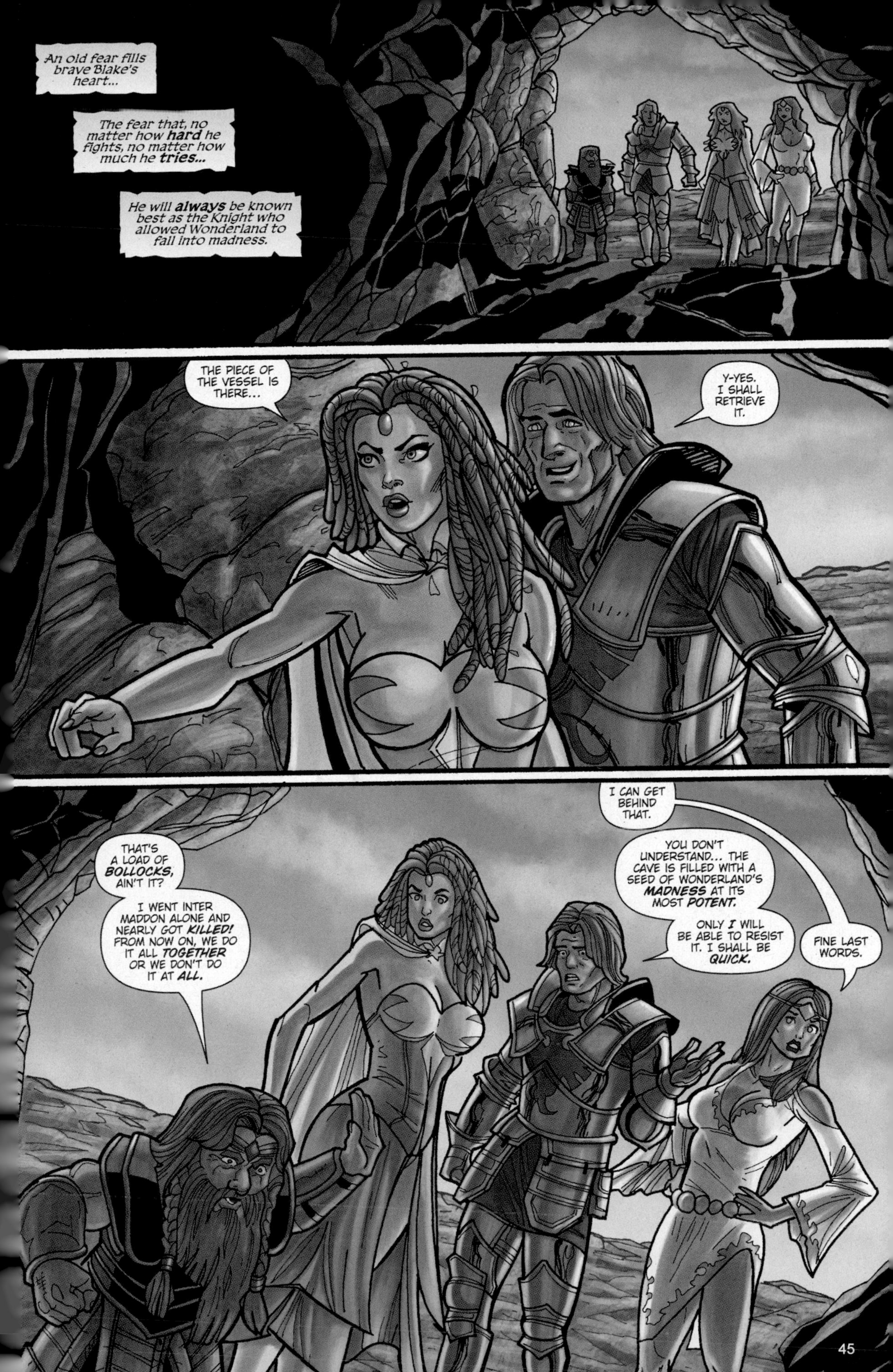
An old fear fills brave Blake's heart...
The fear that, no matter how **hard** he fights, no matter how much he **tries...**
He will **always** be known best as the Knight who allowed Wonderland to fall into madness.
THE PIECE OF THE VESSEL IS THERE...
Y-YES. I SHALL RETRIEVE IT.
THAT'S A LOAD OF **BOLLOCKS,** AIN'T IT?
I WENT INTER MADDON ALONE AND NEARLY GOT **KILLED!** FROM NOW ON, WE DO IT ALL **TOGETHER** OR WE DON'T DO IT AT **ALL.**
YOU DON'T UNDERSTAND... THE CAVE IS FILLED WITH A SEED OF WONDERLAND'S **MADNESS** AT ITS MOST **POTENT.**
ONLY **I** WILL BE ABLE TO RESIST IT. I SHALL BE **QUICK.**
I CAN GET BEHIND THAT.
FINE LAST WORDS.

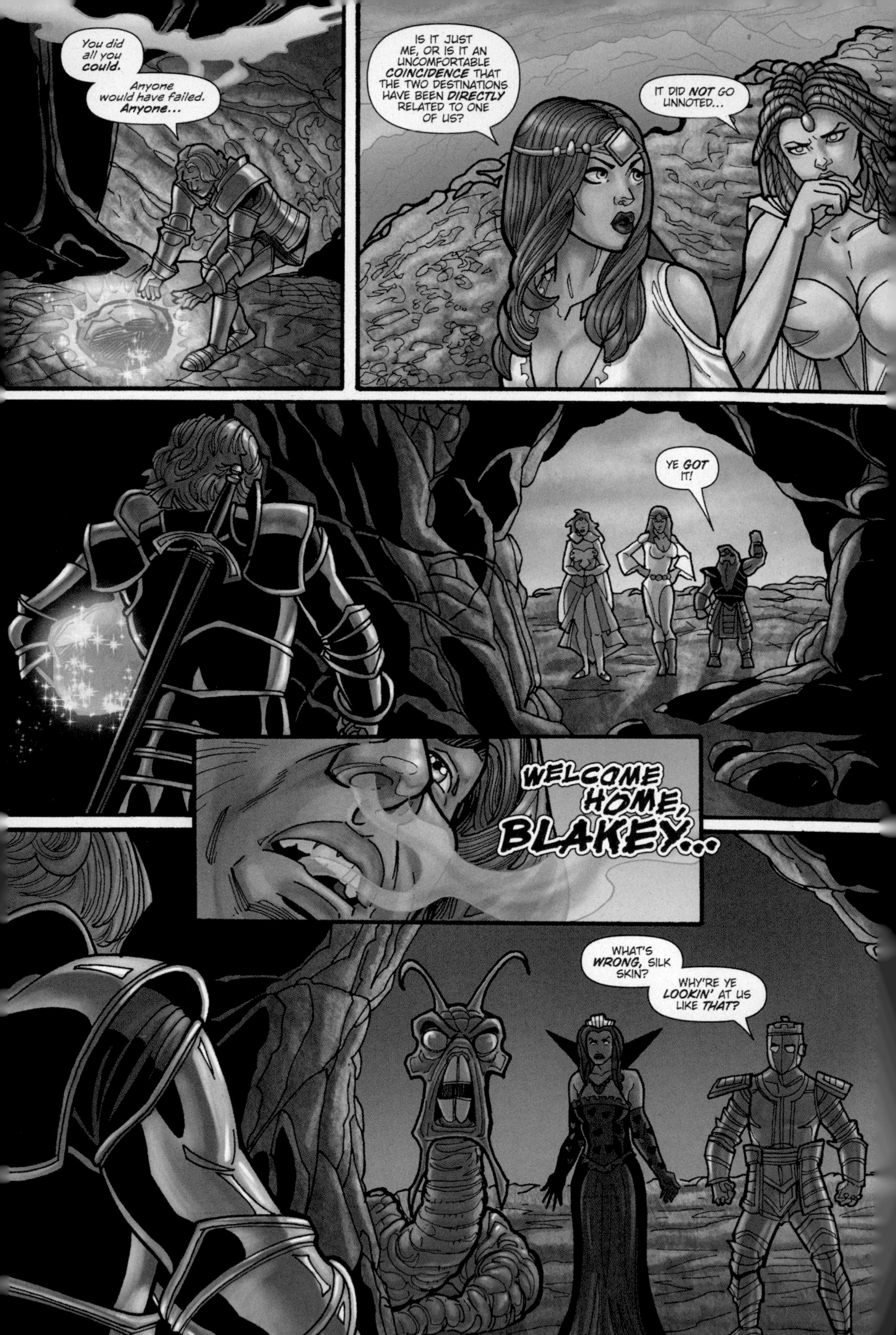
You did all you **could.**
Anyone would have failed. **Anyone...**
IS IT JUST ME, OR IS IT AN UNCOMFORTABLE **COINCIDENCE** THAT THE TWO DESTINATIONS HAVE BEEN **DIRECTLY** RELATED TO ONE OF US?
IT DID **NOT** GO UNNOTED...
YE **GOT** IT!
WELCOME HOME, BLAKEY...
WHAT'S **WRONG,** SILK SKIN?
WHY'RE YE **LOOKIN'** AT US LIKE **THAT?**

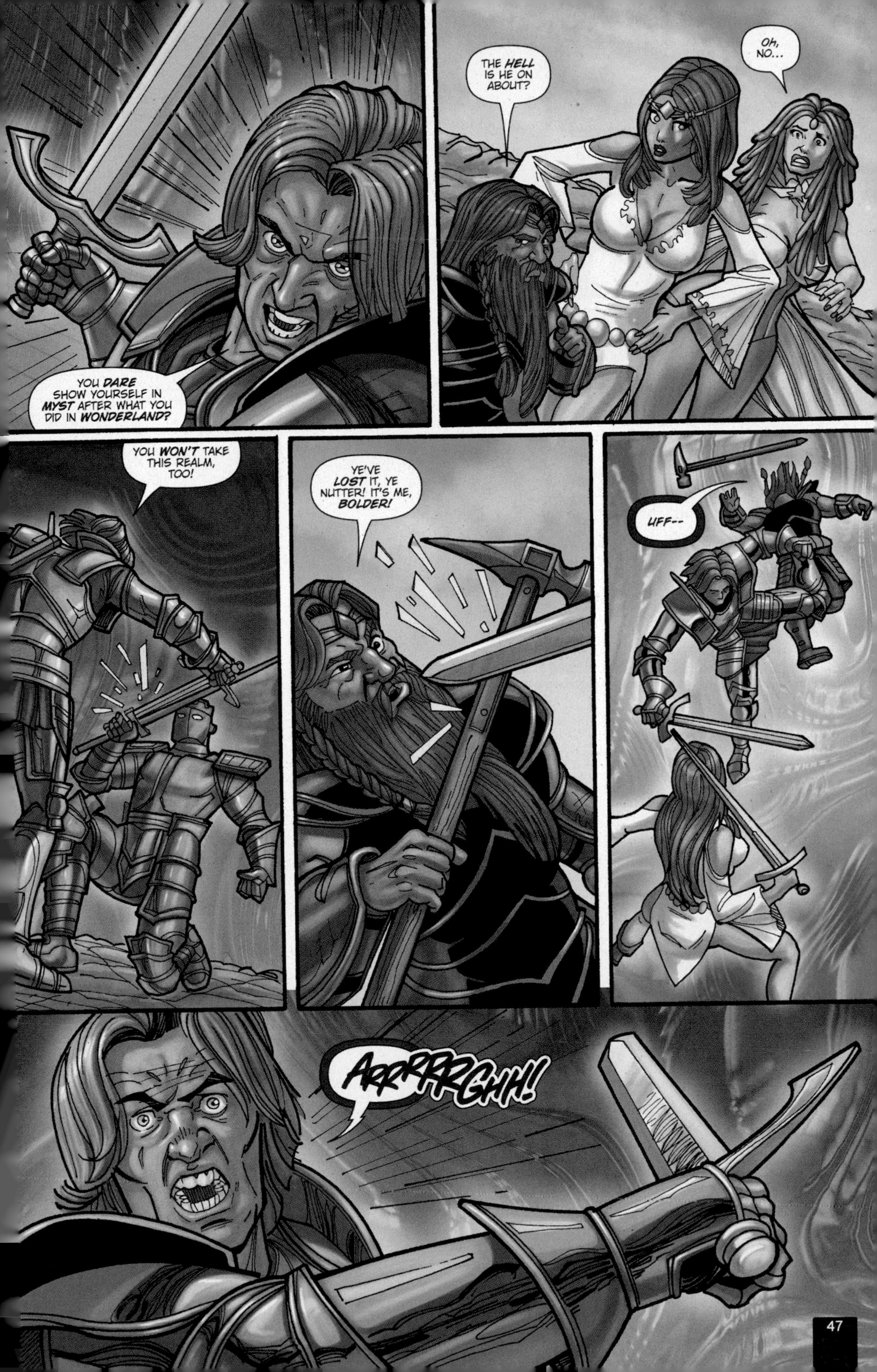

YOU DARE SHOW YOURSELF IN MYST AFTER WHAT YOU DID IN WONDERLAND?
THE HELL IS HE ON ABOUT?
OH, NO...
YOU WON'T TAKE THIS REALM, TOO!
YE'VE LOST IT, YE NUTTER! IT'S ME, BOLDER!
UFF--
ARRRRRGHH!

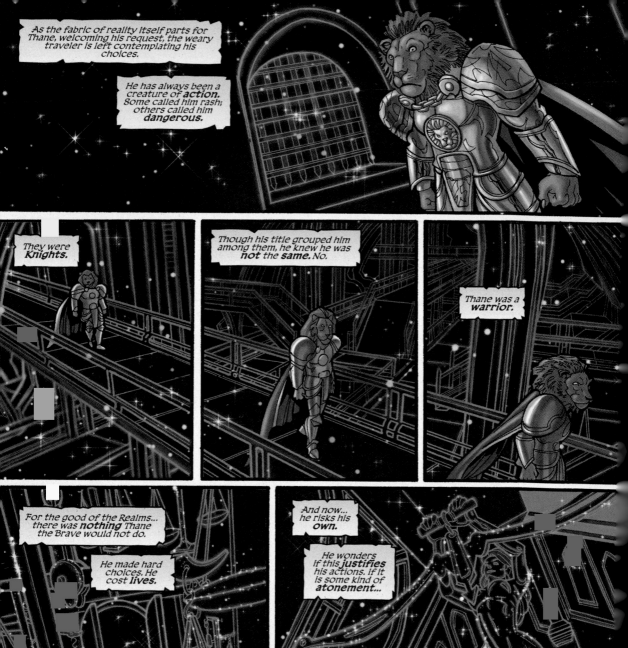

As the fabric of reality itself parts for Thane, welcoming his request, the weary traveler is left contemplating his choices.

He has always been a creature of **action**. Some called him rash; others called him **dangerous**.

They were **Knights**.

Though his title grouped him among them, he knew he was **not** the **same**. No.

Thane was a **warrior**.

For the good of the Realms... there was **nothing** Thane the Brave would not do.

He made hard choices. He cost **lives**.

And now... he risks his **own**.

He wonders if this **justifies** his actions. If it is some kind of **atonement**...

Or if he left the reach of **redemption** long ago.

REST YOUR GAZE **NOT** UPON THE ELDERS, LES YOUR SANITY B ED FREE FRO TS HOLDS

I COME BEFORE YOU WITH A REQUEST. MYST HAS BEEN INVADED BY THE DARK HORDE AND THE HIGH COUNCIL HAS BEEN SHATTERED. I BEG--

AGAIN YOU REMAIN CONFINED TO YOUR WORDS. WE *KNOW* YOUR WISHES.

THEN I *BEG* YOU. THE FATE OF THE REALMS HANGS IN THE *BALANCE*.

ALL HANGS IN THE BALANCE, THANE OF OZ. IF ONE REALM CRUMBLES, ANOTHER WILL *RISE*. IT IS THE *GREAT* BALANCE.

WE ARE *NOT* PROTECTORS. WE DO ONLY WHAT WE *MUST*. WE ARE THE FABRIC THAT BINDS THE THREADS OF THE BALAN--

YES, YES. BALANCE. WITH DUE RESPECT, ELDERS, WHAT YOU CALL BALANCE, I CALL *HOLOCAUST*.

YOU USE THE WORD, YET ITS MEANING ESCAPES YOU.

FOR THE ELDERS TO GIVE...

YOU MUST FIRST PROVE YOURSELF WITH AN OFFERING.

THE HEAD OF OUR CHAMPION...

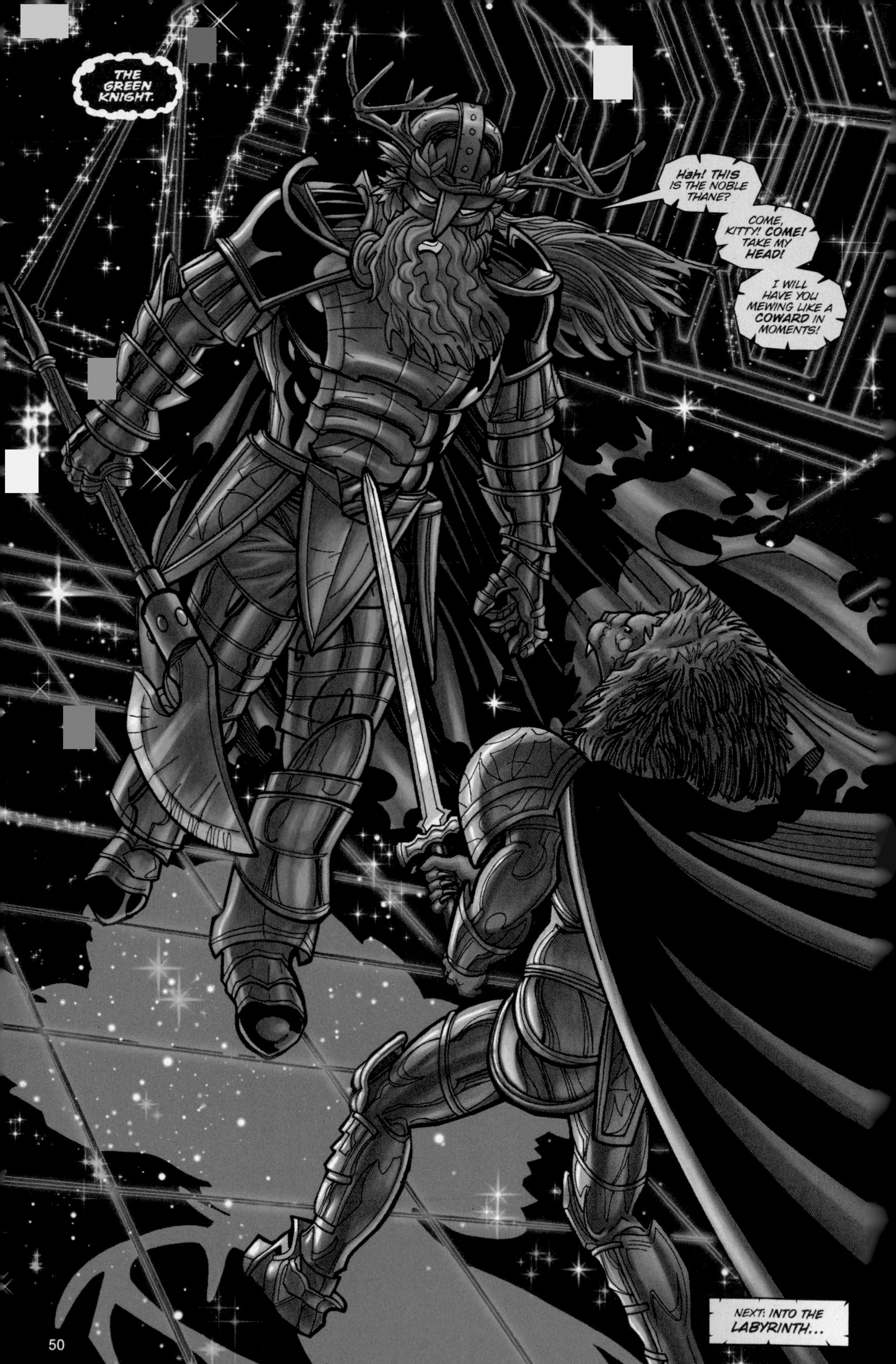
THE GREEN KNIGHT.
Hah! THIS IS THE NOBLE THANE?
COME, KITTY! COME! TAKE MY HEAD!
I WILL HAVE YOU MEWING LIKE A COWARD IN MOMENTS!
NEXT: INTO THE LABYRINTH...

Grimm Fairy Tales presents:

QUEST

AGE OF DARKNESS

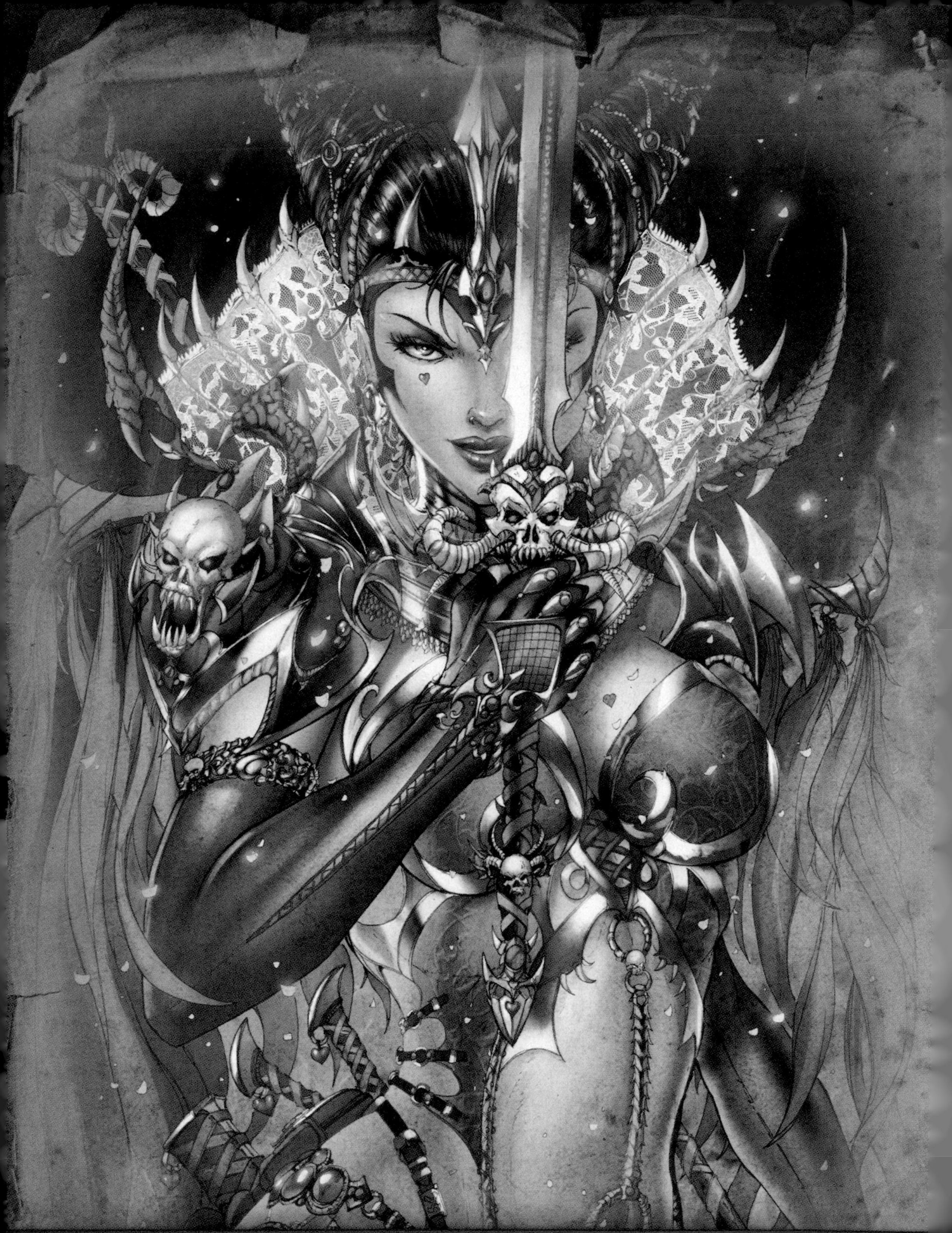

Into the Labyrinth

WRITER PAT SHAND
ARTWORK SERGIO OSUNA
COLORS FRANCESCA ZAMBON
LETTERS JIM CAMPBELL

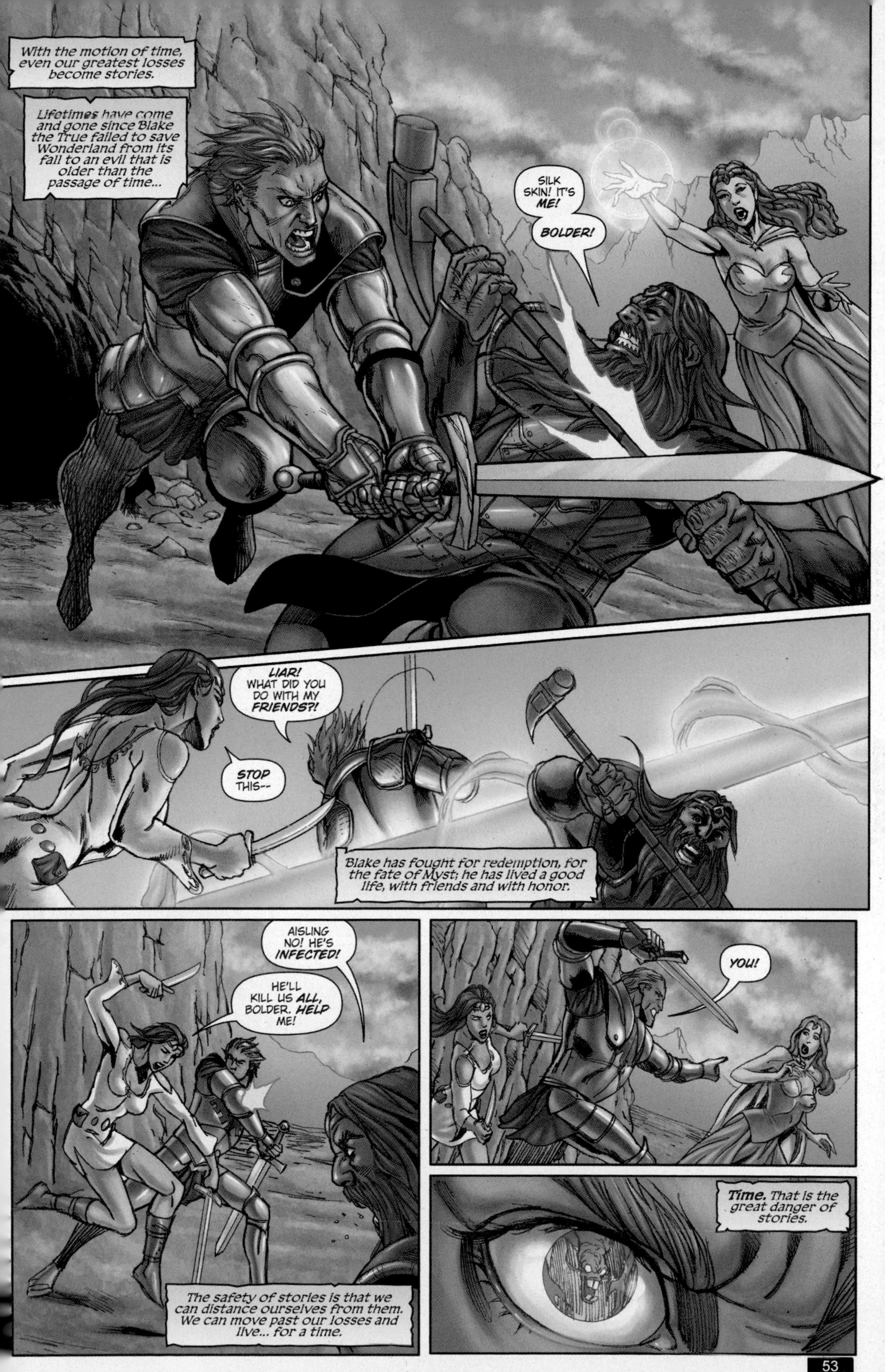
With the motion of time, even our greatest losses become stories.
Lifetimes have come and gone since Blake the True failed to save Wonderland from its fall to an evil that is older than the passage of time...
SILK SKIN! IT'S ME!
BOLDER!
LIAR! WHAT DID YOU DO WITH MY FRIENDS?!
STOP THIS--
Blake has fought for redemption, for the fate of Myst; he has lived a good life, with friends and with honor.
AISLING NO! HE'S INFECTED!
HE'LL KILL US ALL, BOLDER. HELP ME!
The safety of stories is that we can distance ourselves from them. We can move past our losses and live... for a time.
YOU!
Time. That is the great danger of stories.

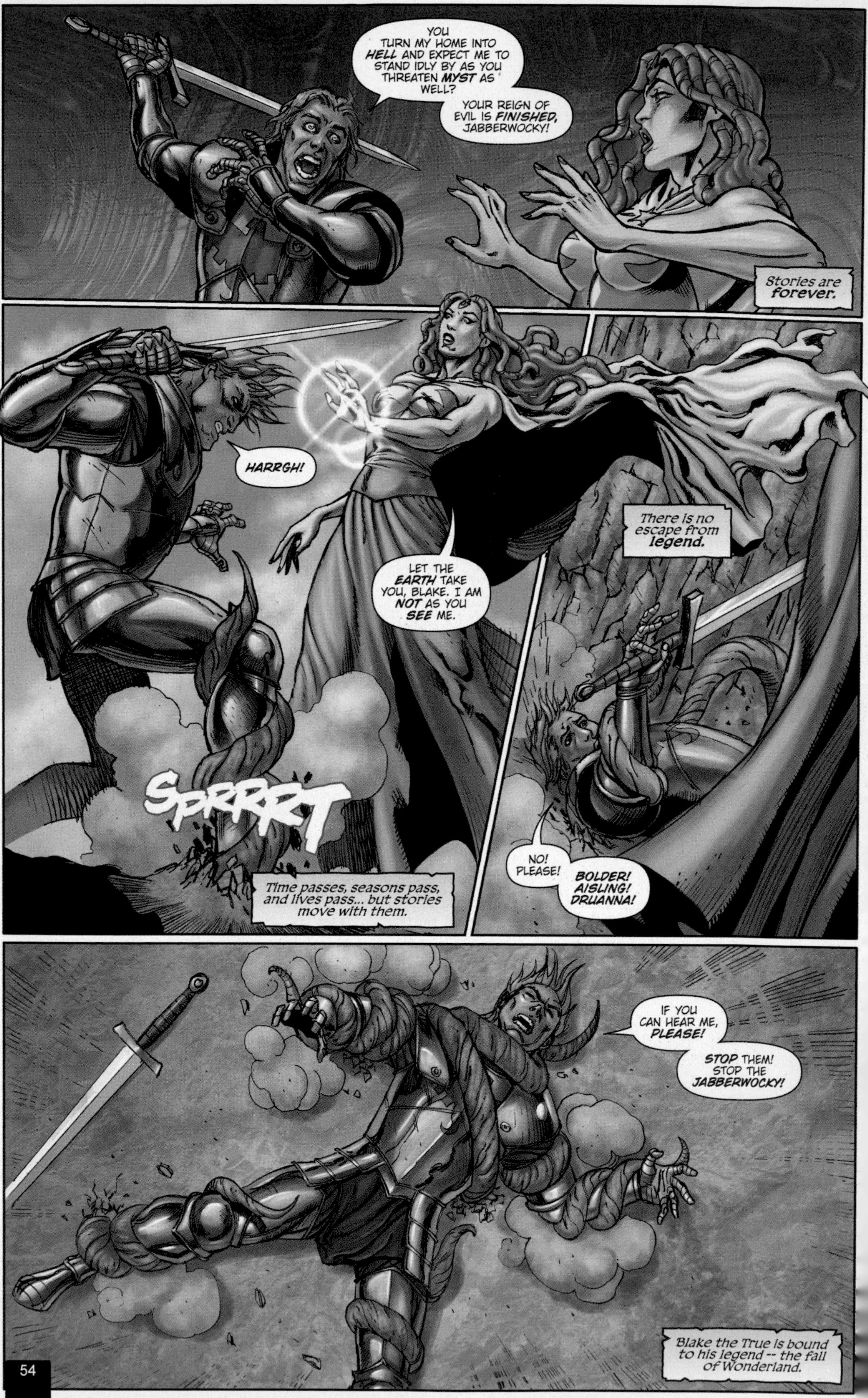
YOU TURN MY HOME INTO HELL AND EXPECT ME TO STAND IDLY BY AS YOU THREATEN MYST AS WELL?
YOUR REIGN OF EVIL IS FINISHED, JABBERWOCKY!
Stories are forever.
HARRGH!
LET THE EARTH TAKE YOU, BLAKE. I AM NOT AS YOU SEE ME.
SPRRRT
Time passes, seasons pass, and lives pass... but stories move with them.
There is no escape from legend.
NO! PLEASE!
BOLDER! AISLING! DRUANNA!
IF YOU CAN HEAR ME, PLEASE!
STOP THEM! STOP THE JABBERWOCKY!
Blake the True is bound to his legend -- the fall of Wonderland.

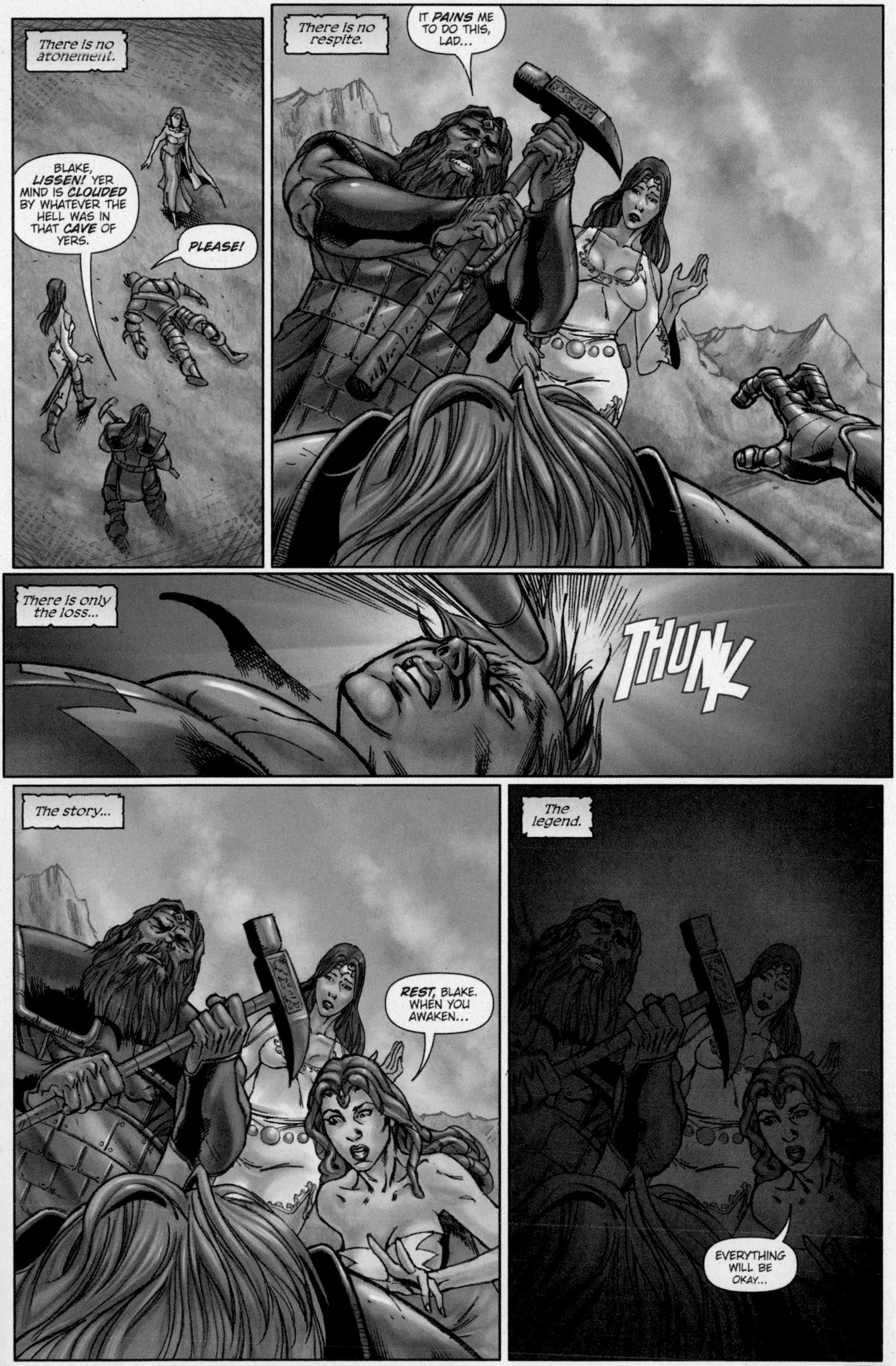
There is no atonement.
BLAKE, LISSEN! YER MIND IS CLOUDED BY WHATEVER THE HELL WAS IN THAT CAVE OF YERS.
PLEASE!
There is no respite.
IT PAINS ME TO DO THIS, LAD...
There is only the loss...
THUNK
The story...
REST, BLAKE. WHEN YOU AWAKEN...
The legend.
EVERYTHING WILL BE OKAY...

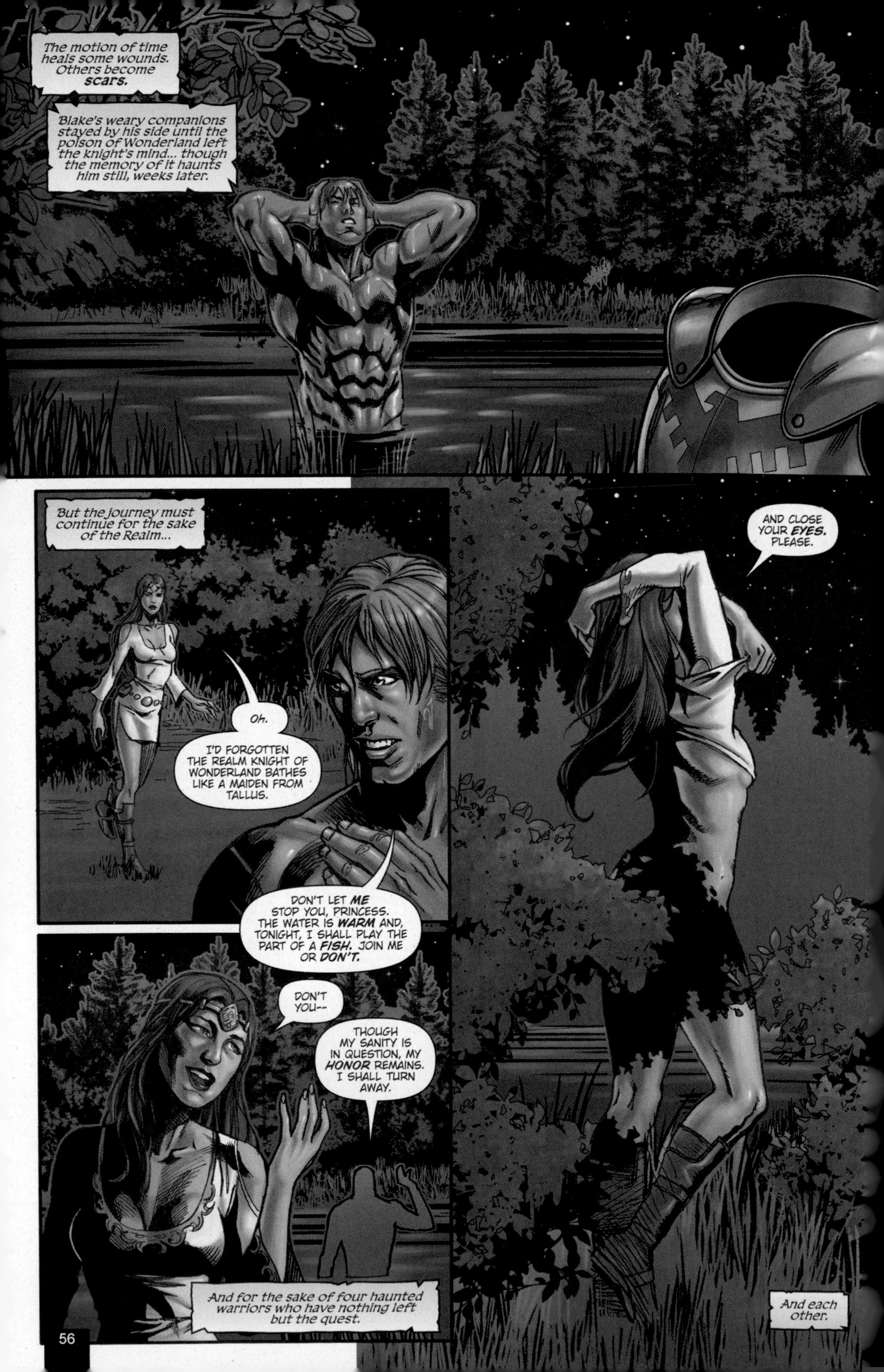
The motion of time heals some wounds. Others become **scars.**
Blake's weary companions stayed by his side until the poison of Wonderland left the knight's mind... though the memory of it haunts him still, weeks later.
But the journey must continue for the sake of the Realm...
Oh.
I'D FORGOTTEN THE REALM KNIGHT OF WONDERLAND BATHES LIKE A MAIDEN FROM TALLUS.
DON'T LET **ME** STOP YOU, PRINCESS. THE WATER IS **WARM** AND, TONIGHT, I SHALL PLAY THE PART OF A **FISH.** JOIN ME OR **DON'T.**
DON'T YOU--
THOUGH MY SANITY IS IN QUESTION, MY **HONOR** REMAINS. I SHALL TURN AWAY.
And for the sake of four haunted warriors who have nothing left but the quest.
AND CLOSE YOUR **EYES.** PLEASE.
And each other.

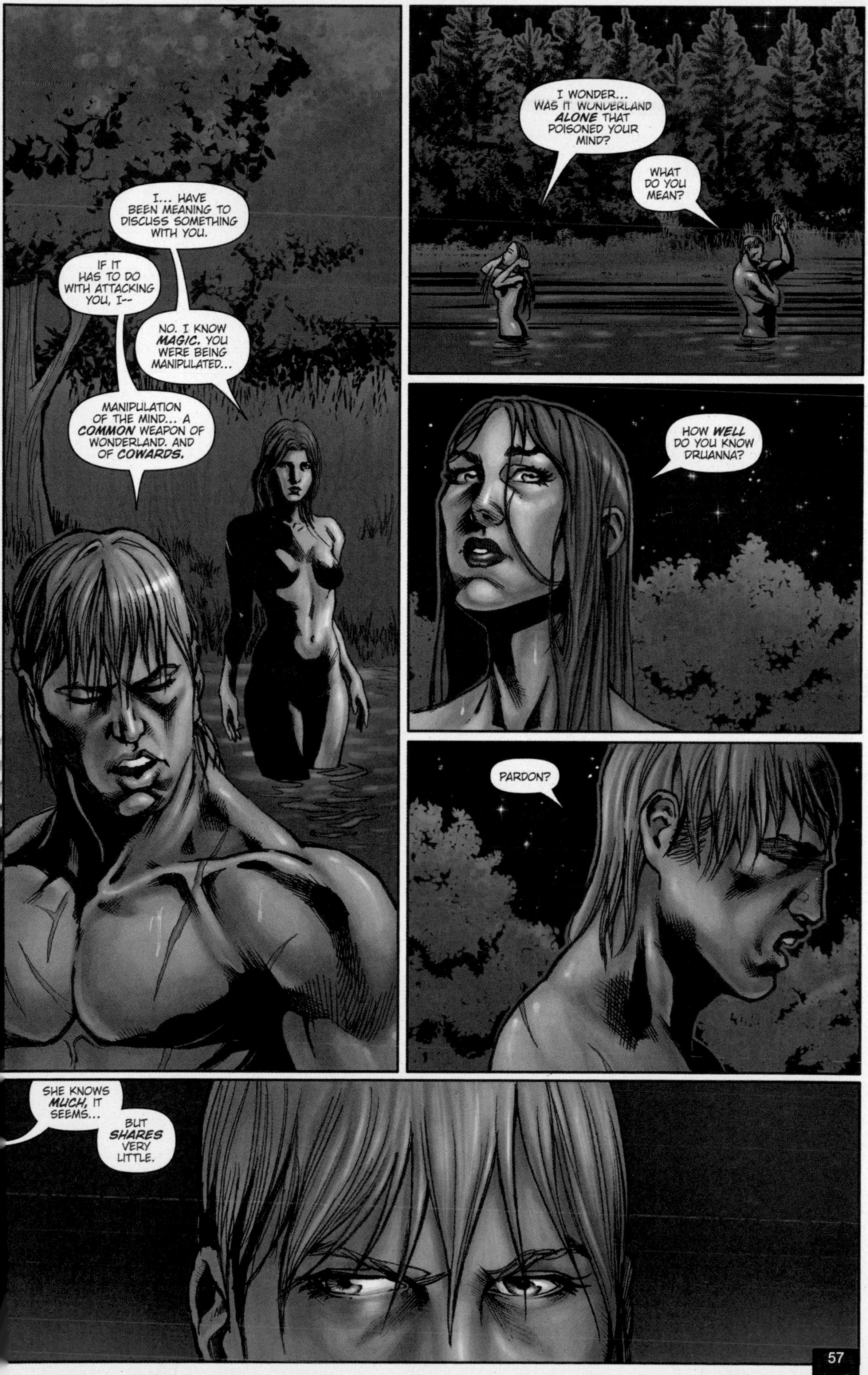
I... HAVE BEEN MEANING TO DISCUSS SOMETHING WITH YOU.
IF IT HAS TO DO WITH ATTACKING YOU, I--
NO. I KNOW MAGIC. YOU WERE BEING MANIPULATED...
MANIPULATION OF THE MIND... A COMMON WEAPON OF WONDERLAND. AND OF COWARDS.
I WONDER... WAS IT WONDERLAND ALONE THAT POISONED YOUR MIND?
WHAT DO YOU MEAN?
HOW WELL DO YOU KNOW DRUANNA?
PARDON?
SHE KNOWS MUCH, IT SEEMS...
BUT SHARES VERY LITTLE.

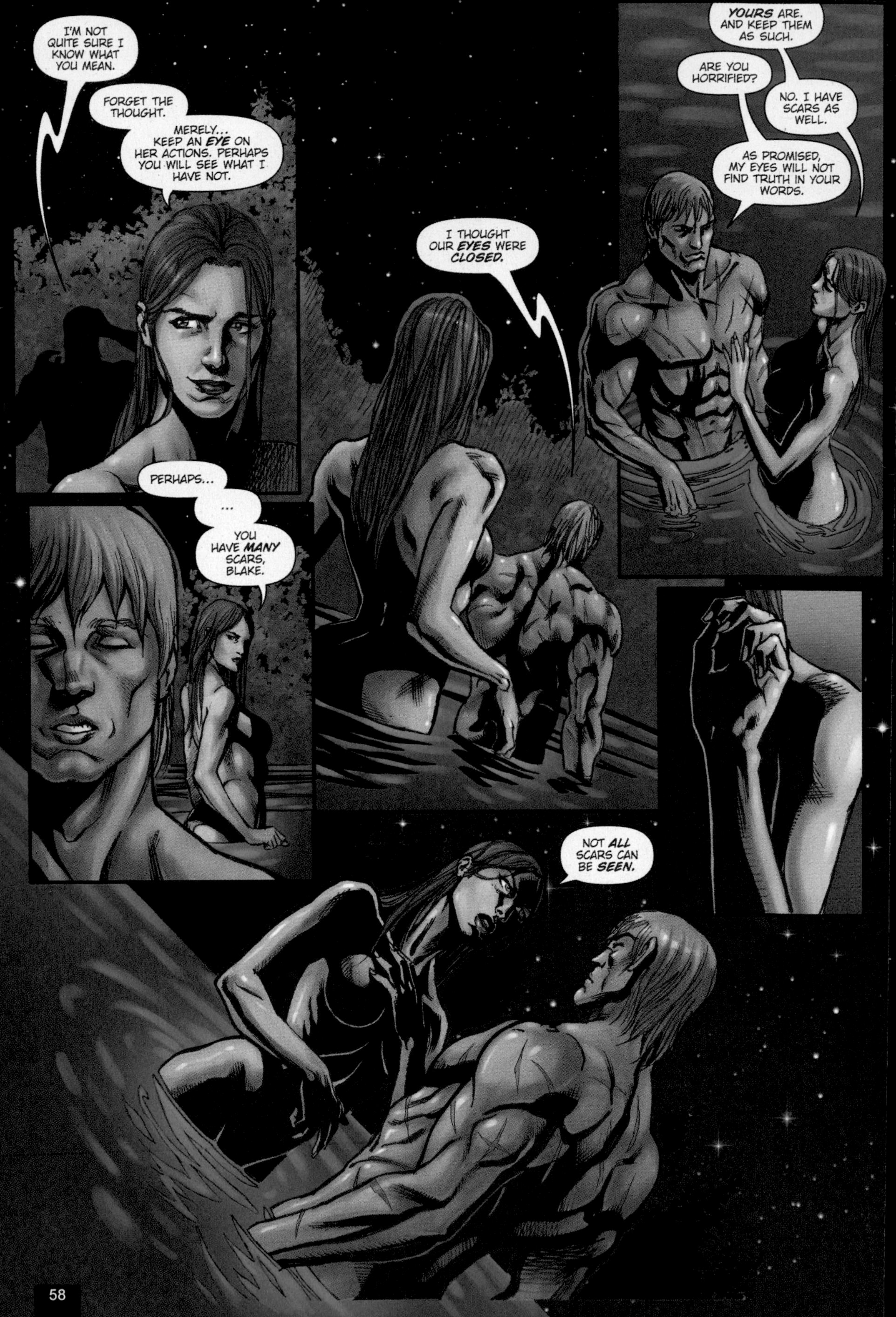
I'M NOT QUITE SURE I KNOW WHAT YOU MEAN.
FORGET THE THOUGHT.
MERELY... KEEP AN EYE ON HER ACTIONS. PERHAPS YOU WILL SEE WHAT I HAVE NOT.
PERHAPS...
...
YOU HAVE MANY SCARS, BLAKE.
I THOUGHT OUR EYES WERE CLOSED.
YOURS ARE. AND KEEP THEM AS SUCH.
ARE YOU HORRIFIED?
NO. I HAVE SCARS AS WELL.
AS PROMISED, MY EYES WILL NOT FIND TRUTH IN YOUR WORDS.
NOT ALL SCARS CAN BE SEEN.

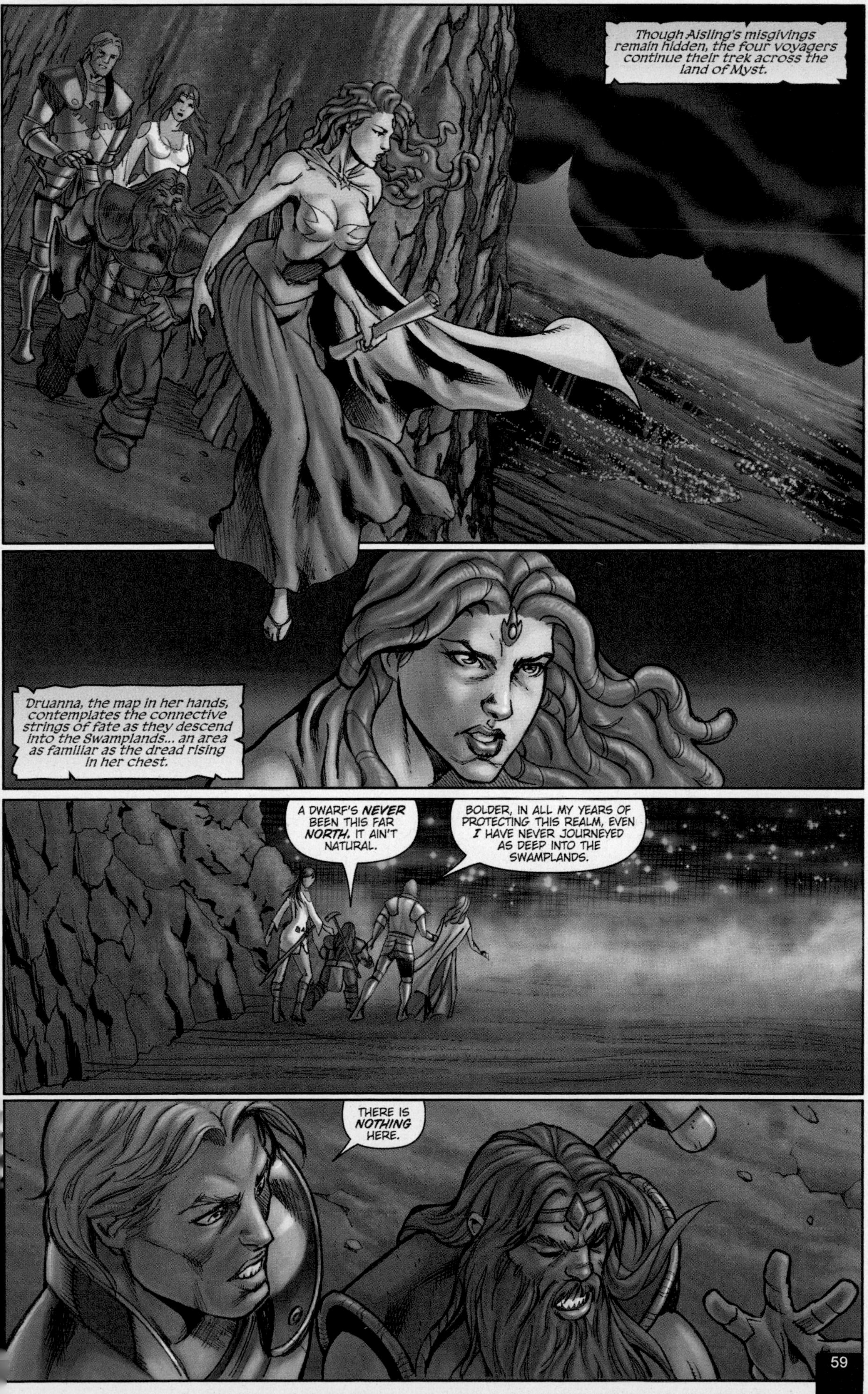
Though Aisling's misgivings remain hidden, the four voyagers continue their trek across the land of Myst.
Druanna, the map in her hands, contemplates the connective strings of fate as they descend into the Swamplands... an area as familiar as the dread rising in her chest.
A DWARF'S NEVER BEEN THIS FAR NORTH. IT AIN'T NATURAL.
BOLDER, IN ALL MY YEARS OF PROTECTING THIS REALM, EVEN I HAVE NEVER JOURNEYED AS DEEP INTO THE SWAMPLANDS.
THERE IS NOTHING HERE.

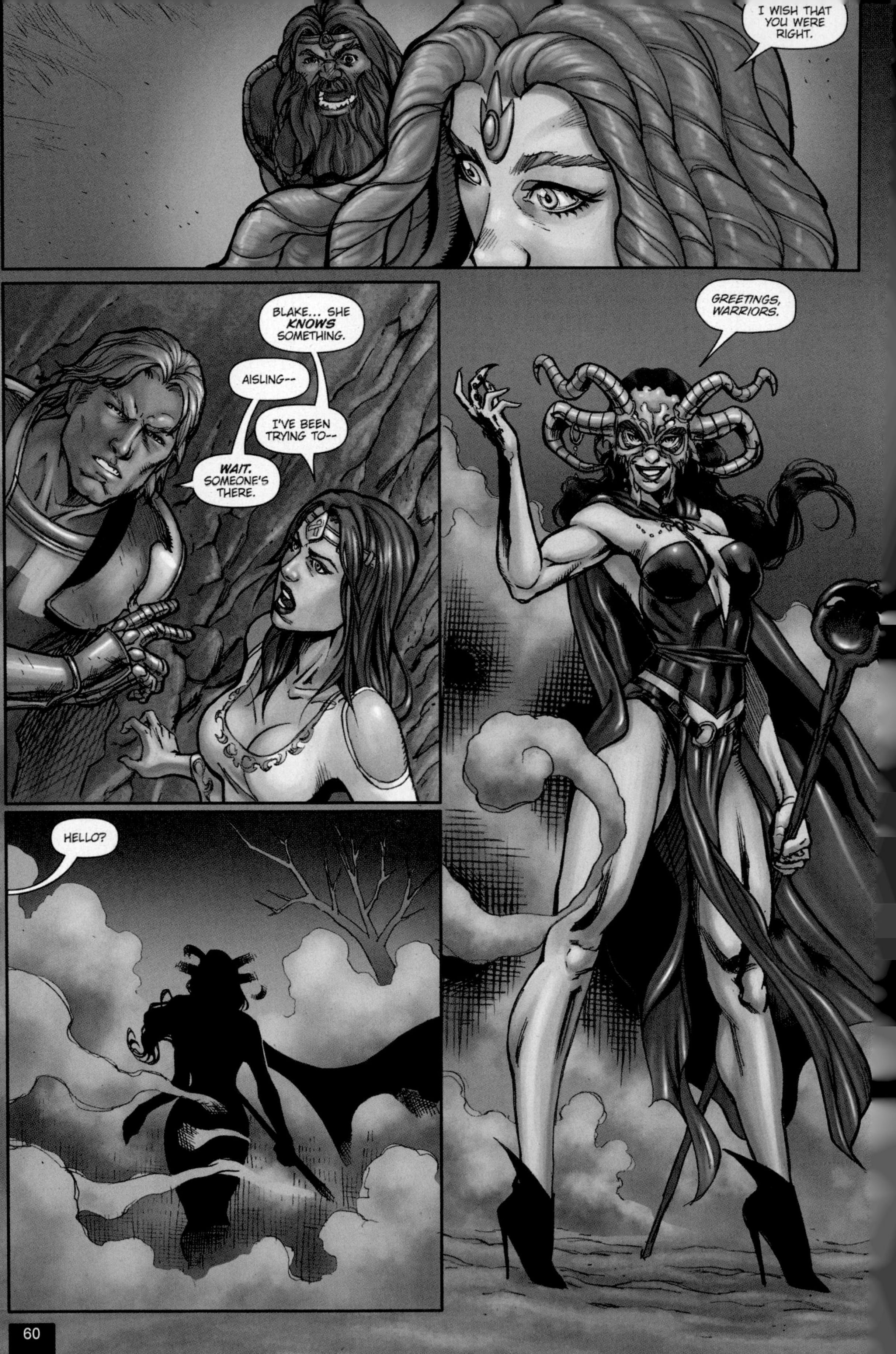
I WISH THAT YOU WERE RIGHT.
BLAKE... SHE **KNOWS** SOMETHING.
AISLING--
I'VE BEEN TRYING TO--
WAIT. SOMEONE'S THERE.
GREETINGS, WARRIORS.
HELLO?

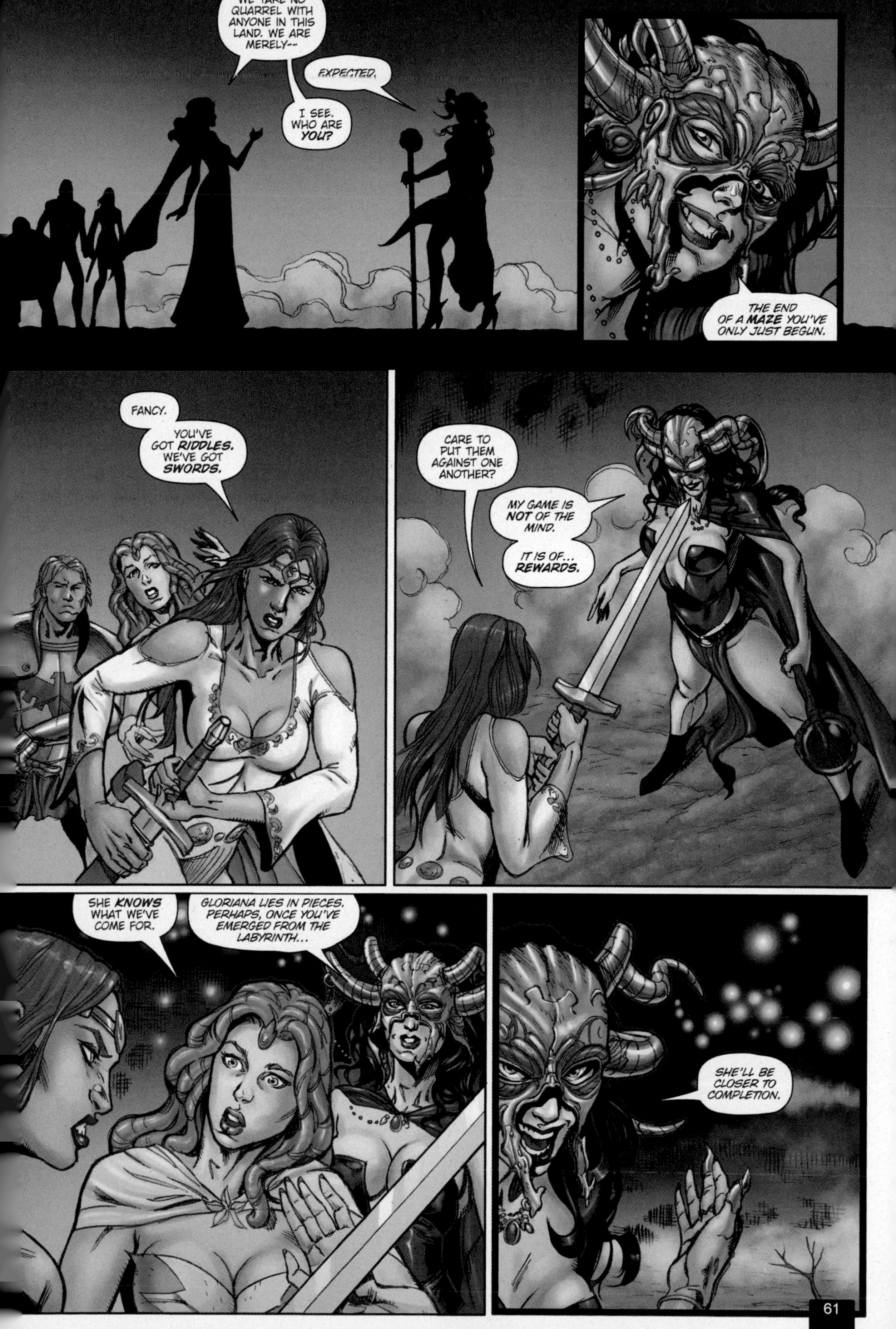
WE TAKE NO QUARREL WITH ANYONE IN THIS LAND. WE ARE MERELY--
EXPECTED.
I SEE. WHO ARE YOU?
THE END OF A MAZE YOU'VE ONLY JUST BEGUN.
FANCY.
YOU'VE GOT RIDDLES. WE'VE GOT SWORDS.
CARE TO PUT THEM AGAINST ONE ANOTHER?
MY GAME IS NOT OF THE MIND.
IT IS OF... REWARDS.
SHE KNOWS WHAT WE'VE COME FOR.
GLORIANA LIES IN PIECES. PERHAPS, ONCE YOU'VE EMERGED FROM THE LABYRINTH...
SHE'LL BE CLOSER TO COMPLETION.

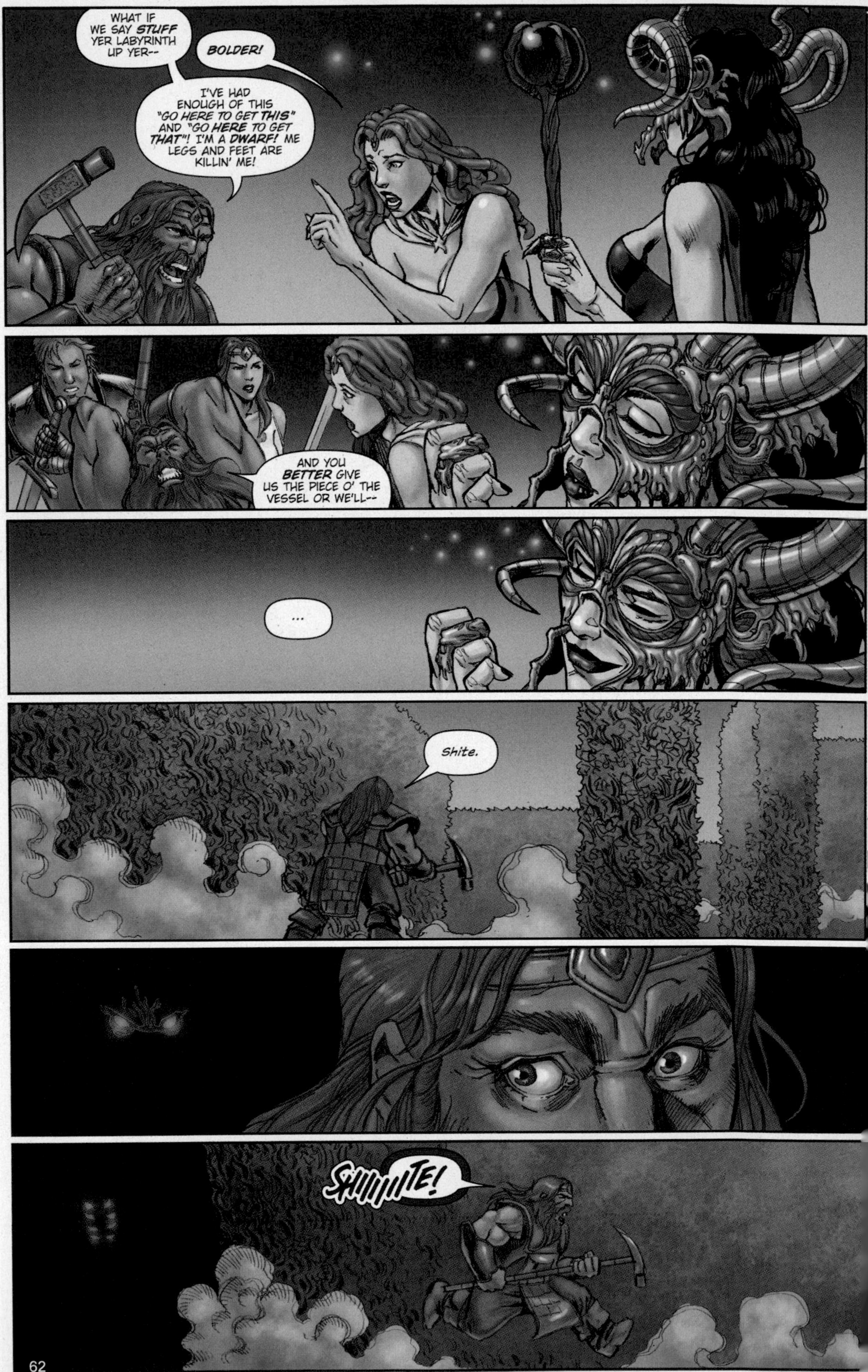
WHAT IF WE SAY STUFF YER LABYRINTH UP YER--
BOLDER!
I'VE HAD ENOUGH OF THIS "GO HERE TO GET THIS" AND "GO HERE TO GET THAT"! I'M A DWARF! ME LEGS AND FEET ARE KILLIN' ME!
AND YOU BETTER GIVE US THE PIECE O' THE VESSEL OR WE'LL--
...
Shite.
SHIIIIIITE!

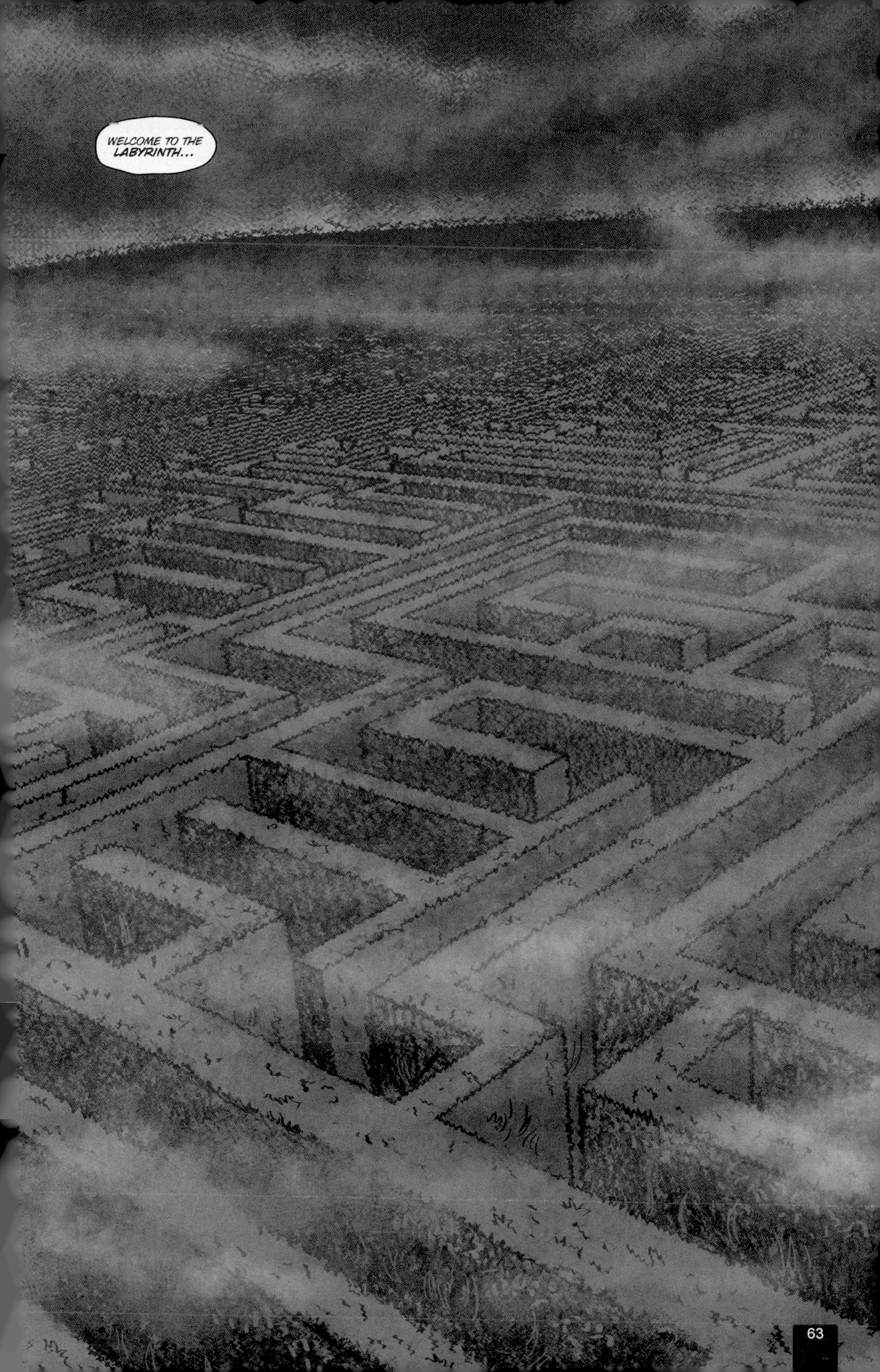
WELCOME TO THE LABYRINTH...

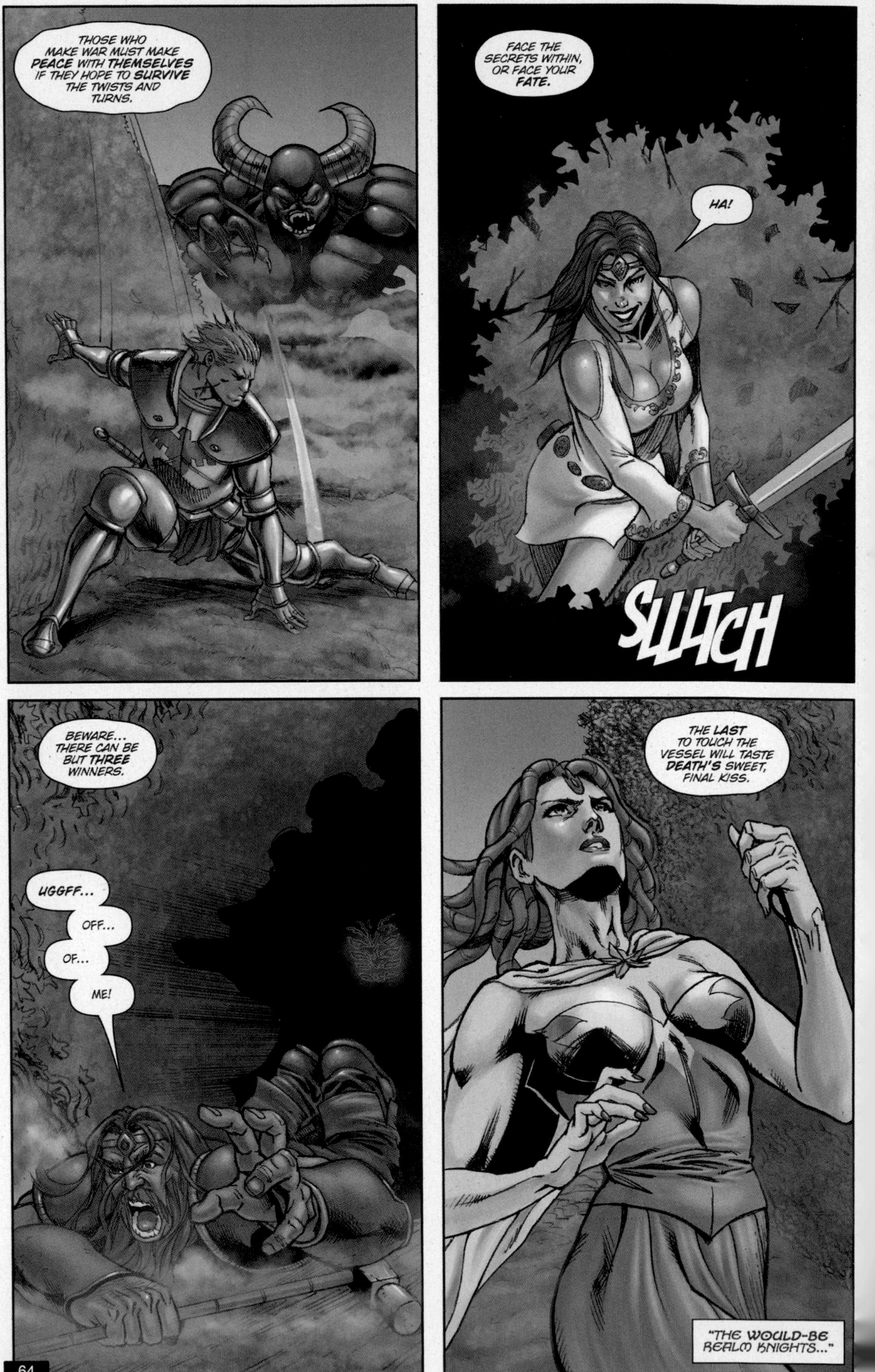
THOSE WHO MAKE WAR MUST MAKE PEACE WITH THEMSELVES IF THEY HOPE TO SURVIVE THE TWISTS AND TURNS.
FACE THE SECRETS WITHIN, OR FACE YOUR FATE.
HA!
SLLLTCH
BEWARE... THERE CAN BE BUT THREE WINNERS.
UGGFF...
OFF...
OF...
ME!
THE LAST TO TOUCH THE VESSEL WILL TASTE DEATH'S SWEET, FINAL KISS.
"THE WOULD-BE REALM KNIGHTS..."

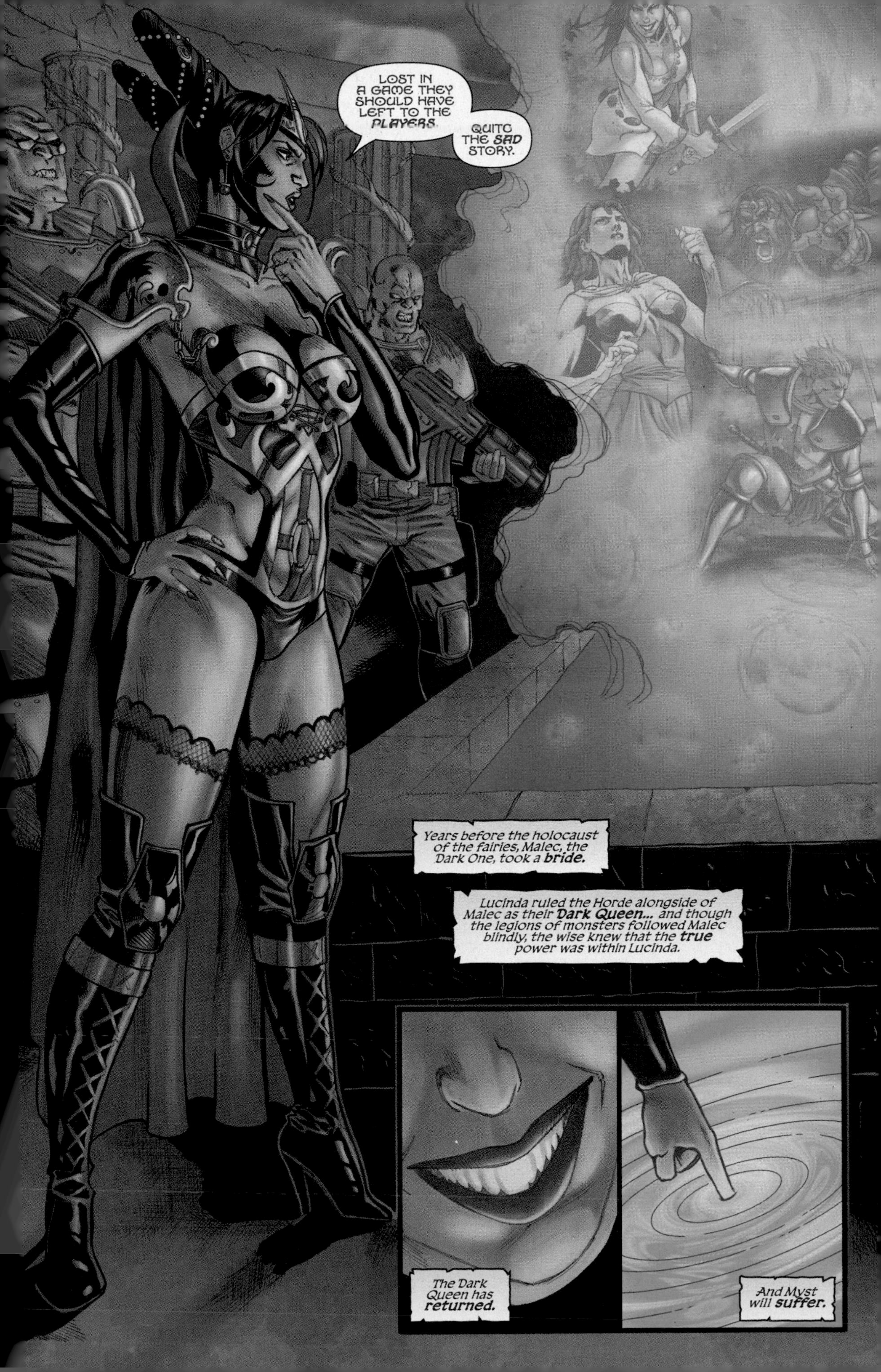
LOST IN A GAME THEY SHOULD HAVE LEFT TO THE *PLAYERS*.
QUITE THE *SAD* STORY.
Years before the holocaust of the fairies, Malec, the Dark One, took a ***bride.***
Lucinda ruled the Horde alongside of Malec as their ***Dark Queen...*** *and though the legions of monsters followed Malec blindly, the wise knew that the* ***true*** *power was within Lucinda.*
The Dark Queen has ***returned.***
And Myst will ***suffer.***

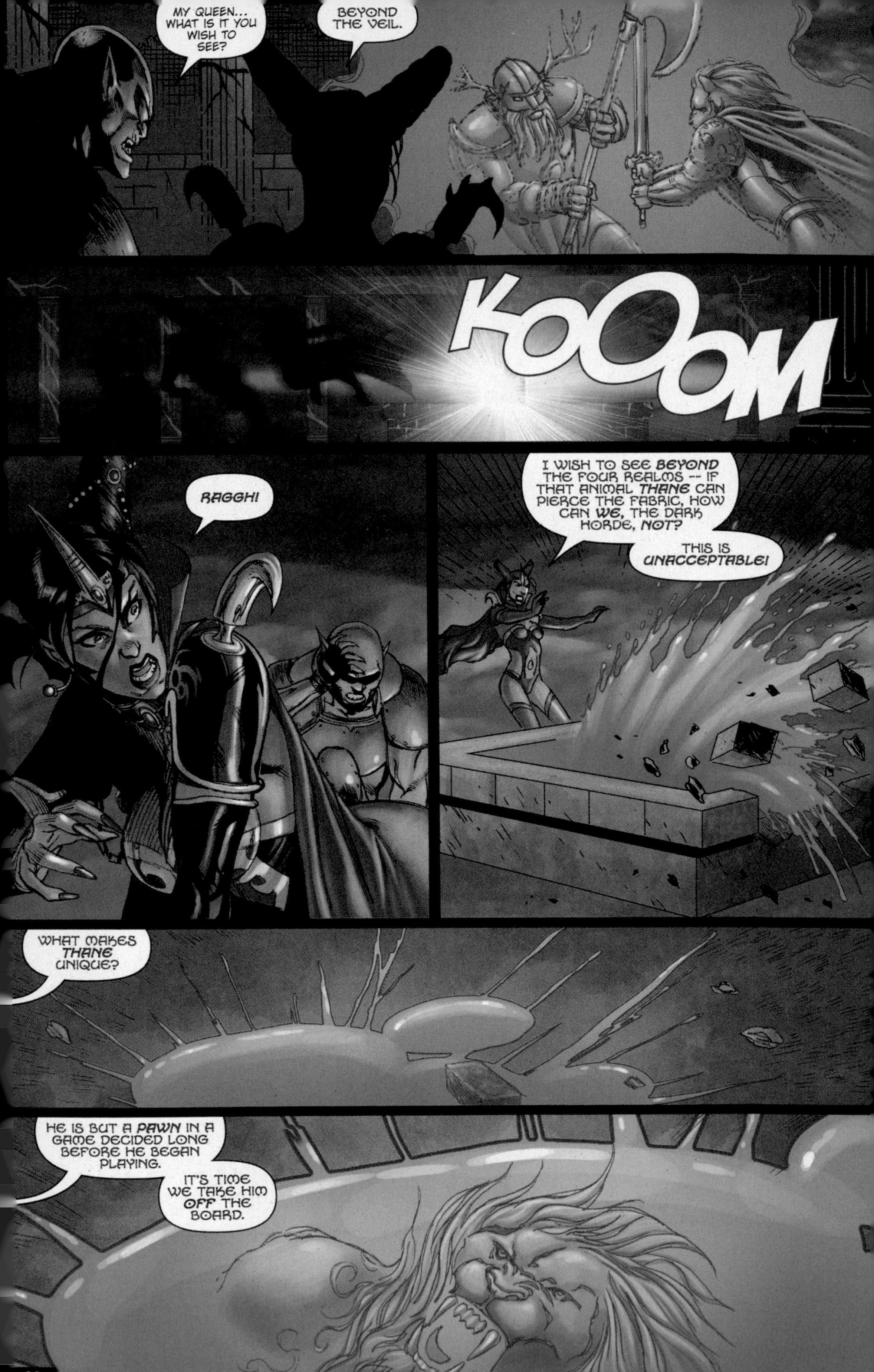
MY QUEEN... WHAT IS IT YOU WISH TO SEE?
BEYOND THE VEIL.
KOOOOM
RAGGH!
I WISH TO SEE BEYOND THE FOUR REALMS -- IF THAT ANIMAL THANE CAN PIERCE THE FABRIC, HOW CAN WE, THE DARK HORDE, NOT?
THIS IS UNACCEPTABLE!
WHAT MAKES THANE UNIQUE?
HE IS BUT A PAWN IN A GAME DECIDED LONG BEFORE HE BEGAN PLAYING.
IT'S TIME WE TAKE HIM OFF THE BOARD.

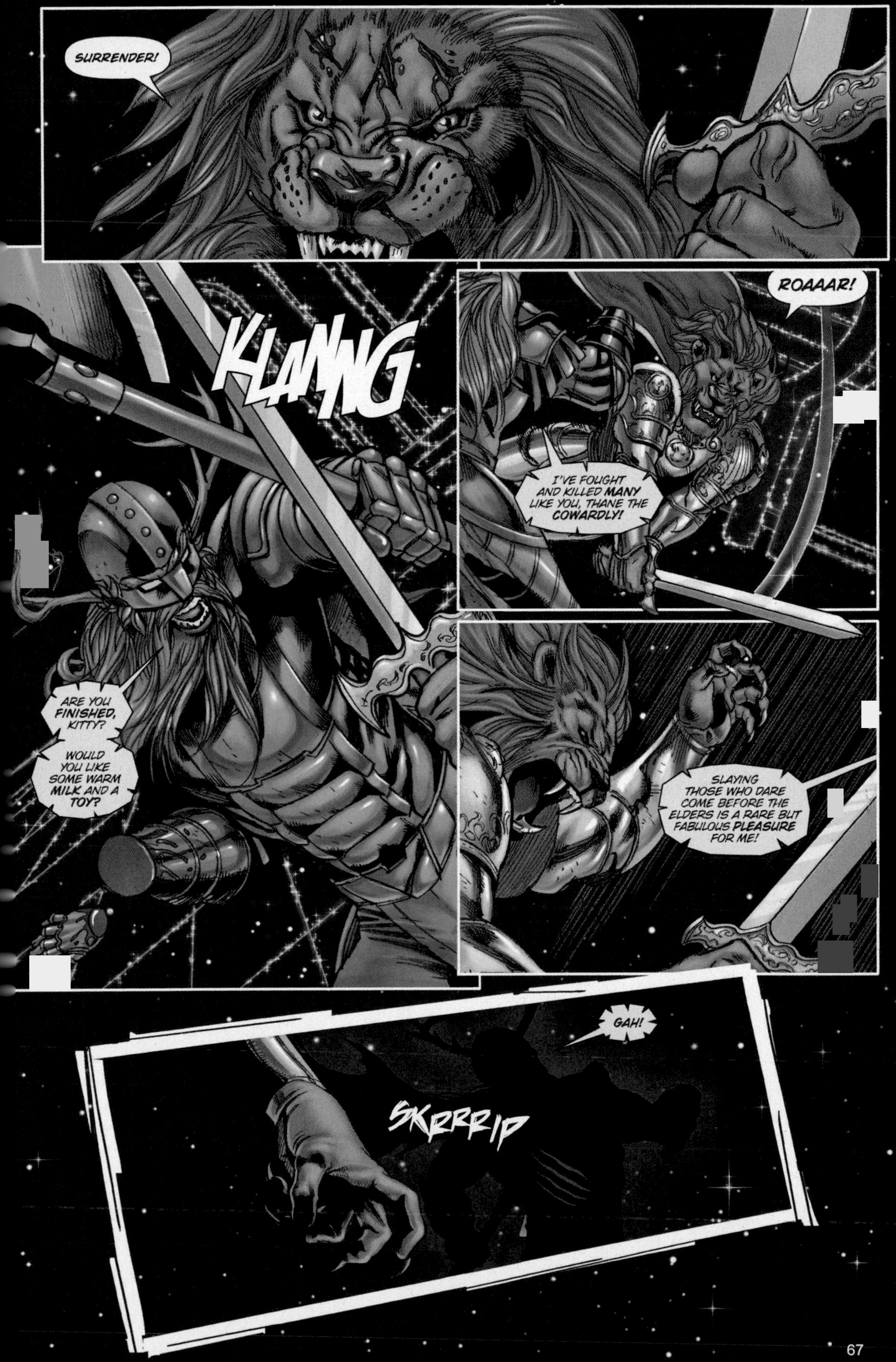
SURRENDER!
KLANNG
ARE YOU FINISHED, KITTY?
WOULD YOU LIKE SOME WARM MILK AND A TOY?
ROAAAR!
I'VE FOUGHT AND KILLED MANY LIKE YOU, THANE THE COWARDLY!
SLAYING THOSE WHO DARE COME BEFORE THE ELDERS IS A RARE BUT FABULOUS PLEASURE FOR ME!
GAH!
SKRRRIP

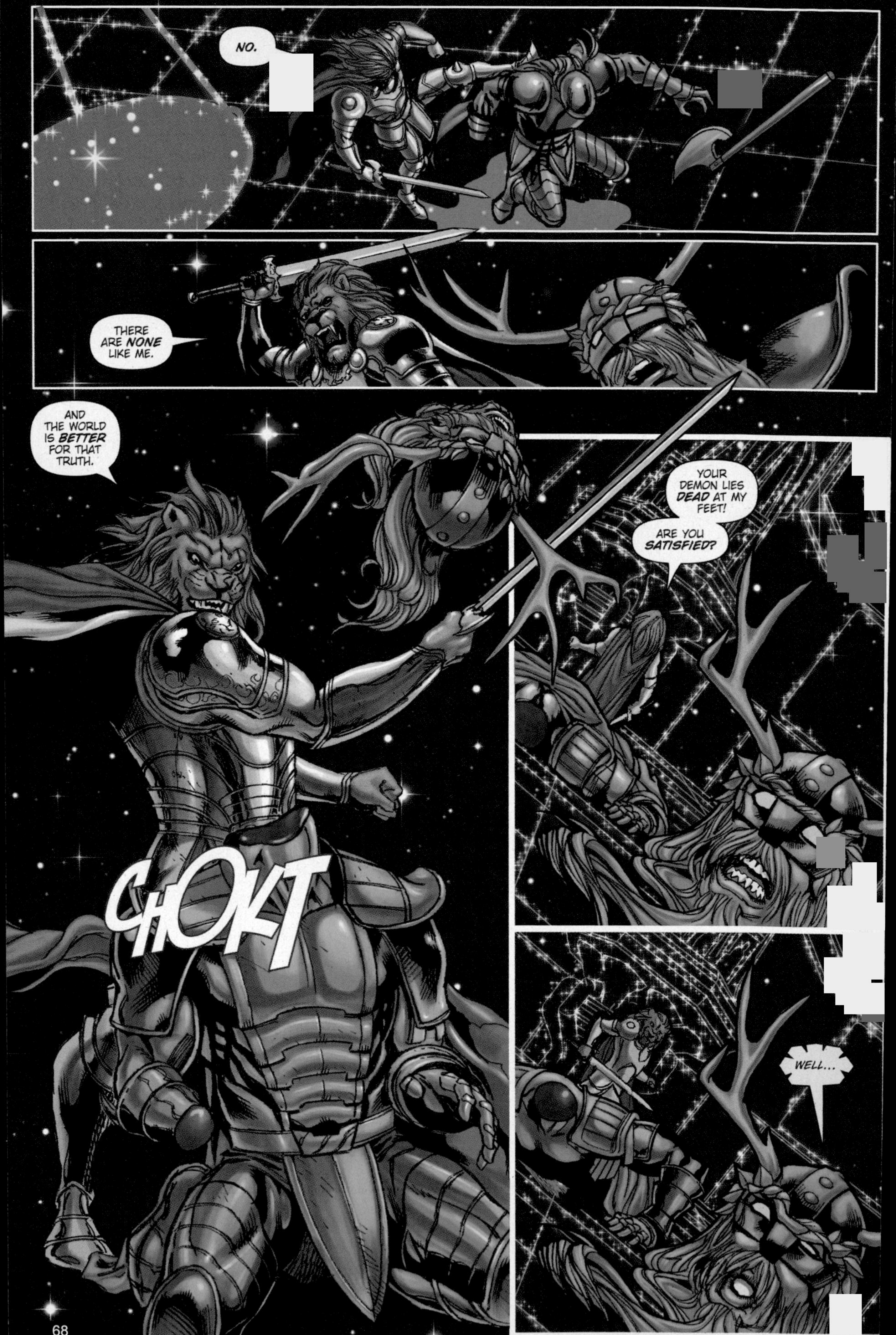
NO.
THERE ARE NONE LIKE ME.
AND THE WORLD IS BETTER FOR THAT TRUTH.
CHOKT
YOUR DEMON LIES DEAD AT MY FEET!
ARE YOU SATISFIED?
WELL...

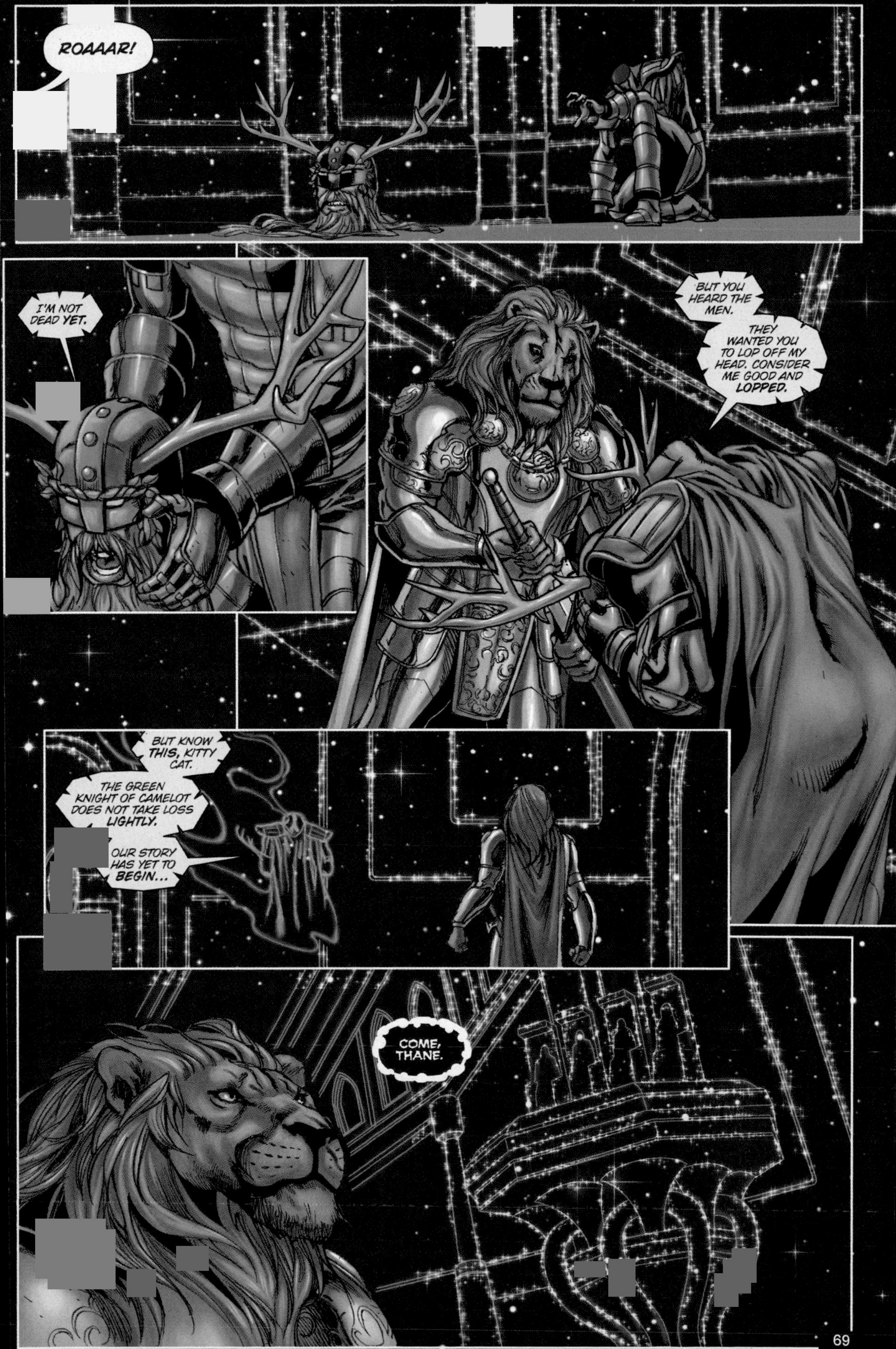
ROAAAR!
I'M NOT DEAD YET.
BUT YOU HEARD THE MEN.
THEY WANTED YOU TO LOP OFF MY HEAD. CONSIDER ME GOOD AND LOPPED.
BUT KNOW THIS, KITTY CAT.
THE GREEN KNIGHT OF CAMELOT DOES NOT TAKE LOSS LIGHTLY.
OUR STORY HAS YET TO BEGIN...
COME, THANE.

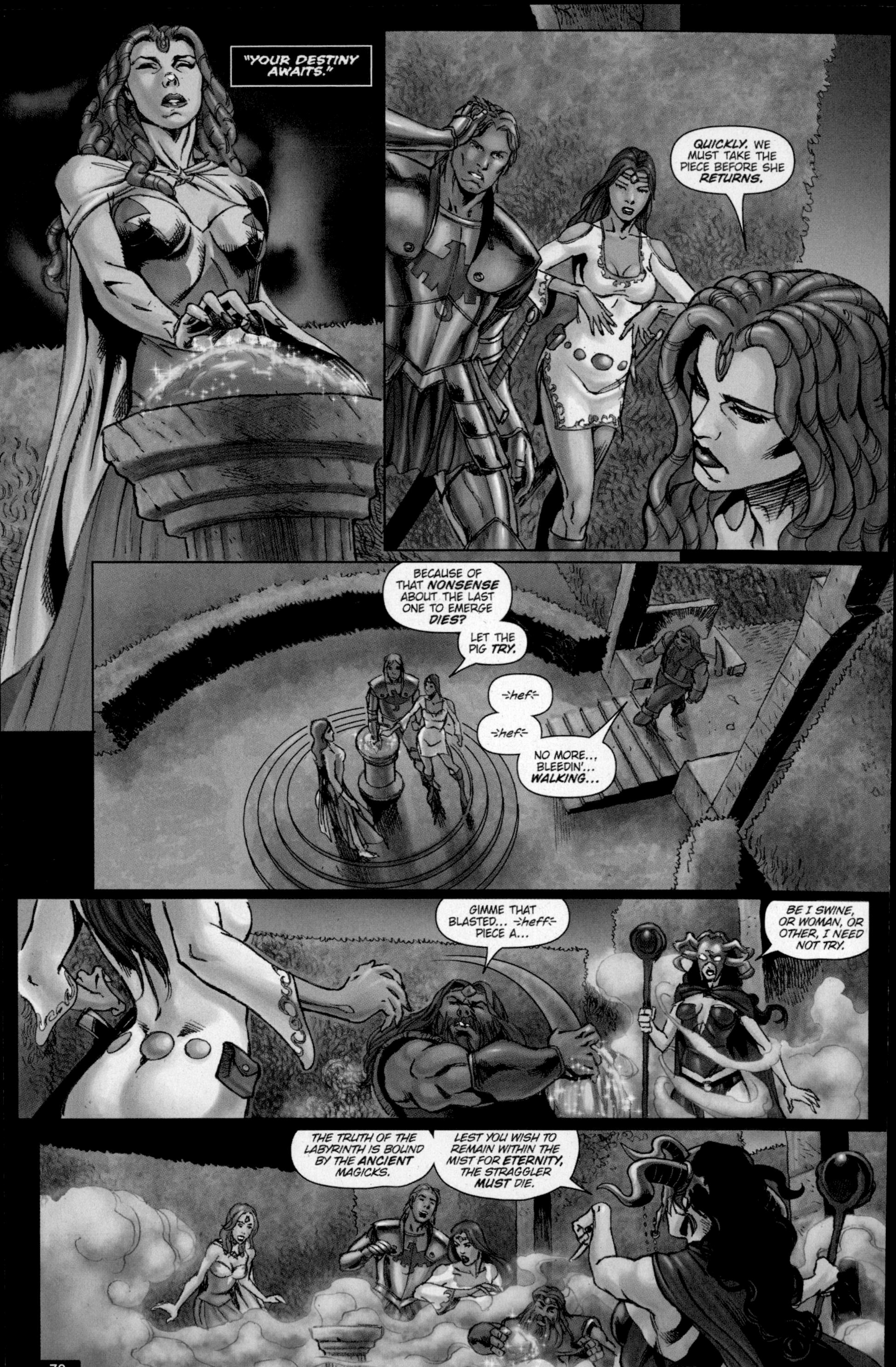
"YOUR DESTINY AWAITS."
QUICKLY. WE MUST TAKE THE PIECE BEFORE SHE RETURNS.
BECAUSE OF THAT NONSENSE ABOUT THE LAST ONE TO EMERGE DIES?
LET THE PIG TRY.
-hef-
-hef-
NO MORE... BLEEDIN'... WALKING...
GIMME THAT BLASTED... -heff- PIECE A...
BE I SWINE, OR WOMAN, OR OTHER, I NEED NOT TRY.
THE TRUTH OF THE LABYRINTH IS BOUND BY THE ANCIENT MAGICKS.
LEST YOU WISH TO REMAIN WITHIN THE MIST FOR ETERNITY, THE STRAGGLER MUST DIE.

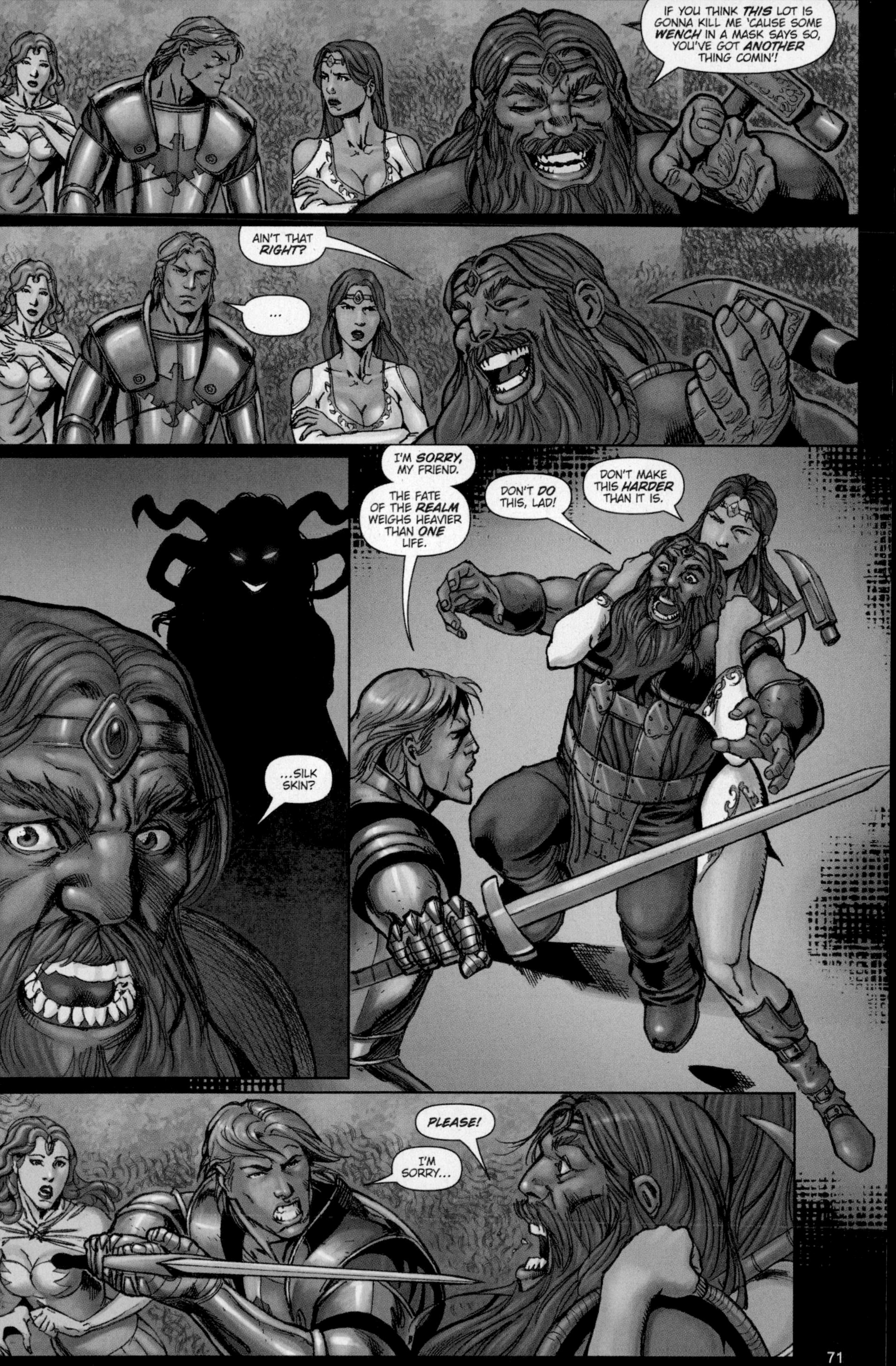

IF YOU THINK THIS LOT IS GONNA KILL ME 'CAUSE SOME WENCH IN A MASK SAYS SO, YOU'VE GOT ANOTHER THING COMIN'!
AIN'T THAT RIGHT?
...
I'M SORRY, MY FRIEND.
THE FATE OF THE REALM WEIGHS HEAVIER THAN ONE LIFE.
DON'T DO THIS, LAD!
DON'T MAKE THIS HARDER THAN IT IS.
...SILK SKIN?
PLEASE!
I'M SORRY...

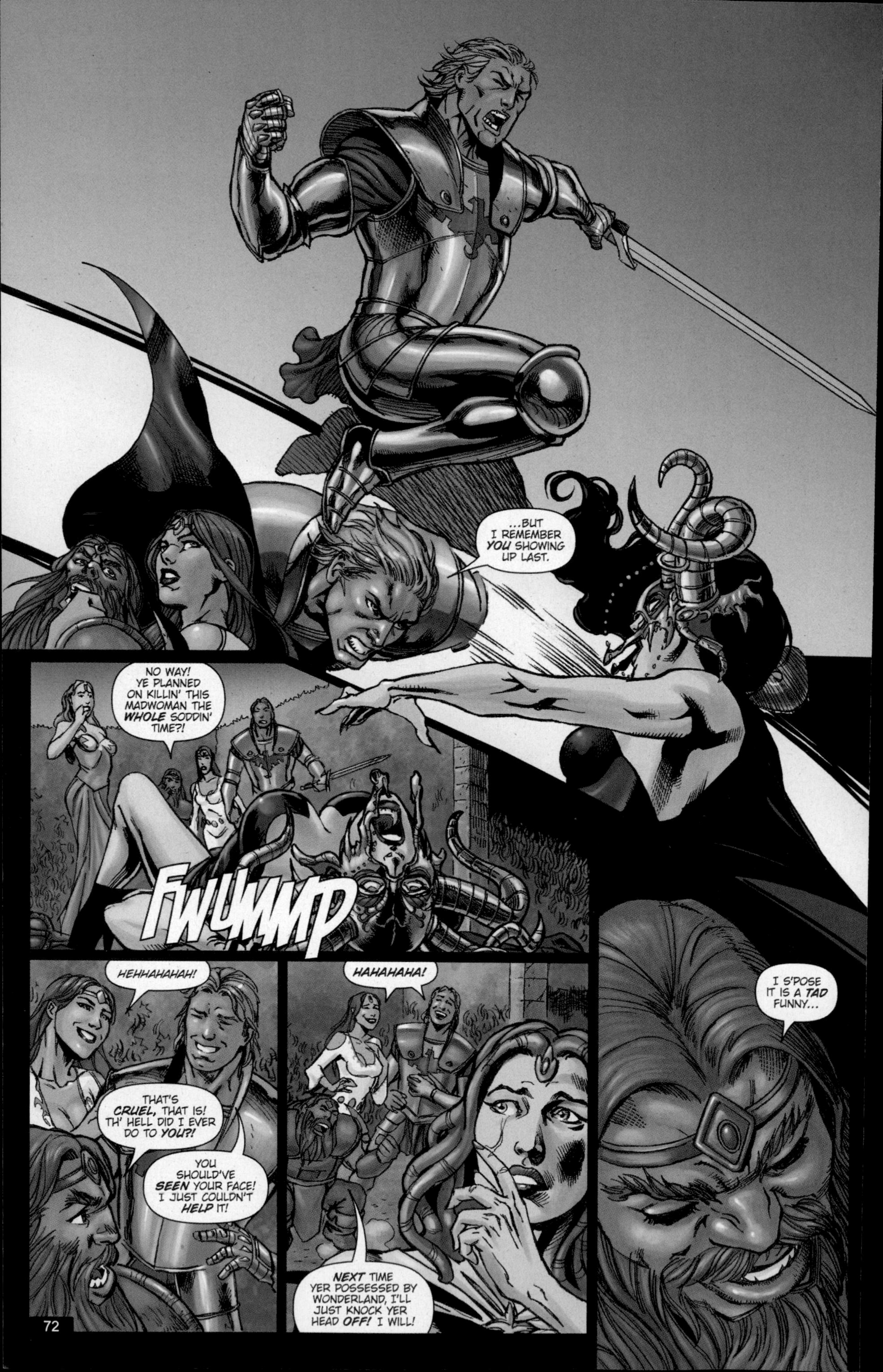
...BUT I REMEMBER YOU SHOWING UP LAST.
NO WAY! YE PLANNED ON KILLIN' THIS MADWOMAN THE WHOLE SODDIN' TIME?!
FWUMMP
HEHHAHAHAH!
THAT'S CRUEL, THAT IS! TH' HELL DID I EVER DO TO YOU?!
YOU SHOULD'VE SEEN YOUR FACE! I JUST COULDN'T HELP IT!
HAHAHAHA!
NEXT TIME YER POSSESSED BY WONDERLAND, I'LL JUST KNOCK YER HEAD OFF! I WILL!
I S'POSE IT IS A TAD FUNNY...

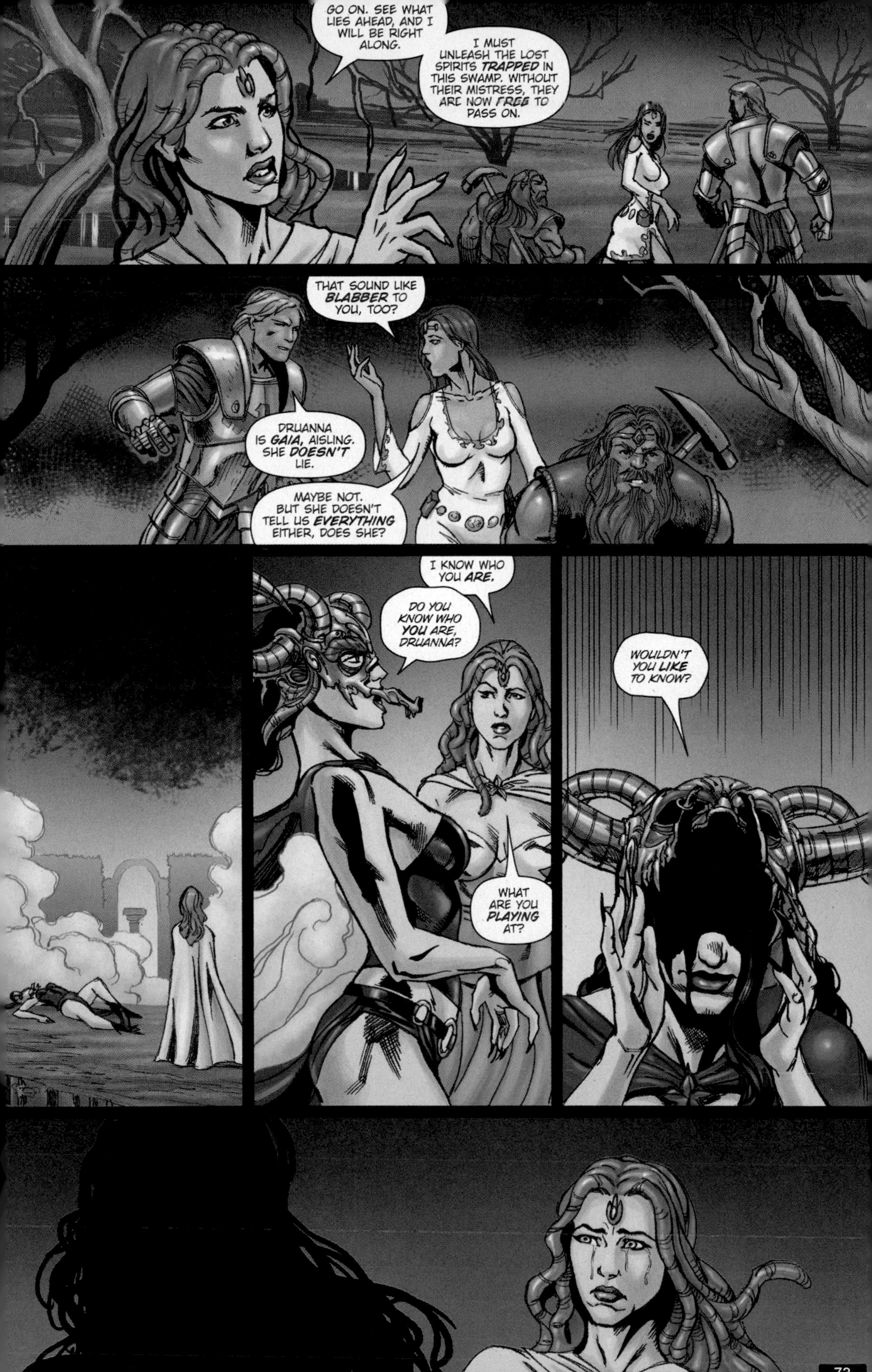
GO ON. SEE WHAT LIES AHEAD, AND I WILL BE RIGHT ALONG.
I MUST UNLEASH THE LOST SPIRITS TRAPPED IN THIS SWAMP. WITHOUT THEIR MISTRESS, THEY ARE NOW FREE TO PASS ON.
THAT SOUND LIKE BLABBER TO YOU, TOO?
DRUANNA IS GAIA, AISLING. SHE DOESN'T LIE.
MAYBE NOT. BUT SHE DOESN'T TELL US EVERYTHING EITHER, DOES SHE?
I KNOW WHO YOU ARE.
DO YOU KNOW WHO YOU ARE, DRUANNA?
WHAT ARE YOU PLAYING AT?
WOULDN'T YOU LIKE TO KNOW?

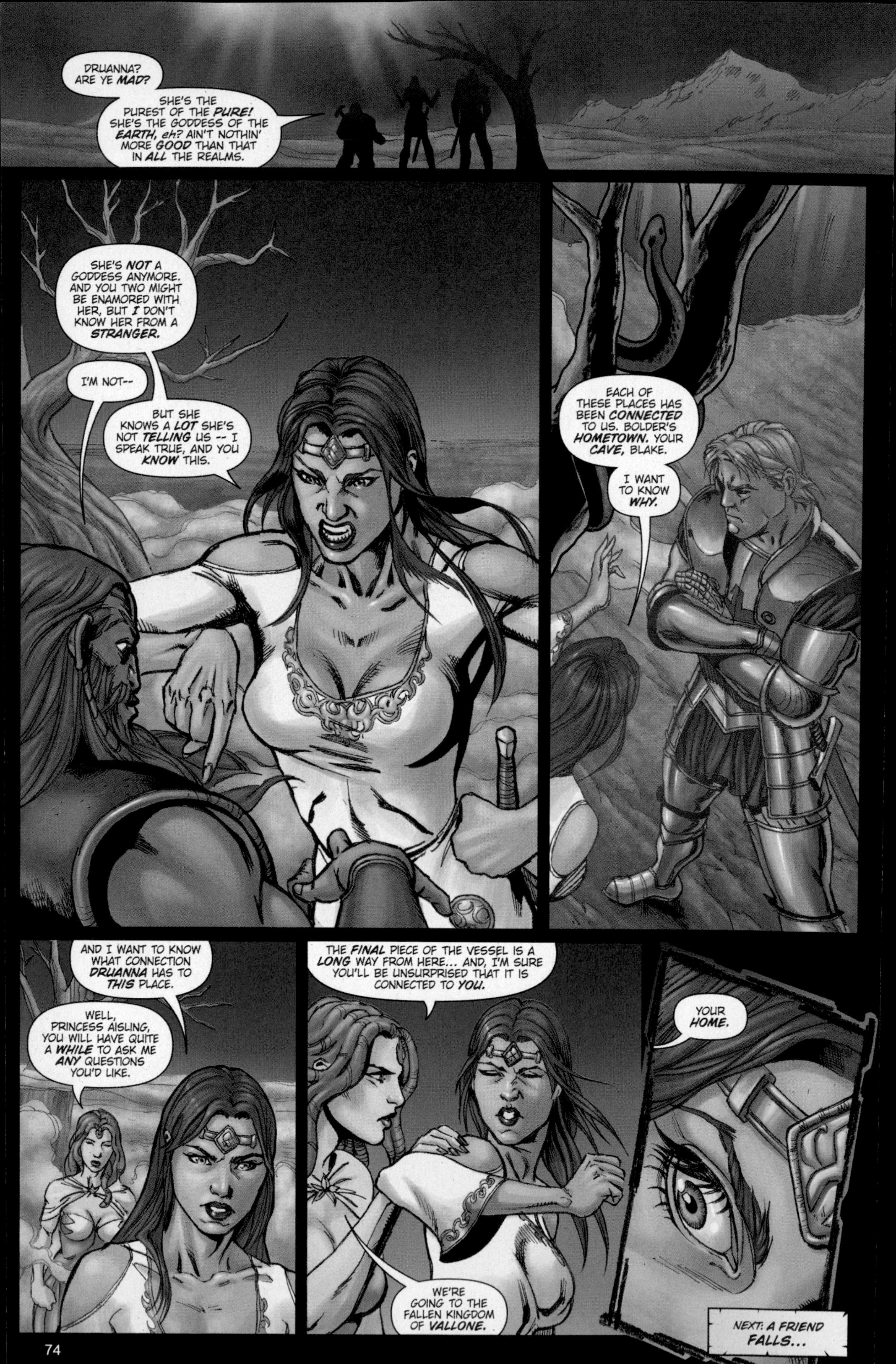
DRUANNA? ARE YE MAD?
SHE'S THE PUREST OF THE PURE! SHE'S THE GODDESS OF THE EARTH, eh? AIN'T NOTHIN' MORE GOOD THAN THAT IN ALL THE REALMS.
SHE'S NOT A GODDESS ANYMORE. AND YOU TWO MIGHT BE ENAMORED WITH HER, BUT I DON'T KNOW HER FROM A STRANGER.
I'M NOT--
BUT SHE KNOWS A LOT SHE'S NOT TELLING US -- I SPEAK TRUE, AND YOU KNOW THIS.
EACH OF THESE PLACES HAS BEEN CONNECTED TO US. BOLDER'S HOMETOWN. YOUR CAVE, BLAKE.
I WANT TO KNOW WHY.
AND I WANT TO KNOW WHAT CONNECTION DRUANNA HAS TO THIS PLACE.
WELL, PRINCESS AISLING, YOU WILL HAVE QUITE A WHILE TO ASK ME ANY QUESTIONS YOU'D LIKE.
THE FINAL PIECE OF THE VESSEL IS A LONG WAY FROM HERE... AND, I'M SURE YOU'LL BE UNSURPRISED THAT IT IS CONNECTED TO YOU.
WE'RE GOING TO THE FALLEN KINGDOM OF VALLONE.
YOUR HOME.
NEXT: A FRIEND FALLS...

Grimm Fairy Tales presents:

QUEST

AGE OF DARKNESS

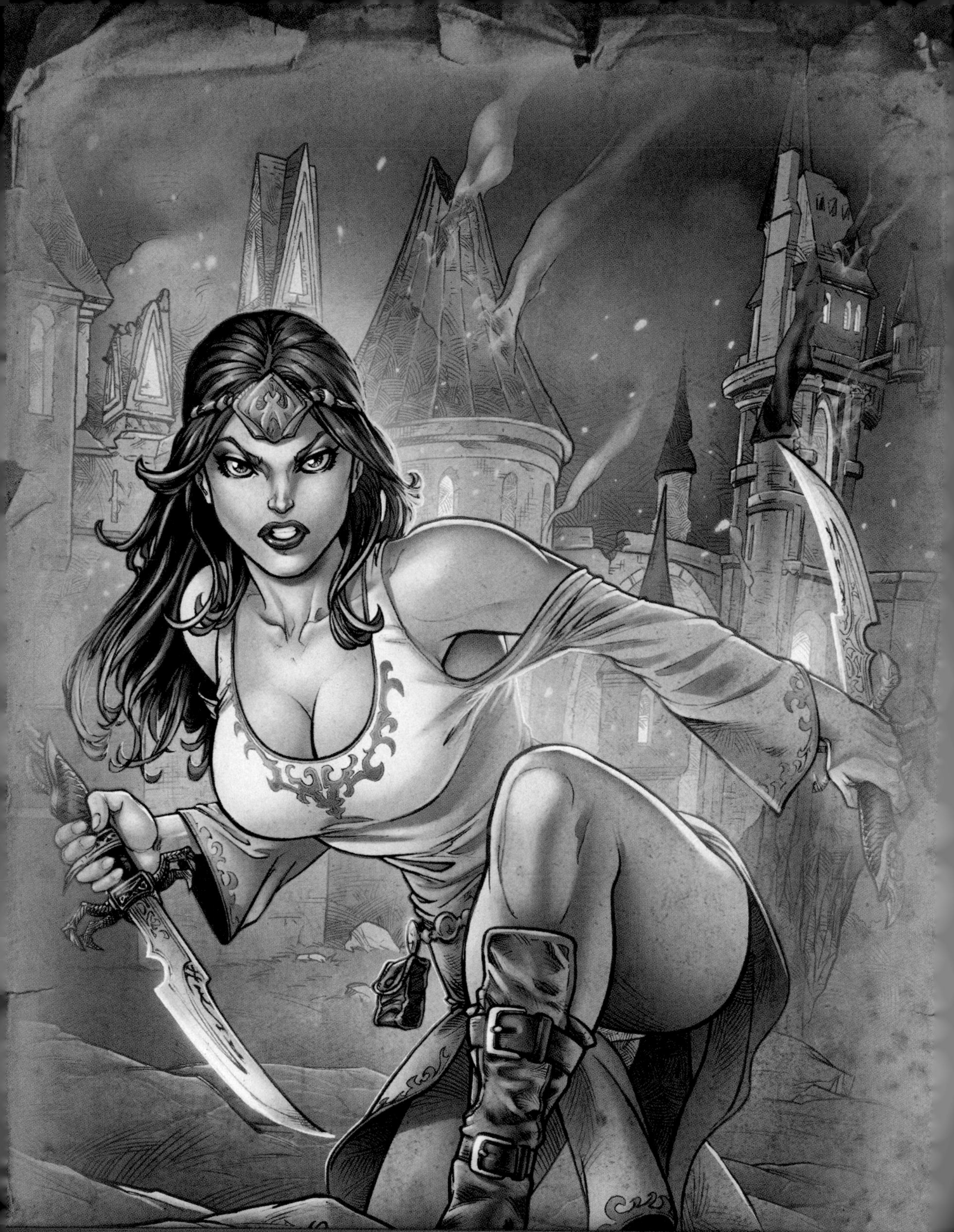

A Friend Falls

WRITER PAT SHAND
ARTWORK SERGIO OSUNA
COLORS FRANCESCA ZAMBON
LETTERS JIM CAMPBELL

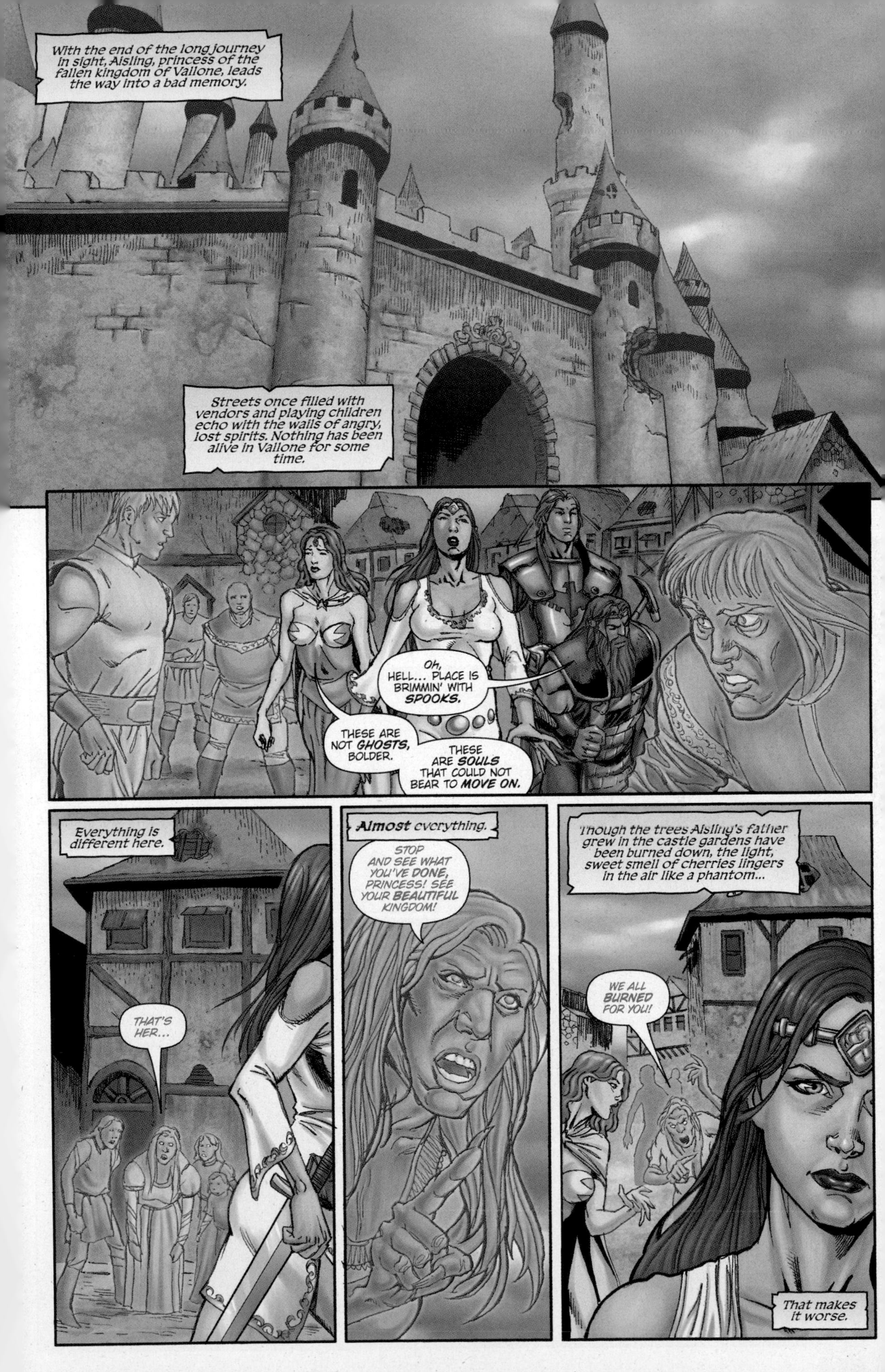
With the end of the long journey in sight, Aisling, princess of the fallen kingdom of Vallone, leads the way into a bad memory.
Streets once filled with vendors and playing children echo with the walls of angry, lost spirits. Nothing has been alive in Vallone for some time.
OH, HELL... PLACE IS BRIMMIN' WITH SPOOKS.
THESE ARE NOT GHOSTS, BOLDER.
THESE ARE SOULS THAT COULD NOT BEAR TO MOVE ON.
Everything is different here.
THAT'S HER...
Almost everything.
STOP AND SEE WHAT YOU'VE DONE, PRINCESS! SEE YOUR BEAUTIFUL KINGDOM!
Though the trees Aisling's father grew in the castle gardens have been burned down, the light, sweet smell of cherries lingers in the air like a phantom...
WE ALL BURNED FOR YOU!
That makes it worse.

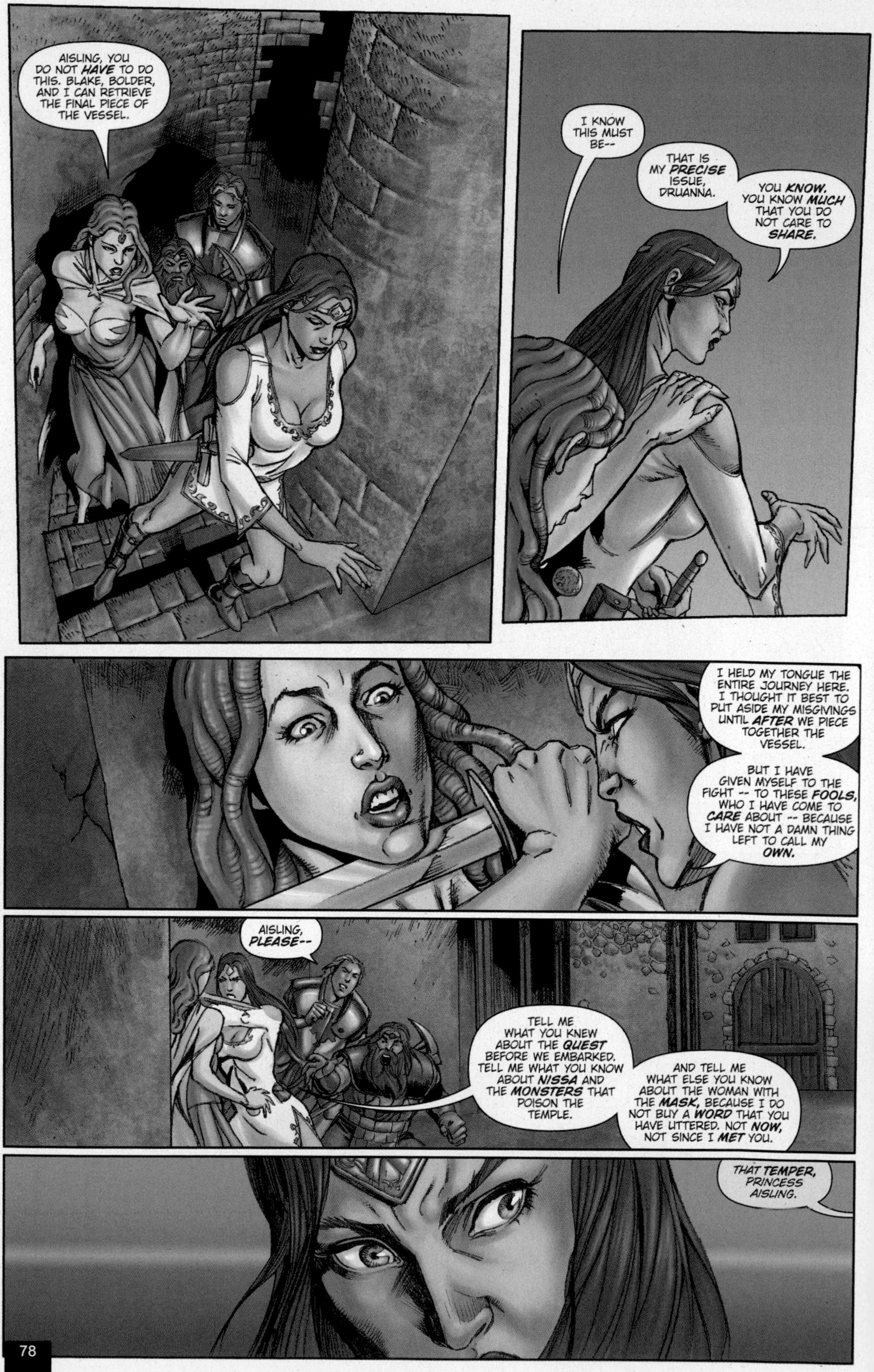
AISLING, YOU DO NOT HAVE TO DO THIS. BLAKE, BOLDER, AND I CAN RETRIEVE THE FINAL PIECE OF THE VESSEL.
I KNOW THIS MUST BE--
THAT IS MY PRECISE ISSUE, DRUANNA.
YOU KNOW. YOU KNOW MUCH THAT YOU DO NOT CARE TO SHARE.
I HELD MY TONGUE THE ENTIRE JOURNEY HERE. I THOUGHT IT BEST TO PUT ASIDE MY MISGIVINGS UNTIL AFTER WE PIECE TOGETHER THE VESSEL.
BUT I HAVE GIVEN MYSELF TO THE FIGHT -- TO THESE FOOLS, WHO I HAVE COME TO CARE ABOUT -- BECAUSE I HAVE NOT A DAMN THING LEFT TO CALL MY OWN.
AISLING, PLEASE--
TELL ME WHAT YOU KNEW ABOUT THE QUEST BEFORE WE EMBARKED. TELL ME WHAT YOU KNOW ABOUT NISSA AND THE MONSTERS THAT POISON THE TEMPLE.
AND TELL ME WHAT ELSE YOU KNOW ABOUT THE WOMAN WITH THE MASK, BECAUSE I DO NOT BUY A WORD THAT YOU HAVE UTTERED. NOT NOW, NOT SINCE I MET YOU.
THAT TEMPER, PRINCESS AISLING.

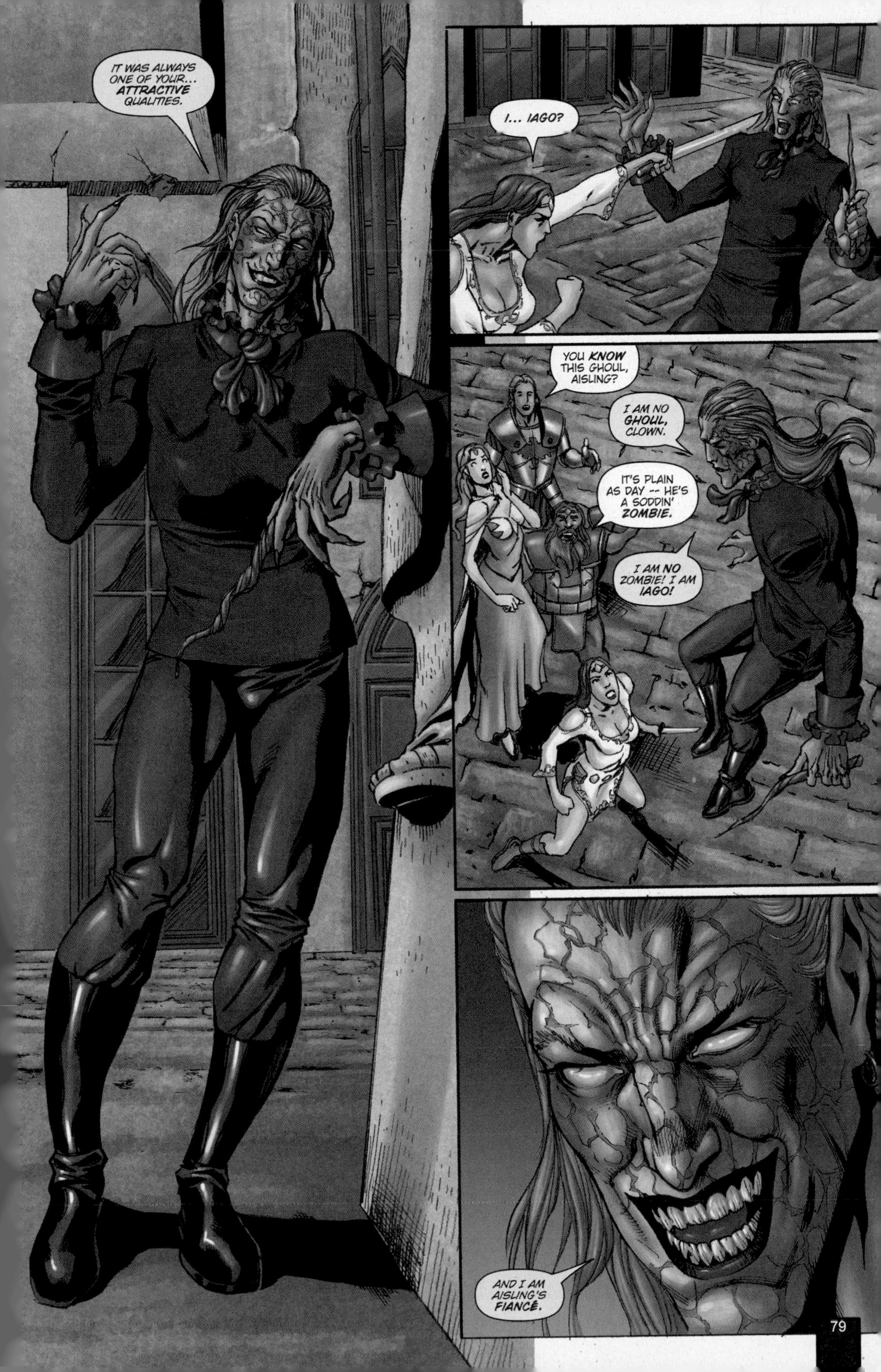
IT WAS ALWAYS ONE OF YOUR... ATTRACTIVE QUALITIES.
I... IAGO?
YOU KNOW THIS GHOUL, AISLING?
I AM NO GHOUL, CLOWN.
IT'S PLAIN AS DAY -- HE'S A SODDIN' ZOMBIE.
I AM NO ZOMBIE! I AM IAGO!
AND I AM AISLING'S FIANCÉ.

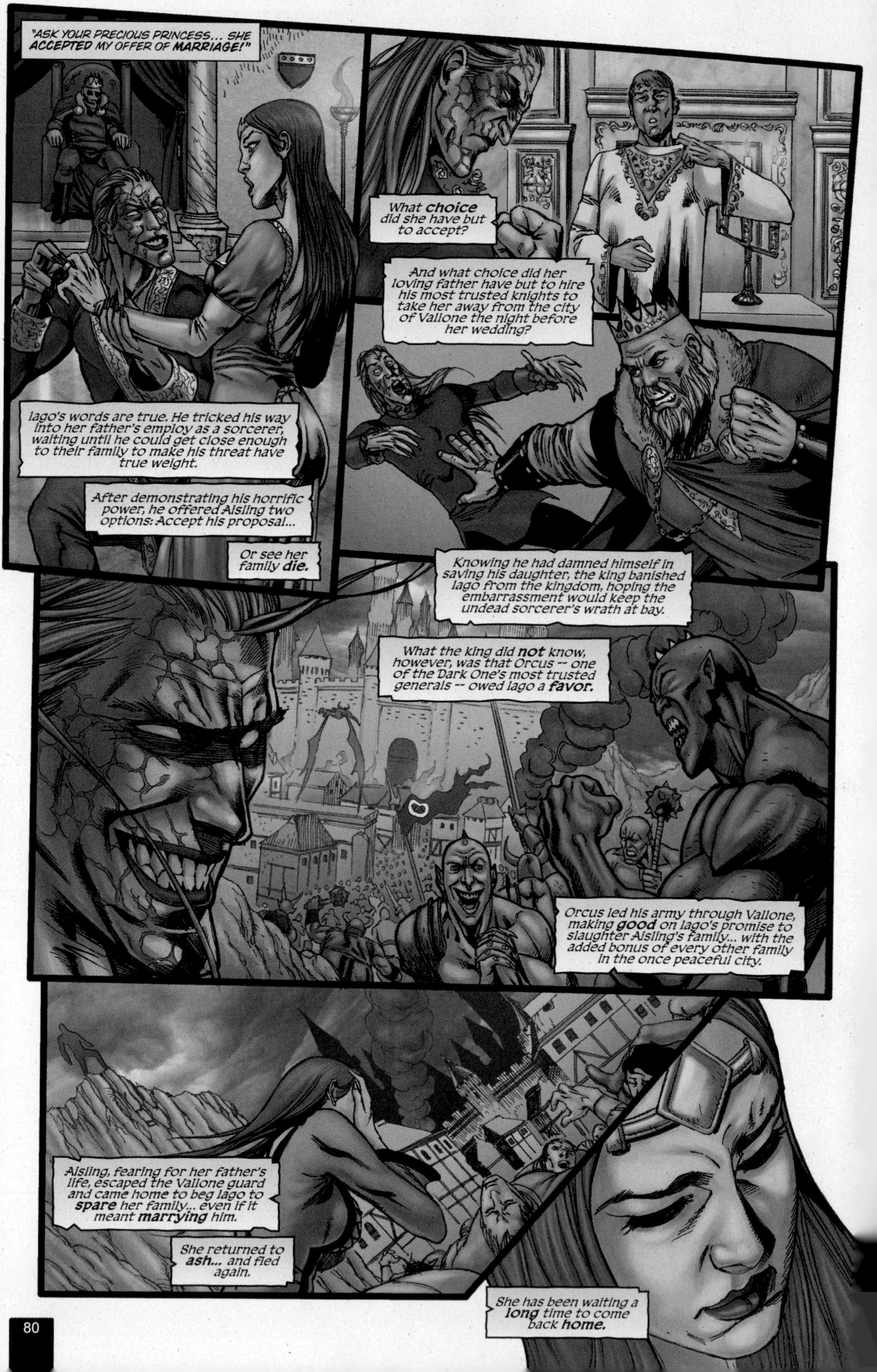

"ASK YOUR PRECIOUS PRINCESS... SHE ACCEPTED MY OFFER OF MARRIAGE!"
What choice did she have but to accept?
And what choice did her loving father have but to hire his most trusted knights to take her away from the city of Vallone the night before her wedding?
Iago's words are true. He tricked his way into her father's employ as a sorcerer, waiting until he could get close enough to their family to make his threat have true weight.
After demonstrating his horrific power, he offered Aisling two options: Accept his proposal...
Or see her family die.
Knowing he had damned himself in saving his daughter, the king banished Iago from the kingdom, hoping the embarrassment would keep the undead sorcerer's wrath at bay.
What the king did not know, however, was that Orcus -- one of the Dark One's most trusted generals -- owed Iago a favor.
Orcus led his army through Vallone, making good on Iago's promise to slaughter Aisling's family... with the added bonus of every other family in the once peaceful city.
Aisling, fearing for her father's life, escaped the Vallone guard and came home to beg Iago to spare her family... even if it meant marrying him.
She returned to ash... and fled again.
She has been waiting a long time to come back home.

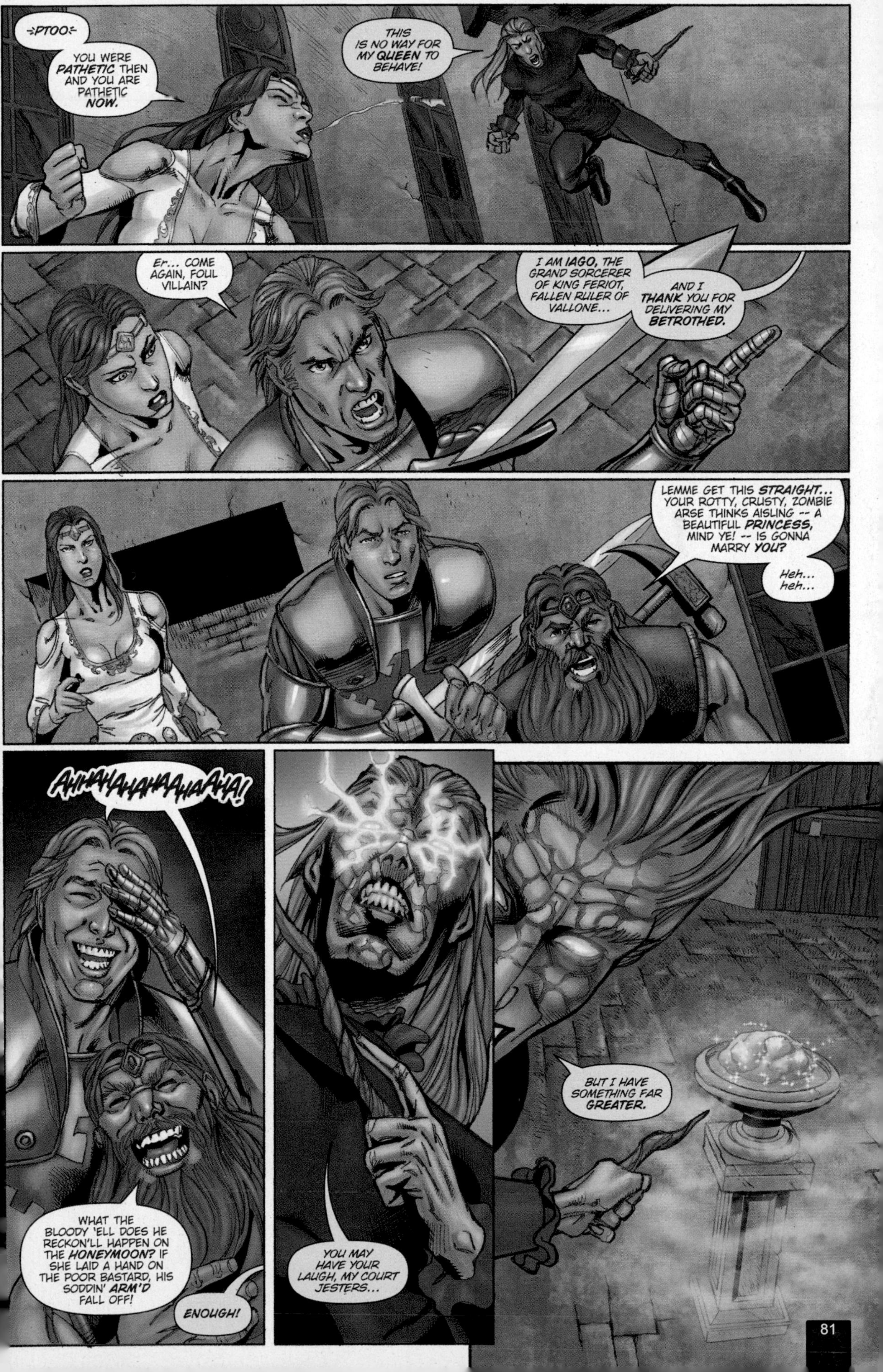

-PTOO-
YOU WERE PATHETIC THEN AND YOU ARE PATHETIC NOW.
THIS IS NO WAY FOR MY QUEEN TO BEHAVE!
Er... COME AGAIN, FOUL VILLAIN?
I AM IAGO, THE GRAND SORCERER OF KING FERIOT, FALLEN RULER OF VALLONE...
AND I THANK YOU FOR DELIVERING MY BETROTHED.
LEMME GET THIS STRAIGHT... YOUR ROTTY, CRUSTY, ZOMBIE ARSE THINKS AISLING -- A BEAUTIFUL PRINCESS, MIND YE! -- IS GONNA MARRY YOU?
Heh... heh...
AHHAHAHAHAHAHAHA!
WHAT THE BLOODY 'ELL DOES HE RECKON'LL HAPPEN ON THE HONEYMOON? IF SHE LAID A HAND ON THE POOR BASTARD, HIS SODDIN' ARM'D FALL OFF!
ENOUGH!
YOU MAY HAVE YOUR LAUGH, MY COURT JESTERS...
BUT I HAVE SOMETHING FAR GREATER.

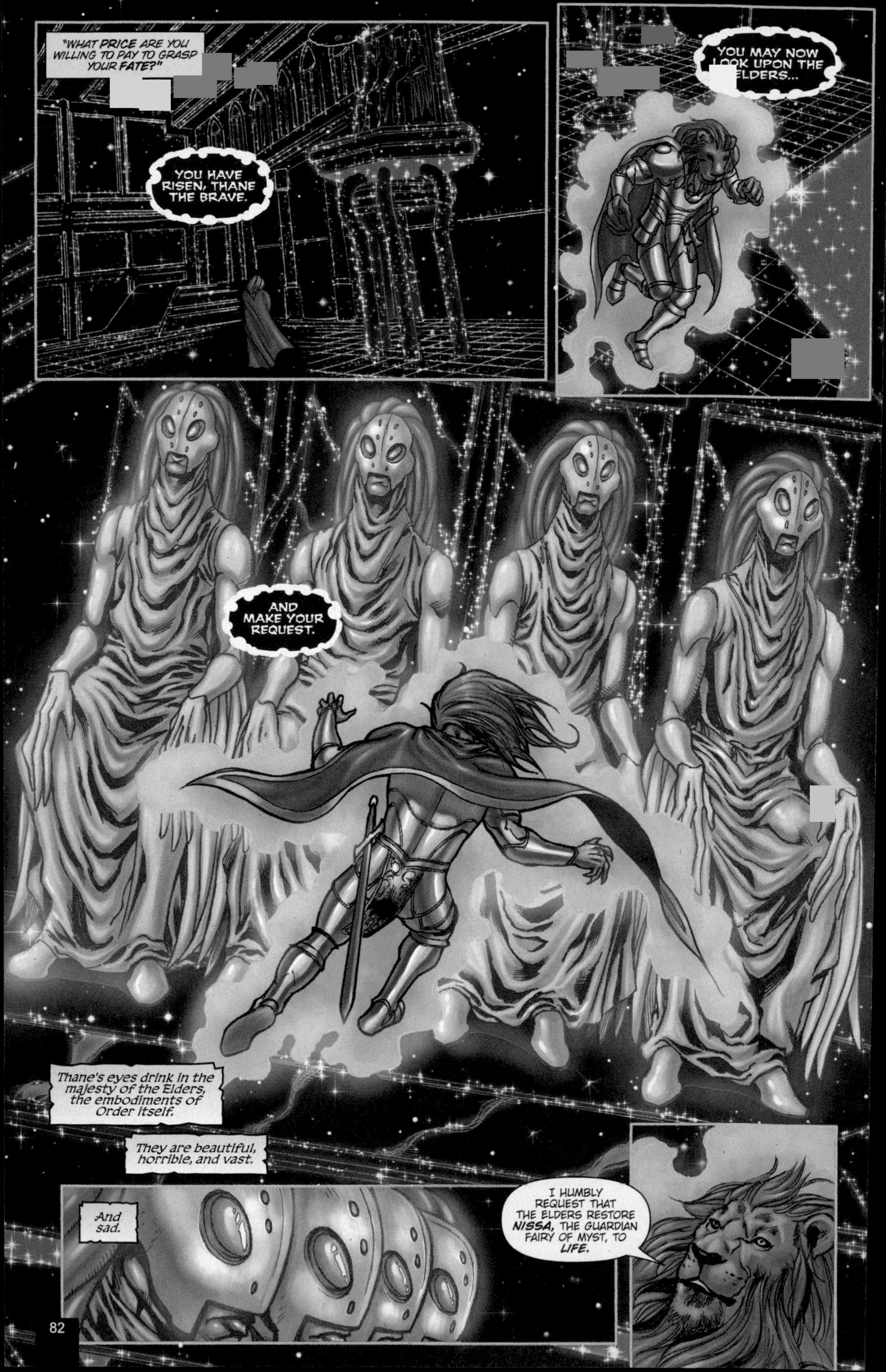
"WHAT PRICE ARE YOU WILLING TO PAY TO GRASP YOUR FATE?"
YOU HAVE RISEN, THANE THE BRAVE.
YOU MAY NOW LOOK UPON THE ELDERS...
AND MAKE YOUR REQUEST.
Thane's eyes drink in the majesty of the Elders, the embodiments of Order itself.
They are beautiful, horrible, and vast.
And sad.
I HUMBLY REQUEST THAT THE ELDERS RESTORE NISSA, THE GUARDIAN FAIRY OF MYST, TO LIFE.

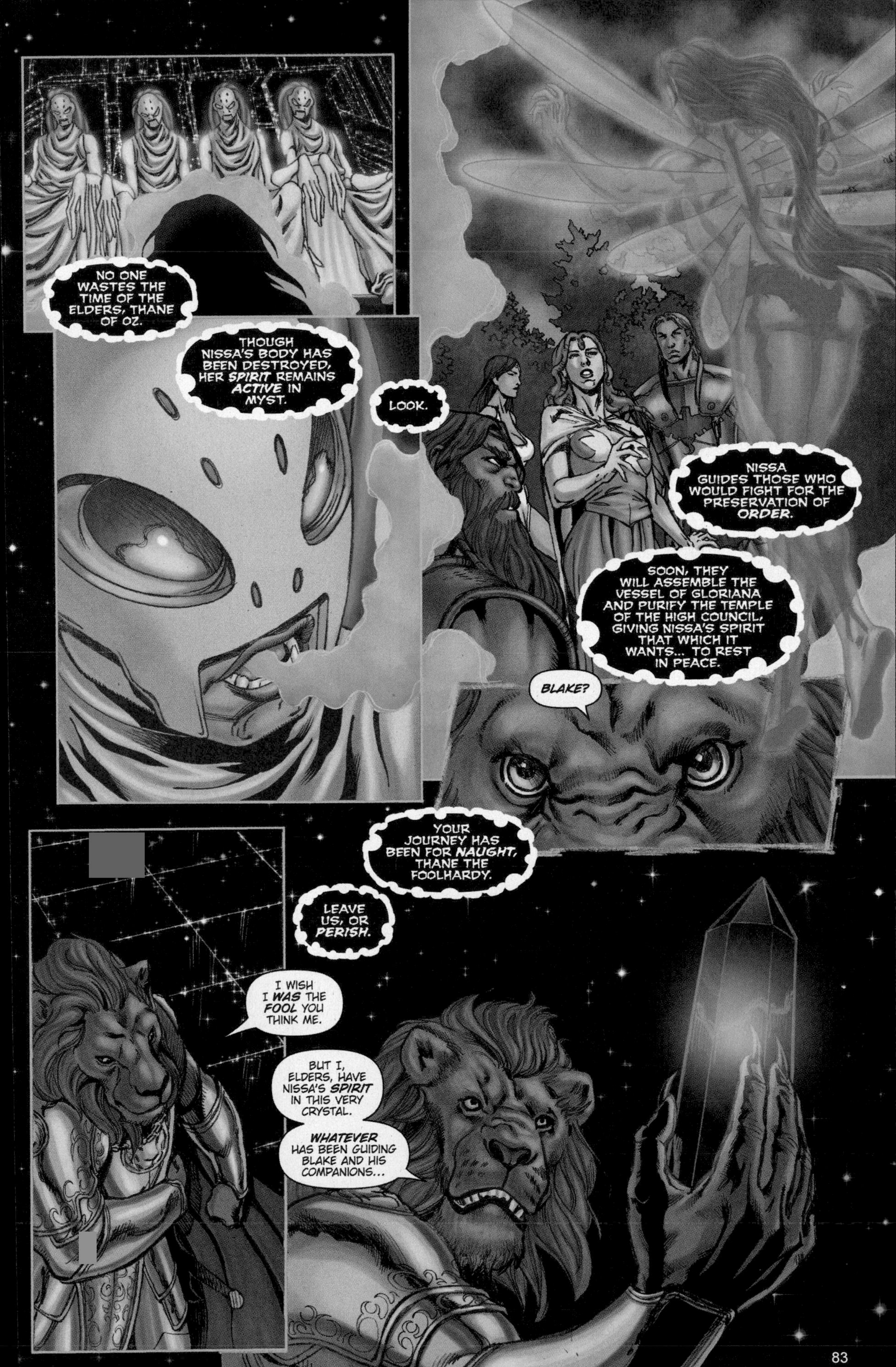
NO ONE WASTES THE TIME OF THE ELDERS, THANE OF OZ.
THOUGH NISSA'S BODY HAS BEEN DESTROYED, HER SPIRIT REMAINS ACTIVE IN MYST.
LOOK.
NISSA GUIDES THOSE WHO WOULD FIGHT FOR THE PRESERVATION OF ORDER.
SOON, THEY WILL ASSEMBLE THE VESSEL OF GLORIANA AND PURIFY THE TEMPLE OF THE HIGH COUNCIL, GIVING NISSA'S SPIRIT THAT WHICH IT WANTS... TO REST IN PEACE.
BLAKE?
YOUR JOURNEY HAS BEEN FOR NAUGHT, THANE THE FOOLHARDY.
LEAVE US, OR PERISH.
I WISH I WAS THE FOOL YOU THINK ME.
BUT I, ELDERS, HAVE NISSA'S SPIRIT IN THIS VERY CRYSTAL.
WHATEVER HAS BEEN GUIDING BLAKE AND HIS COMPANIONS...

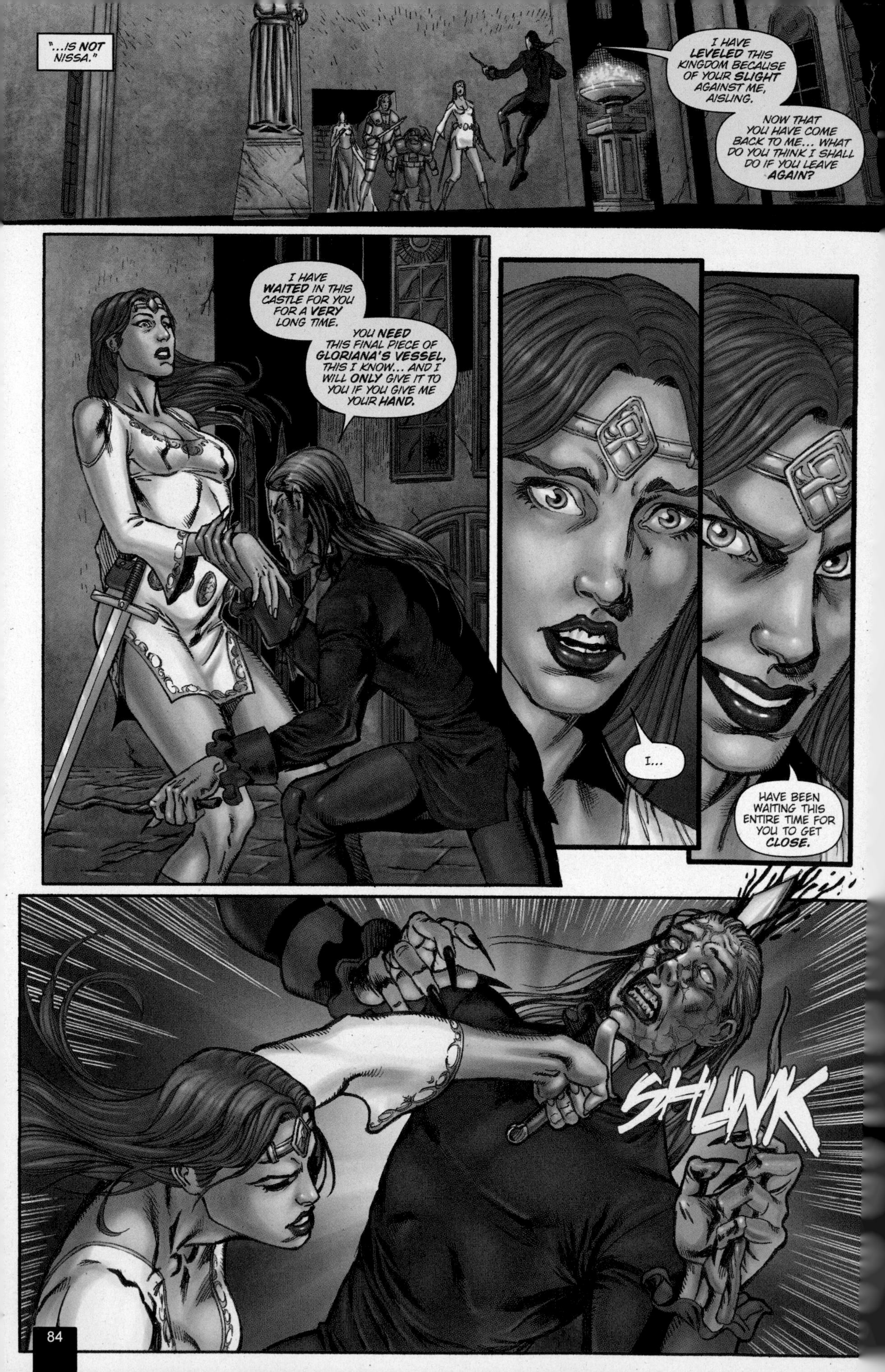
"...IS NOT NISSA."
I HAVE LEVELED THIS KINGDOM BECAUSE OF YOUR SLIGHT AGAINST ME, AISLING.
NOW THAT YOU HAVE COME BACK TO ME... WHAT DO YOU THINK I SHALL DO IF YOU LEAVE AGAIN?
I HAVE WAITED IN THIS CASTLE FOR YOU FOR A VERY LONG TIME.
YOU NEED THIS FINAL PIECE OF GLORIANA'S VESSEL, THIS I KNOW... AND I WILL ONLY GIVE IT TO YOU IF YOU GIVE ME YOUR HAND.
I...
HAVE BEEN WAITING THIS ENTIRE TIME FOR YOU TO GET CLOSE.
SHUNK

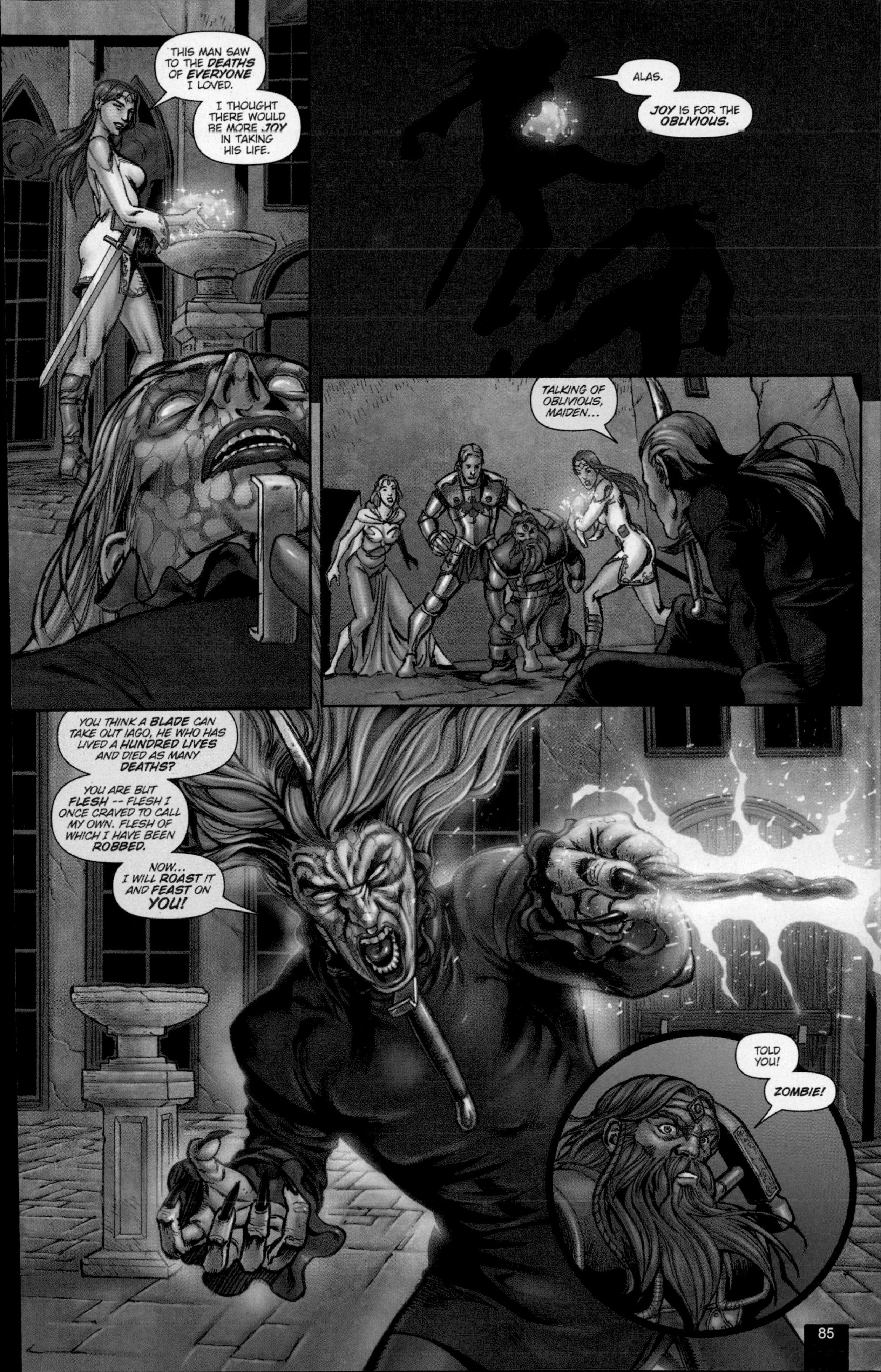
THIS MAN SAW TO THE DEATHS OF EVERYONE I LOVED.
I THOUGHT THERE WOULD BE MORE JOY IN TAKING HIS LIFE.
ALAS.
JOY IS FOR THE OBLIVIOUS.
TALKING OF OBLIVIOUS, MAIDEN...
YOU THINK A BLADE CAN TAKE OUT IAGO, HE WHO HAS LIVED A HUNDRED LIVES AND DIED AS MANY DEATHS?
YOU ARE BUT FLESH -- FLESH I ONCE CRAVED TO CALL MY OWN. FLESH OF WHICH I HAVE BEEN ROBBED.
NOW... I WILL ROAST IT AND FEAST ON YOU!
TOLD YOU!
ZOMBIE!

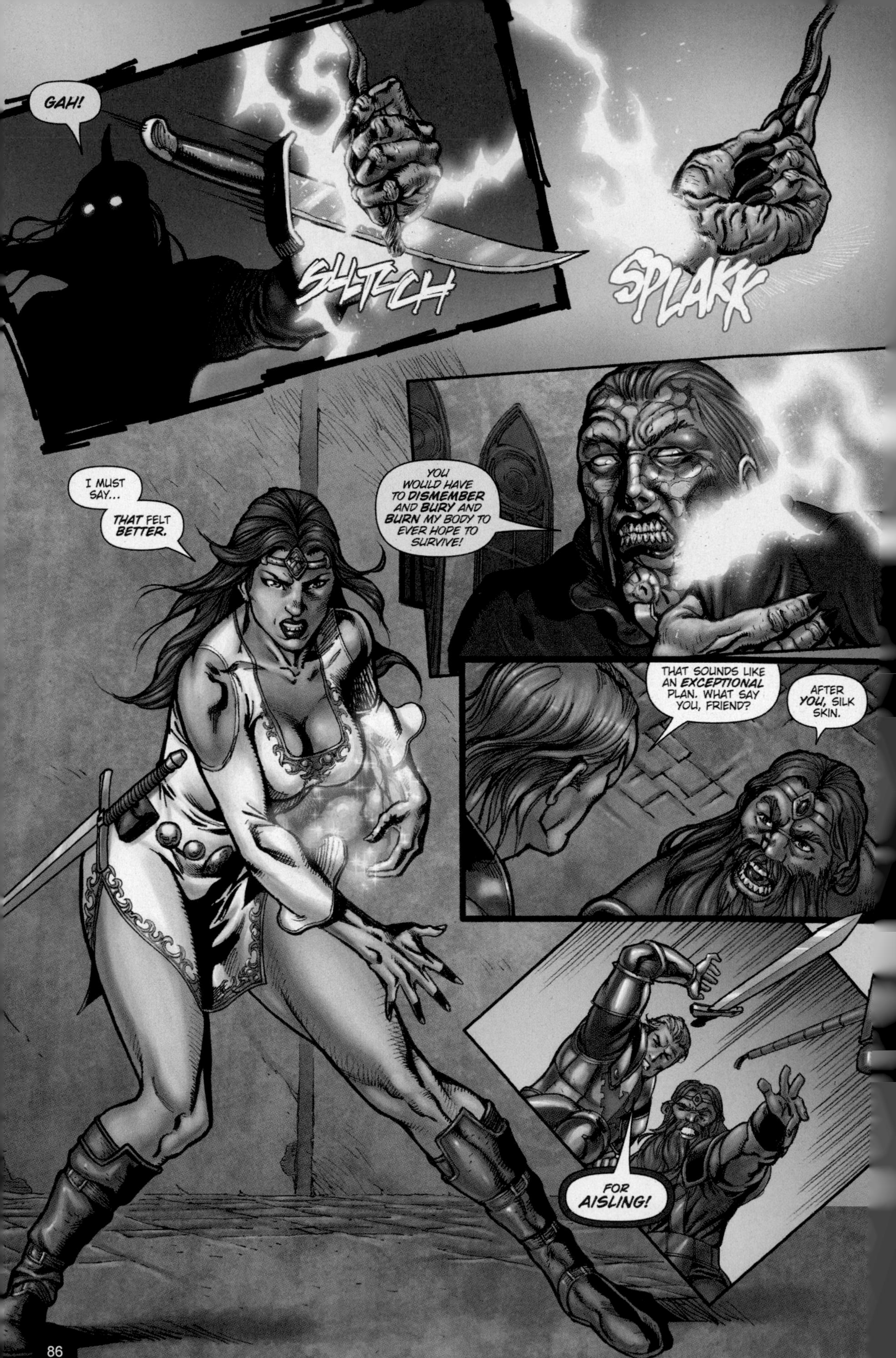
GAH!
SLLTCH
SPLAKK
I MUST SAY... THAT FELT BETTER.
YOU WOULD HAVE TO DISMEMBER AND BURY AND BURN MY BODY TO EVER HOPE TO SURVIVE!
THAT SOUNDS LIKE AN EXCEPTIONAL PLAN. WHAT SAY YOU, FRIEND?
AFTER YOU, SILK SKIN.
FOR AISLING!

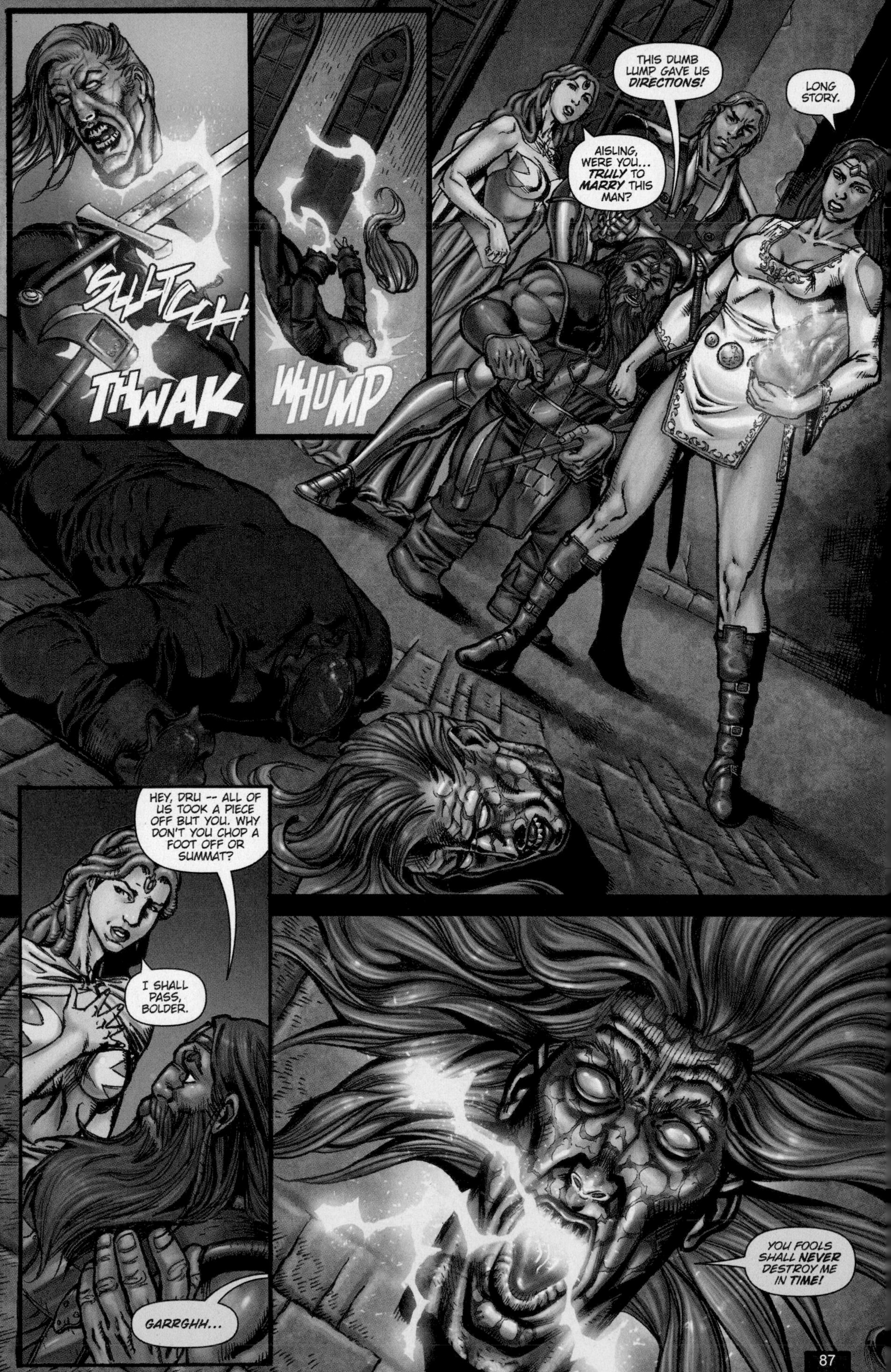
SLLLTCCH
THWAK
WHUMP
THIS DUMB LUMP GAVE US DIRECTIONS!
LONG STORY.
AISLING, WERE YOU... TRULY TO MARRY THIS MAN?
HEY, DRU -- ALL OF US TOOK A PIECE OFF BUT YOU. WHY DON'T YOU CHOP A FOOT OFF OR SUMMAT?
I SHALL PASS, BOLDER.
GARRGHH...
YOU FOOLS SHALL NEVER DESTROY ME IN TIME!

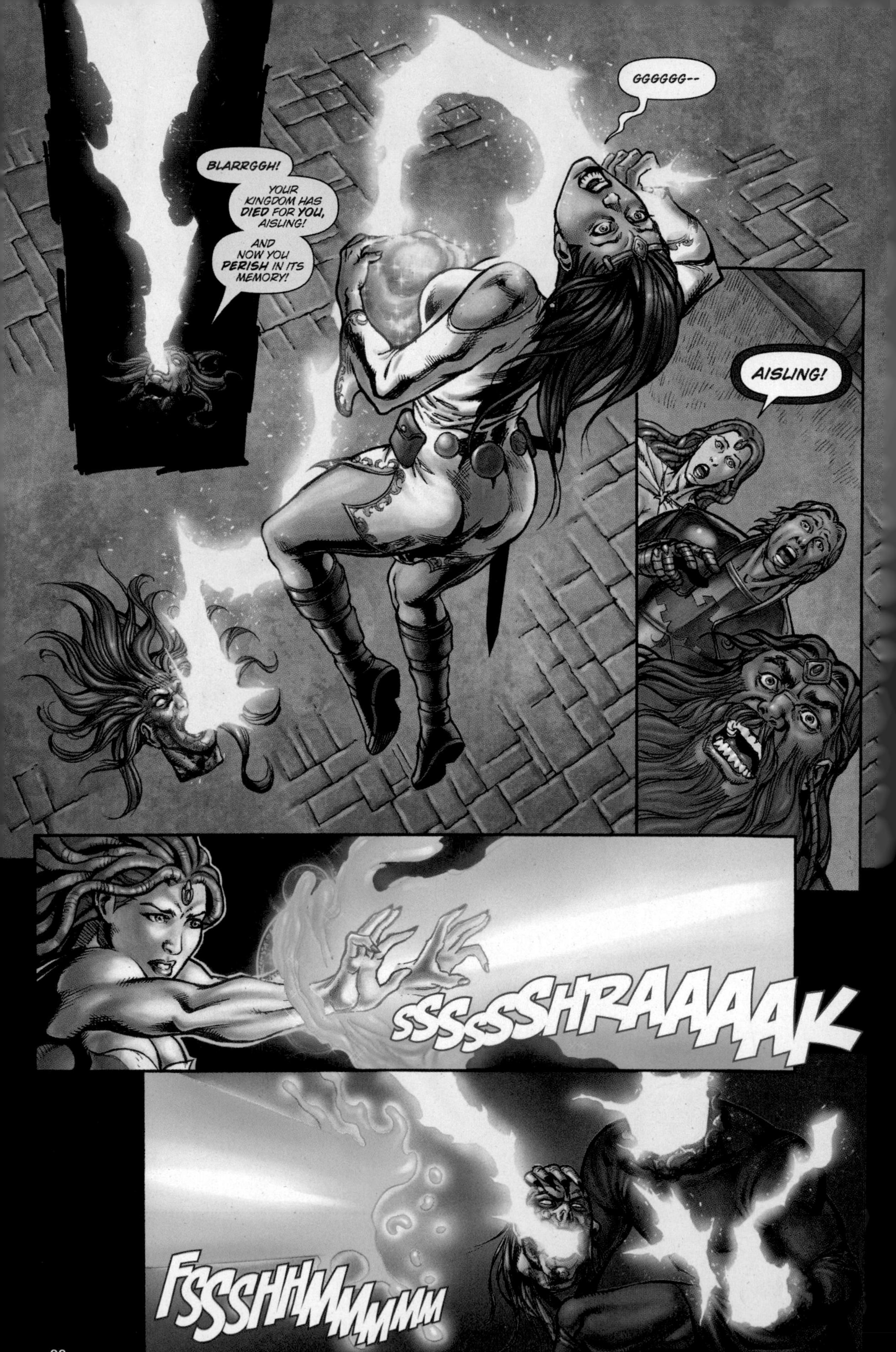
GGGGGG--
BLARRGGH!
YOUR KINGDOM HAS DIED FOR YOU, AISLING!
AND NOW YOU PERISH IN ITS MEMORY!
AISLING!
SSSSSHRAAAAK
FSSSHHMMMMMM

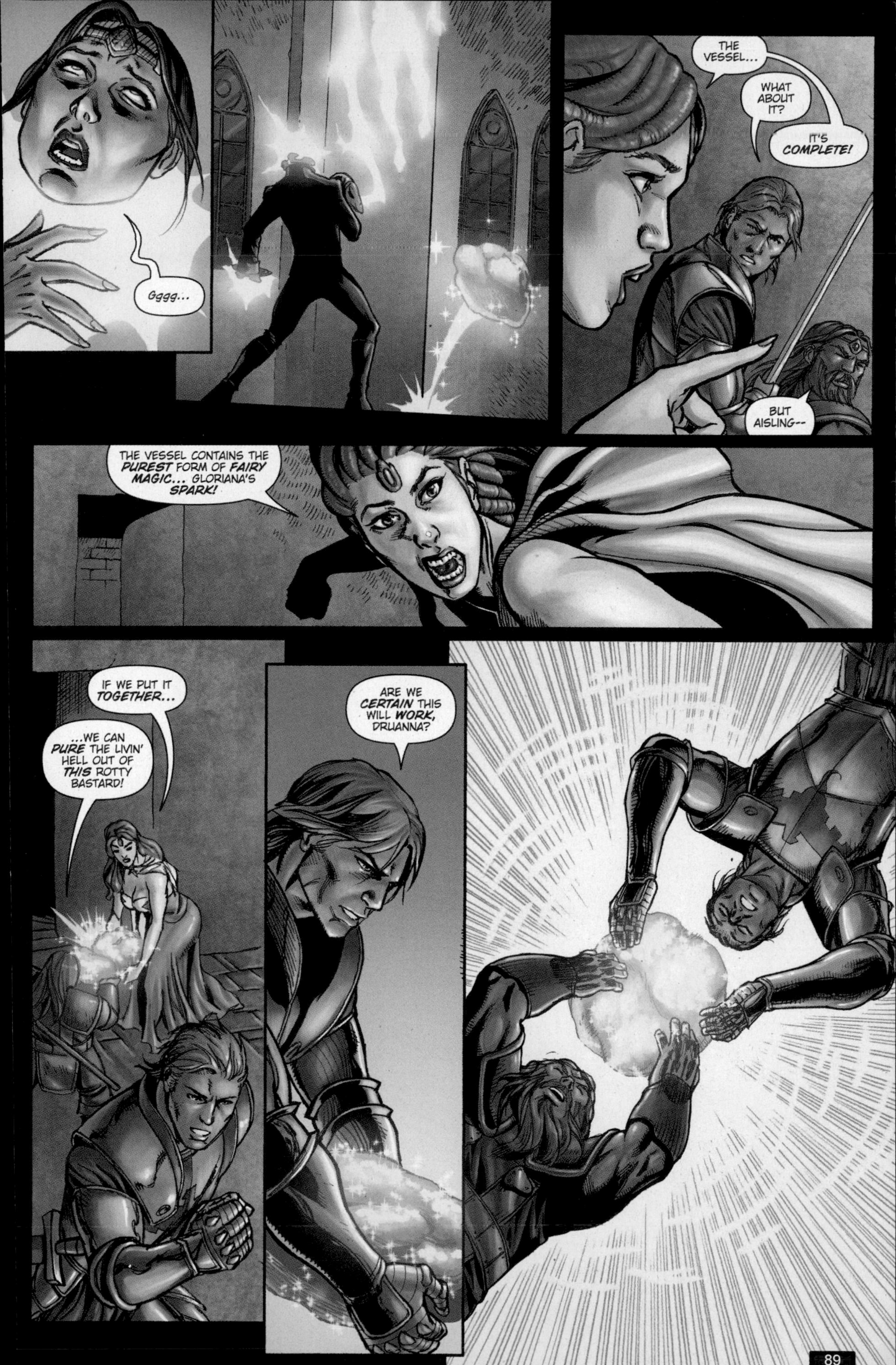
Gggg...
THE VESSEL...
WHAT ABOUT IT?
IT'S COMPLETE!
BUT AISLING--
THE VESSEL CONTAINS THE PUREST FORM OF FAIRY MAGIC... GLORIANA'S SPARK!
IF WE PUT IT TOGETHER...
...WE CAN PURE THE LIVIN' HELL OUT OF THIS ROTTY BASTARD!
ARE WE CERTAIN THIS WILL WORK, DRUANNA?

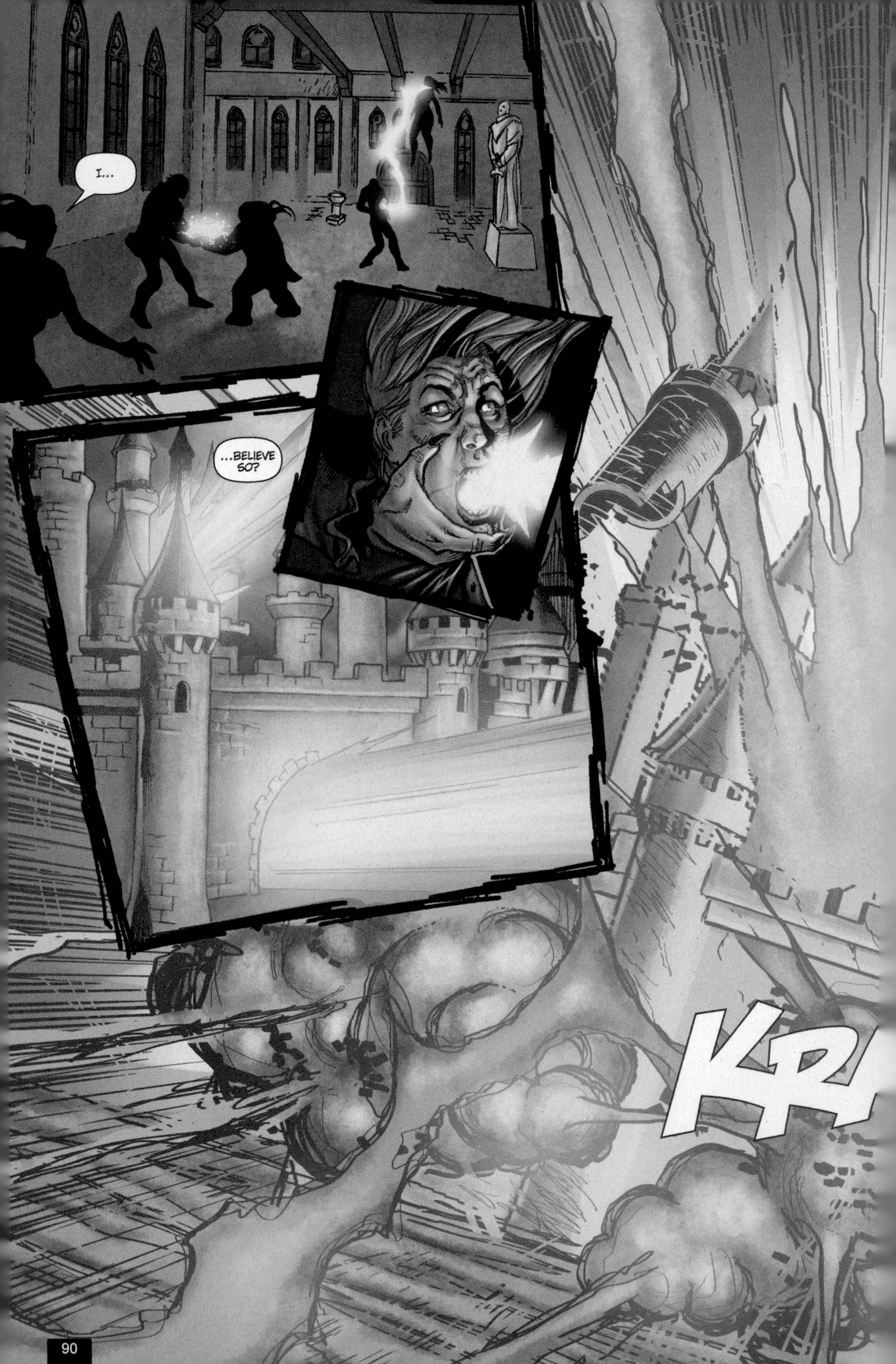
I...
...BELIEVE SO?
KR

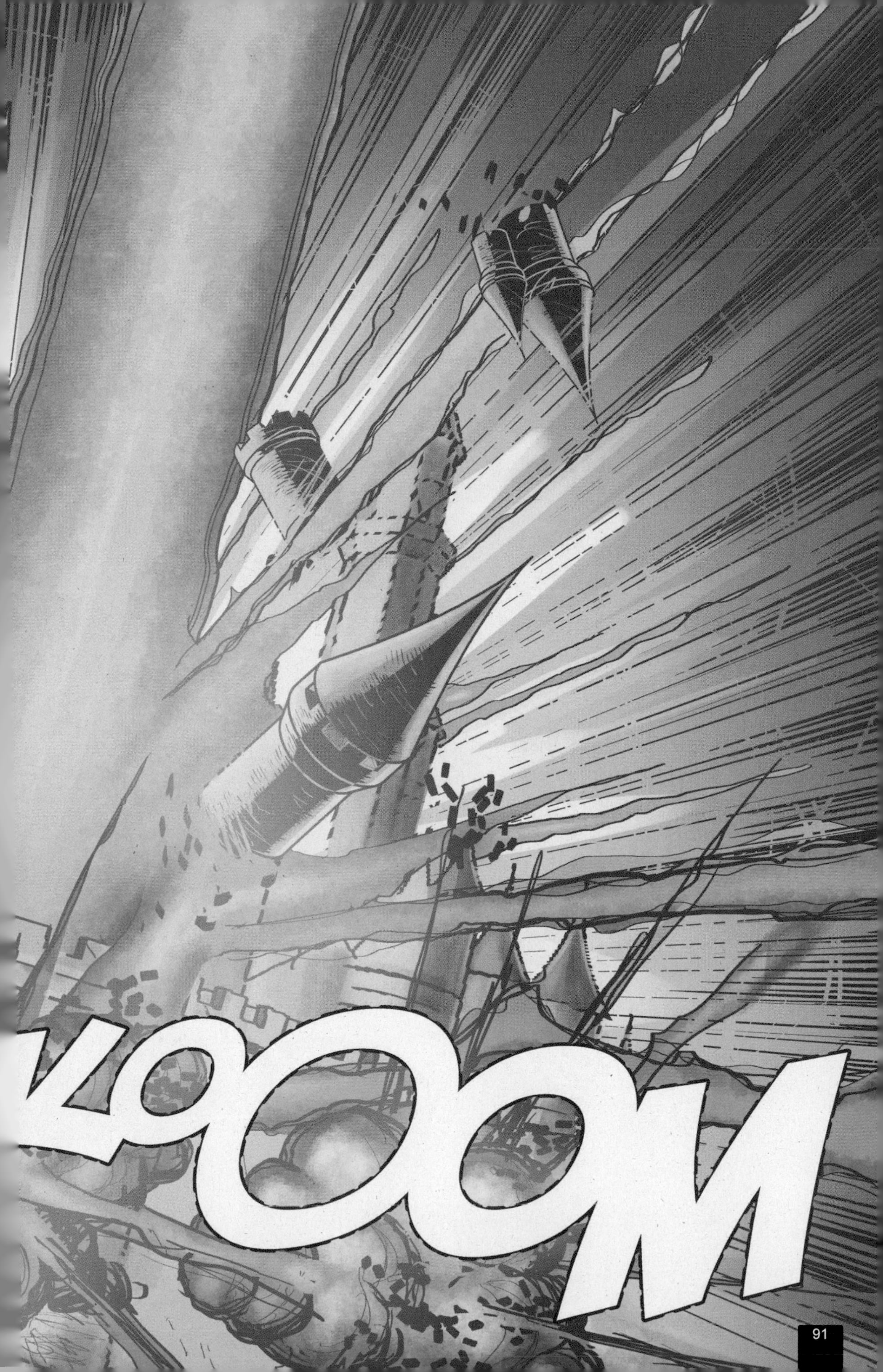
OOOM

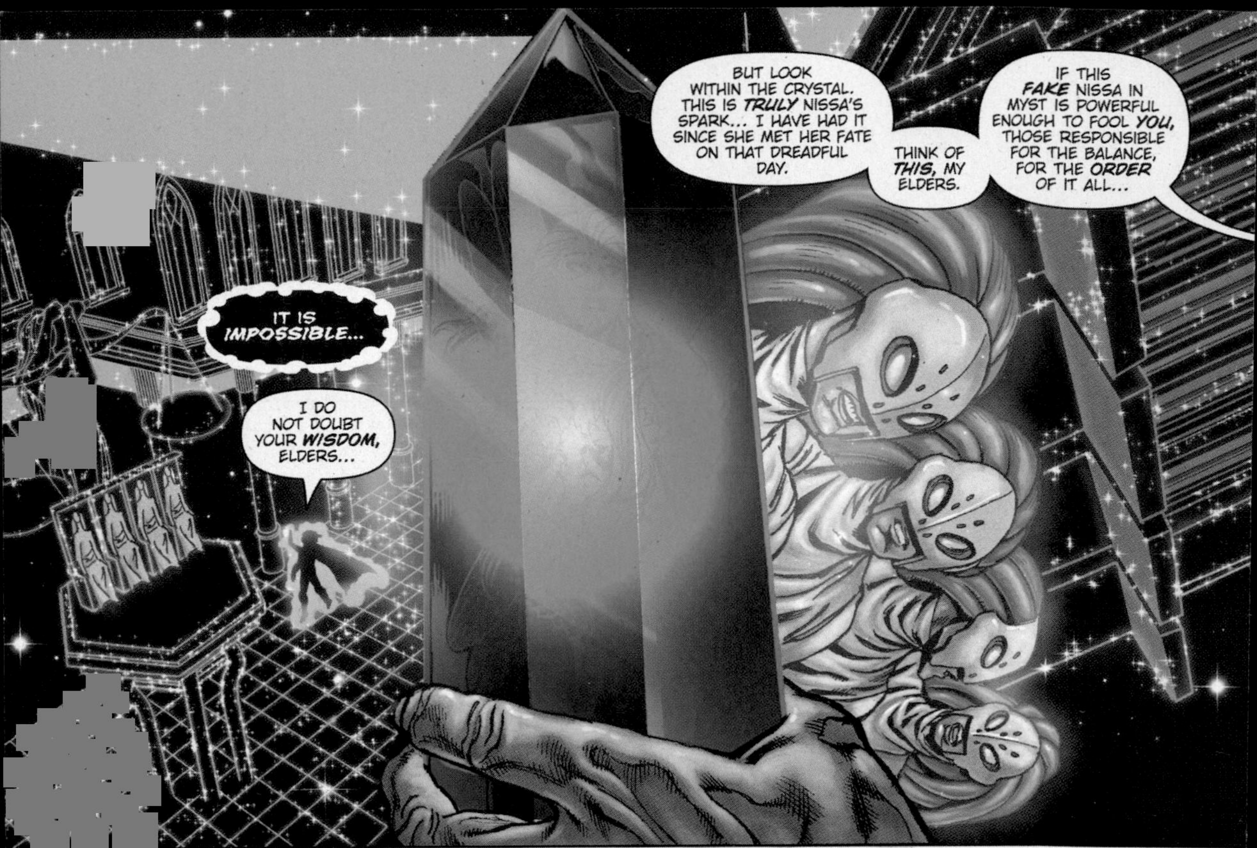
BUT LOOK WITHIN THE CRYSTAL. THIS IS TRULY NISSA'S SPARK... I HAVE HAD IT SINCE SHE MET HER FATE ON THAT DREADFUL DAY.
THINK OF THIS, MY ELDERS.
IF THIS FAKE NISSA IN MYST IS POWERFUL ENOUGH TO FOOL YOU, THOSE RESPONSIBLE FOR THE BALANCE, FOR THE ORDER OF IT ALL...
IT IS IMPOSSIBLE...
I DO NOT DOUBT YOUR WISDOM, ELDERS...

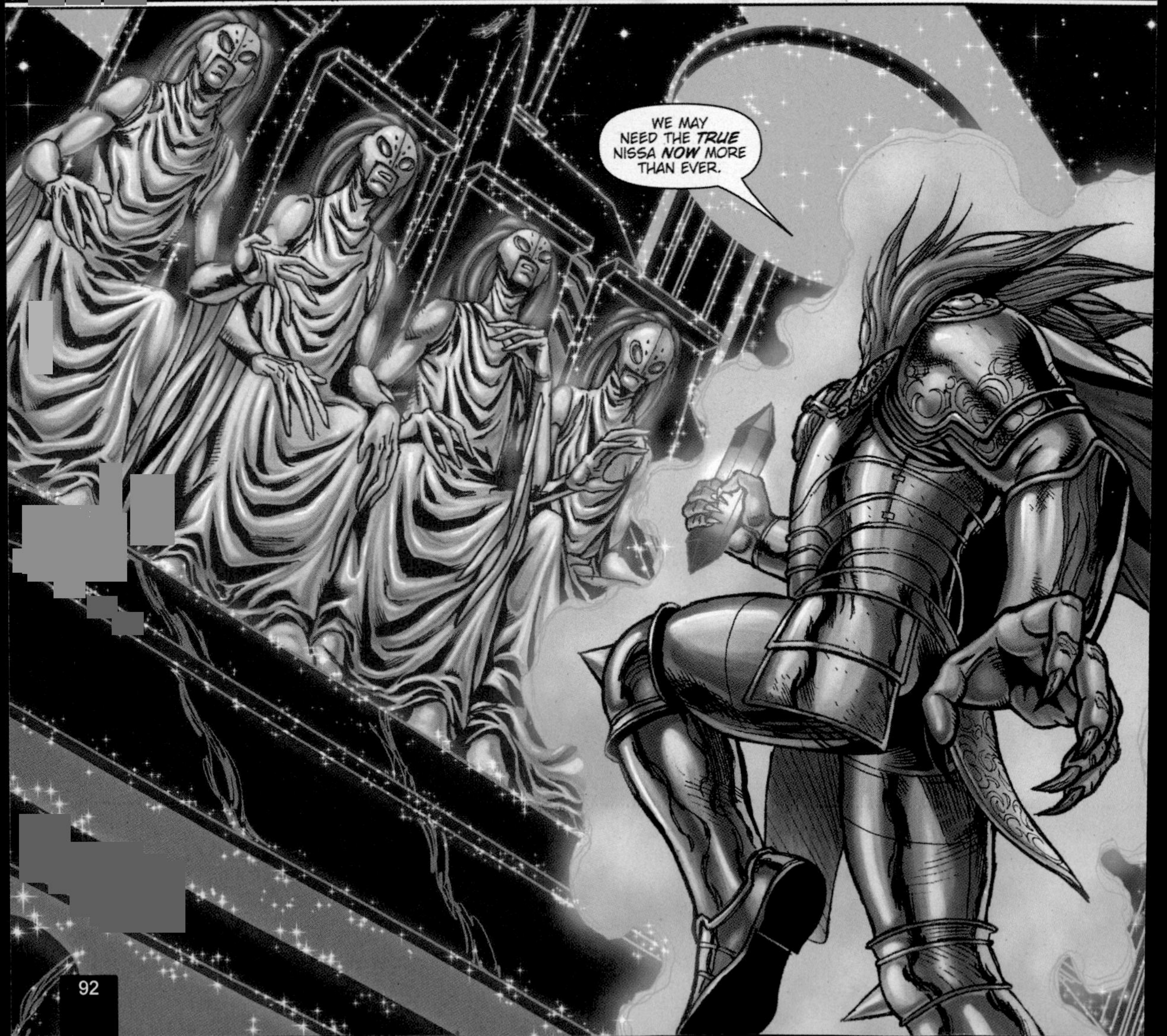
WE MAY NEED THE TRUE NISSA NOW MORE THAN EVER.

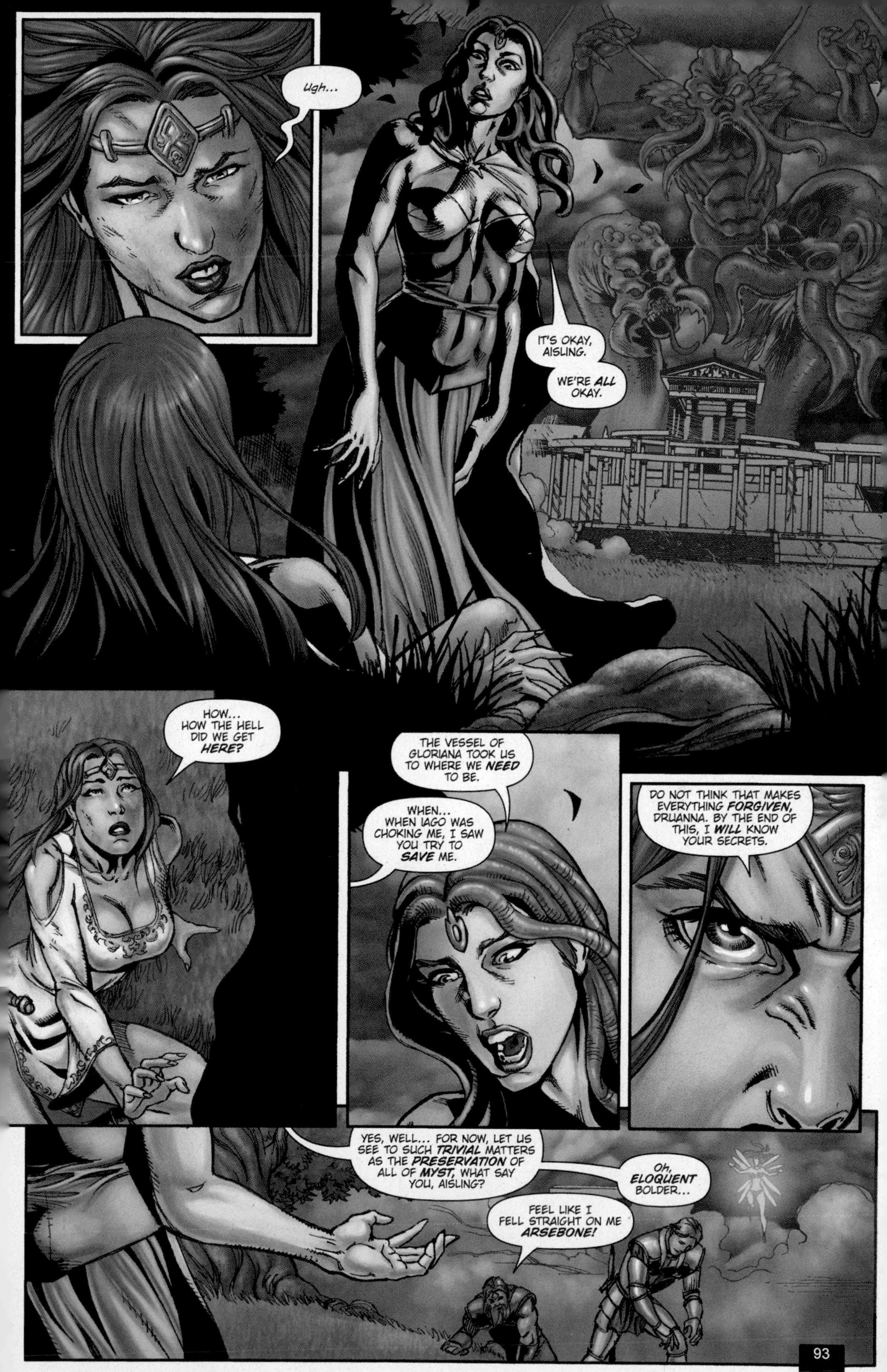
Ugh...
IT'S OKAY, AISLING.
WE'RE ALL OKAY.
HOW... HOW THE HELL DID WE GET HERE?
THE VESSEL OF GLORIANA TOOK US TO WHERE WE NEED TO BE.
WHEN... WHEN IAGO WAS CHOKING ME, I SAW YOU TRY TO SAVE ME.
DO NOT THINK THAT MAKES EVERYTHING FORGIVEN, DRUANNA. BY THE END OF THIS, I WILL KNOW YOUR SECRETS.
YES, WELL... FOR NOW, LET US SEE TO SUCH TRIVIAL MATTERS AS THE PRESERVATION OF ALL OF MYST, WHAT SAY YOU, AISLING?
Oh, ELOQUENT BOLDER...
FEEL LIKE I FELL STRAIGHT ON ME ARSEBONE!

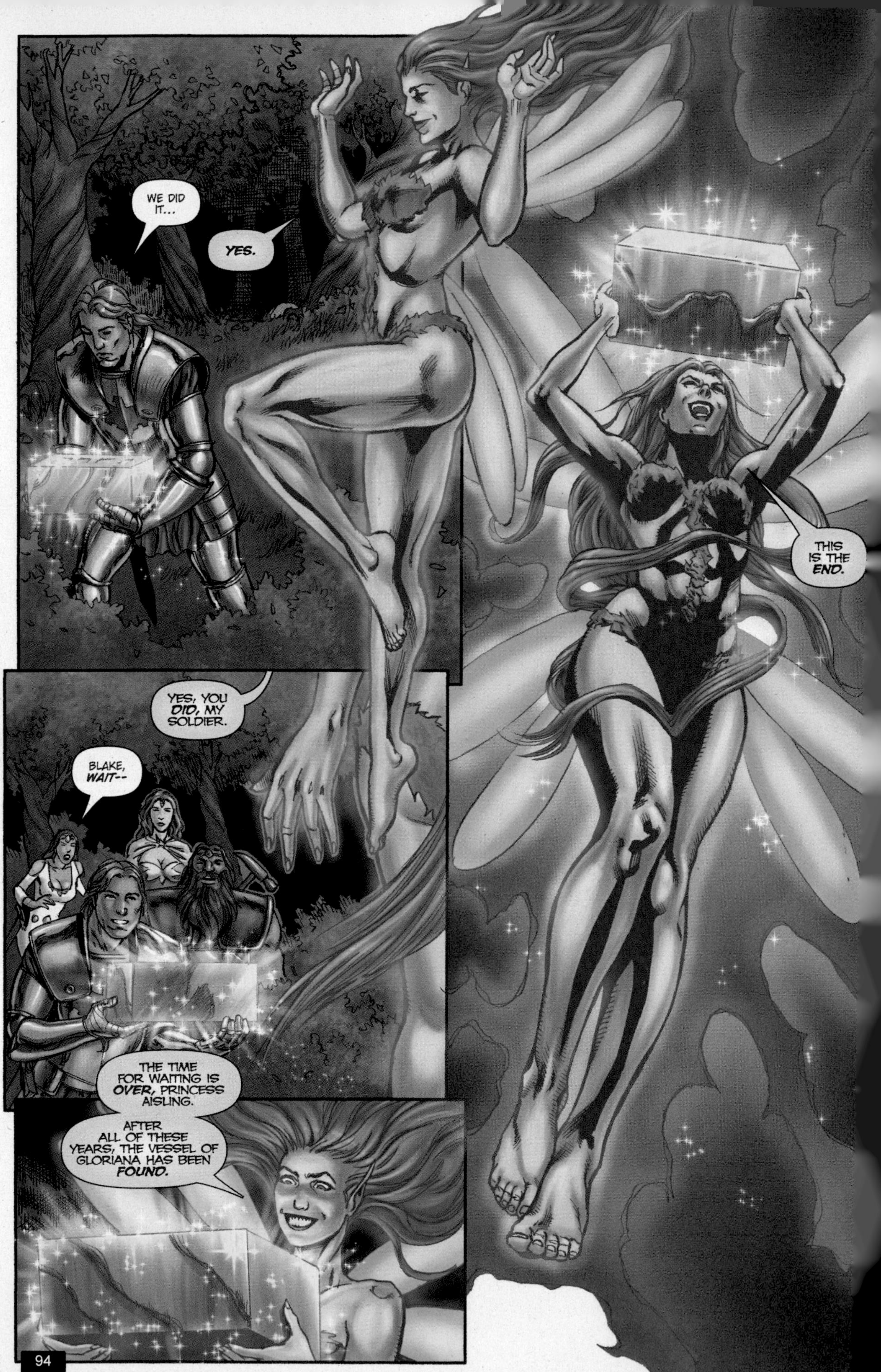
WE DID IT...
YES.
THIS IS THE END.
YES, YOU DID, MY SOLDIER.
BLAKE, WAIT--
THE TIME FOR WAITING IS OVER, PRINCESS AISLING.
AFTER ALL OF THESE YEARS, THE VESSEL OF GLORIANA HAS BEEN FOUND.

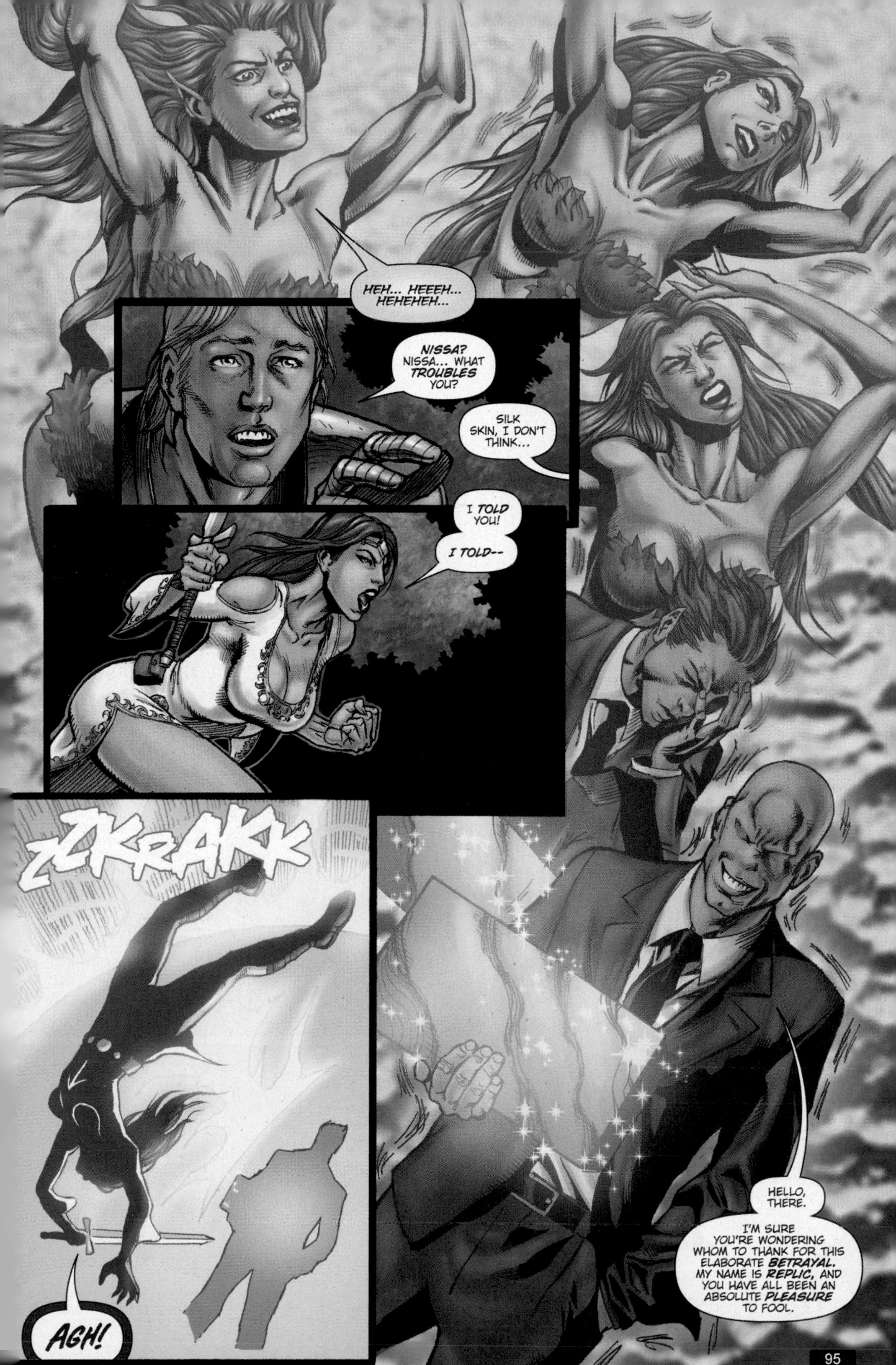

HEH... HEEEH... HEHEHEH...
NISSA? NISSA... WHAT TROUBLES YOU?
SILK SKIN, I DON'T THINK...
I TOLD YOU!
I TOLD--
ZZKRAKK
AGH!
HELLO, THERE.
I'M SURE YOU'RE WONDERING WHOM TO THANK FOR THIS ELABORATE BETRAYAL. MY NAME IS REPLIC, AND YOU HAVE ALL BEEN AN ABSOLUTE PLEASURE TO FOOL.

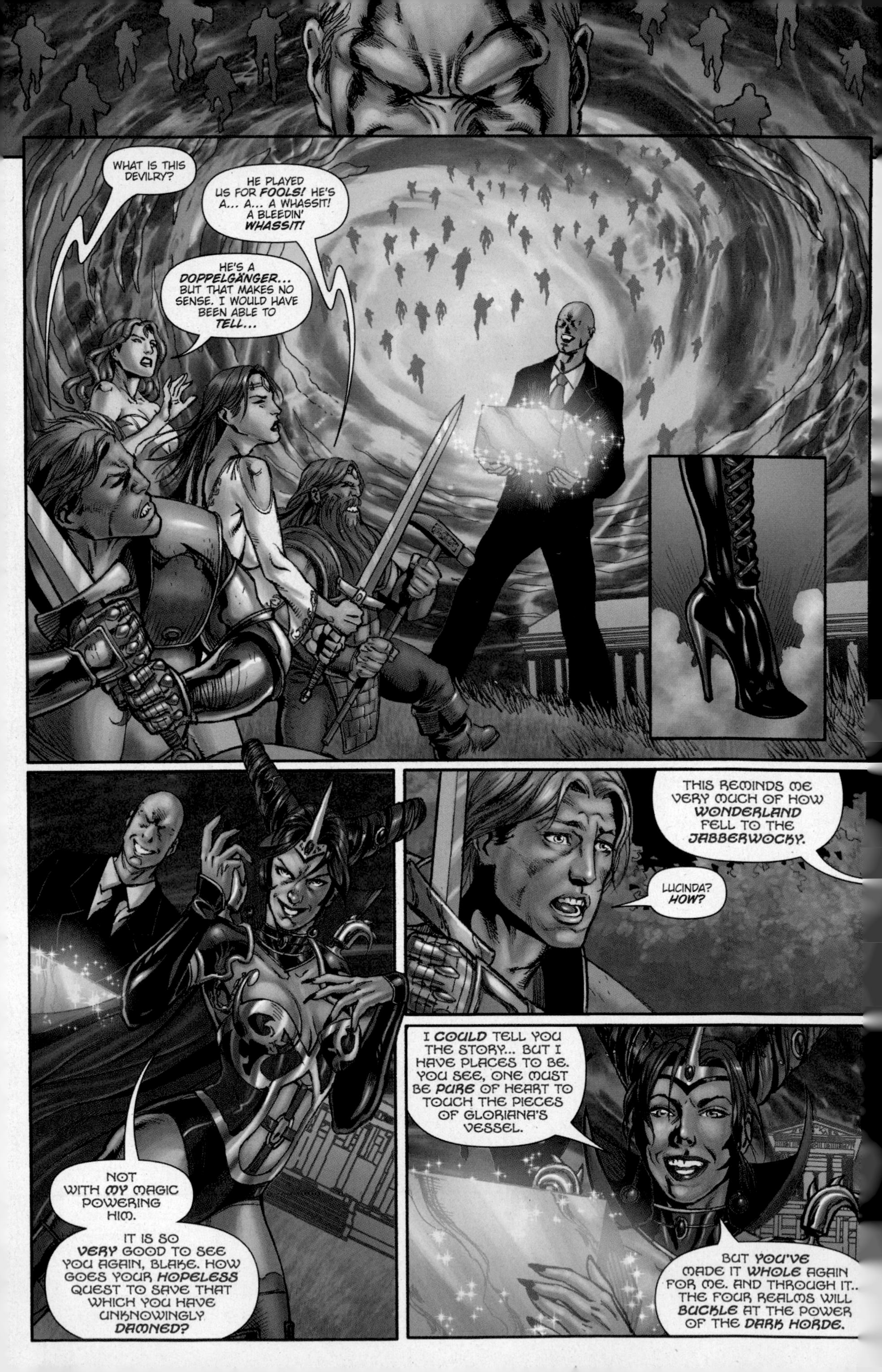
WHAT IS THIS DEVILRY?
HE PLAYED US FOR FOOLS! HE'S A... A... A WHASSIT! A BLEEDIN' WHASSIT!
HE'S A DOPPELGÄNGER... BUT THAT MAKES NO SENSE. I WOULD HAVE BEEN ABLE TO TELL...
THIS REMINDS ME VERY MUCH OF HOW WONDERLAND FELL TO THE JABBERWOCKY.
LUCINDA? HOW?
NOT WITH MY MAGIC POWERING HIM.
IT IS SO VERY GOOD TO SEE YOU AGAIN, BLAKE. HOW GOES YOUR HOPELESS QUEST TO SAVE THAT WHICH YOU HAVE UNKNOWINGLY DAMNED?
I COULD TELL YOU THE STORY... BUT I HAVE PLACES TO BE. YOU SEE, ONE MUST BE PURE OF HEART TO TOUCH THE PIECES OF GLORIANA'S VESSEL.
BUT YOU'VE MADE IT WHOLE AGAIN FOR ME. AND THROUGH IT... THE FOUR REALMS WILL BUCKLE AT THE POWER OF THE DARK HORDE.

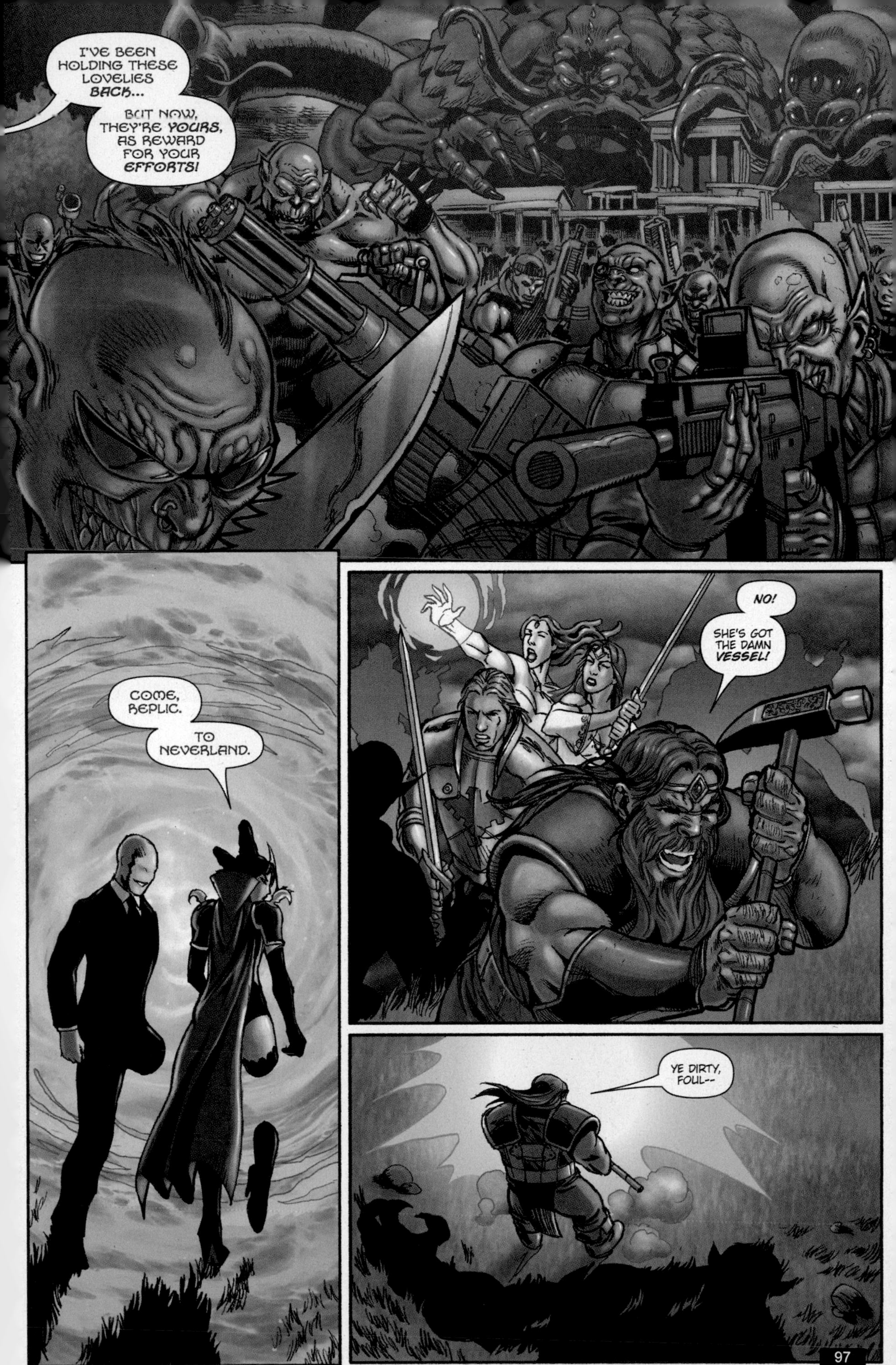
I'VE BEEN HOLDING THESE LOVELIES BACK...
BUT NOW, THEY'RE YOURS, AS REWARD FOR YOUR EFFORTS!
COME, REPLIC.
TO NEVERLAND.
NO!
SHE'S GOT THE DAMN VESSEL!
YE DIRTY, FOUL--

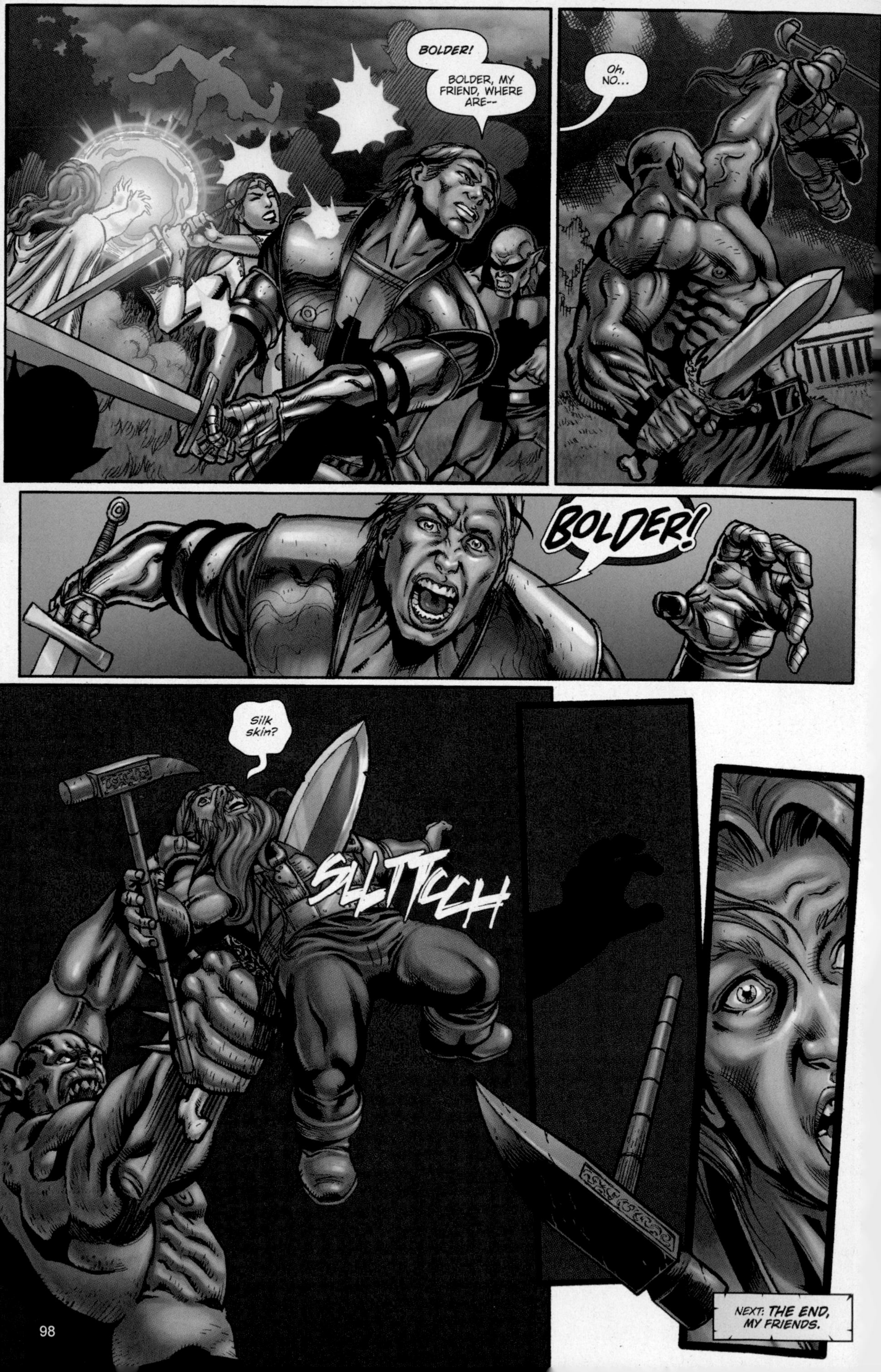
BOLDER!
BOLDER, MY FRIEND, WHERE ARE--
Oh, NO...
BOLDER!
Silk skin?
SLLTTCCH
NEXT: THE END, MY FRIENDS.

Grimm Fairy Tales presents:

QUEST

AGE OF DARKNESS

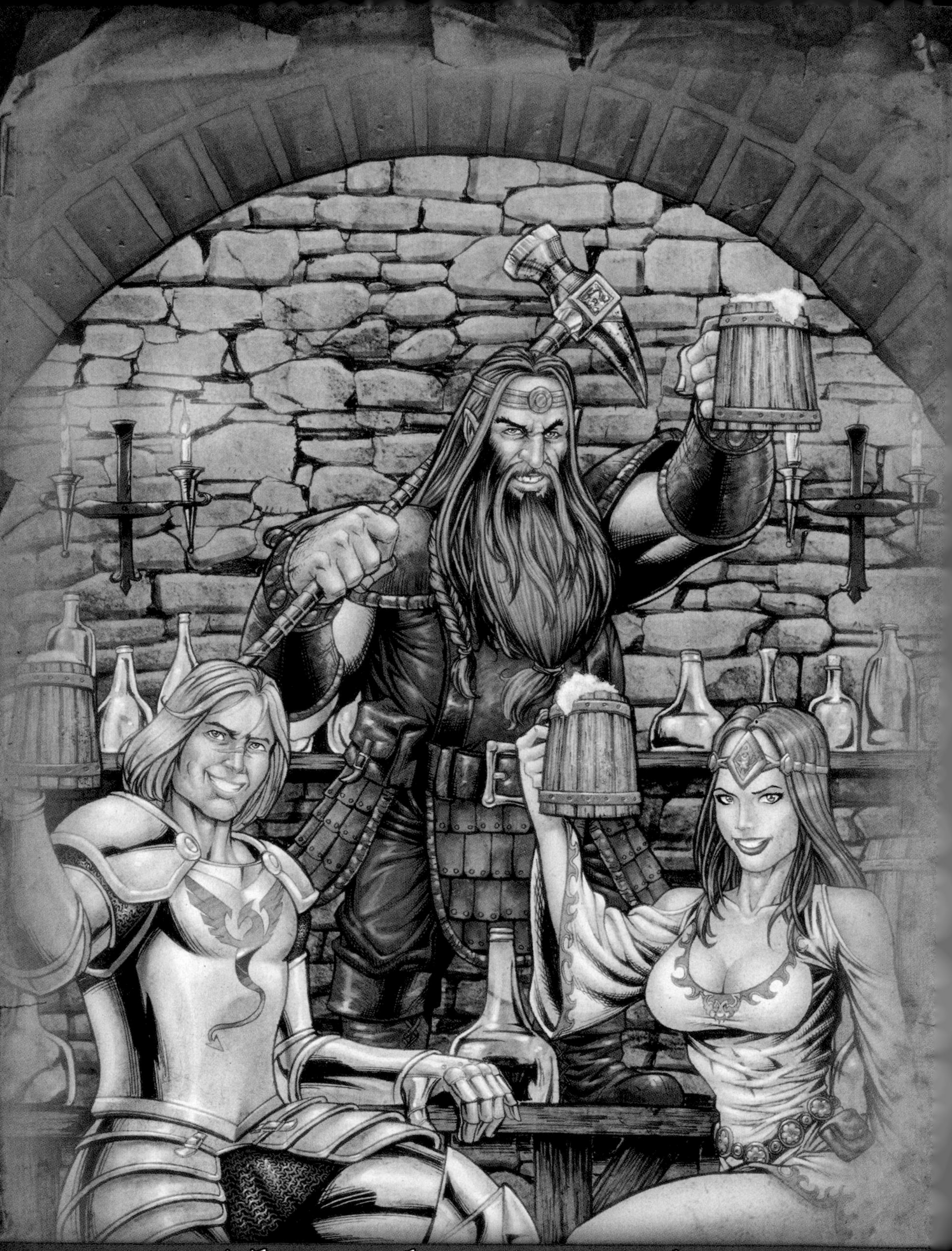

The End, My Friends

WRITER PAT SHAND
ARTWORK NOAH SALONGA
COLORS FRANCESCA ZAMBON
LETTERS JIM CAMPBELL

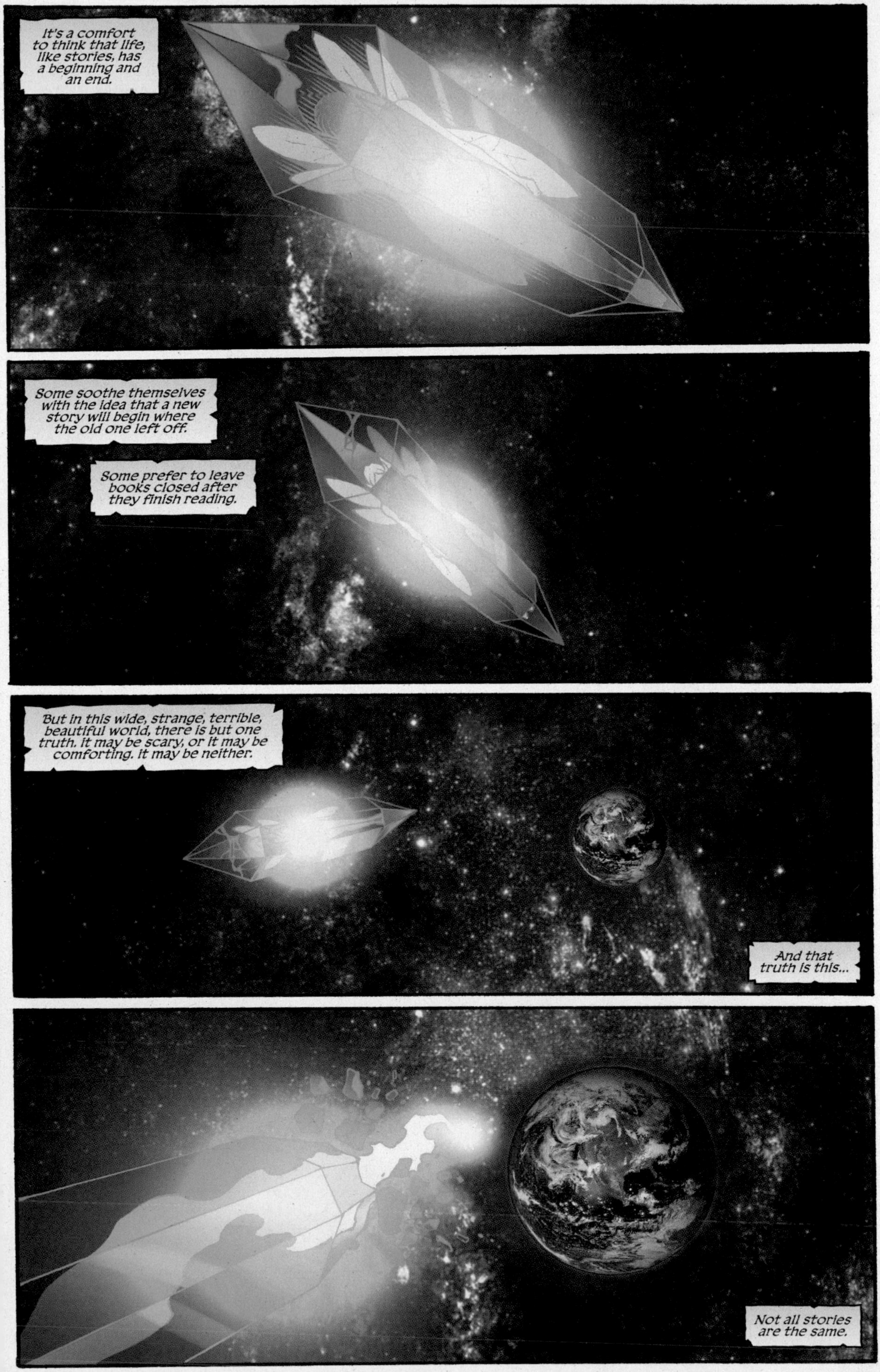
It's a comfort to think that life, like stories, has a beginning and an end.
Some soothe themselves with the idea that a new story will begin where the old one left off.
Some prefer to leave books closed after they finish reading.
But in this wide, strange, terrible, beautiful world, there is but one truth. It may be scary, or it may be comforting. It may be neither.
And that truth is this...
Not all stories are the same.

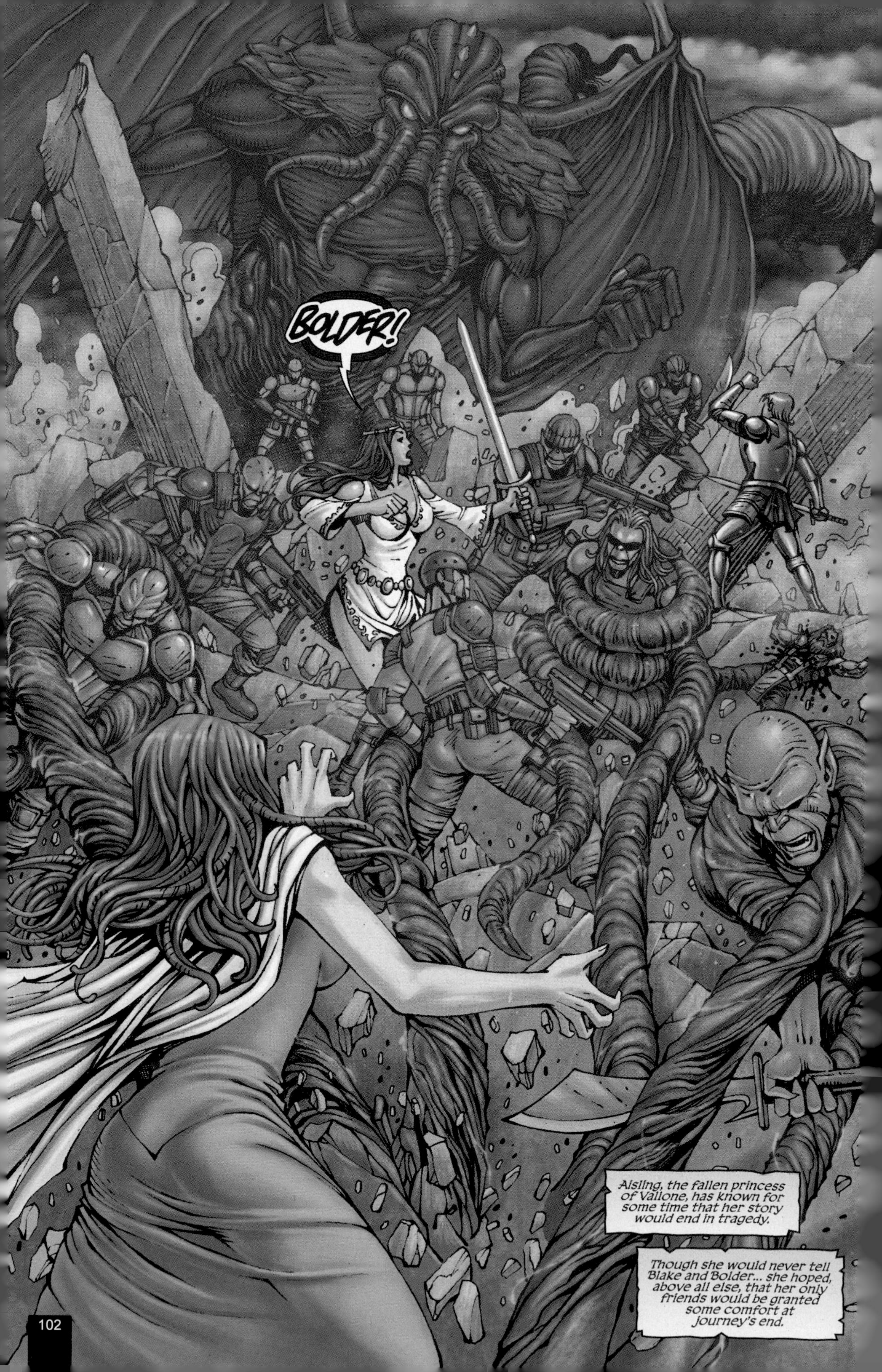
BOLDER!
Aisling, the fallen princess of Vallone, has known for some time that her story would end in tragedy.
Though she would never tell Blake and Bolder... she hoped, above all else, that her only friends would be granted some comfort at journey's end.

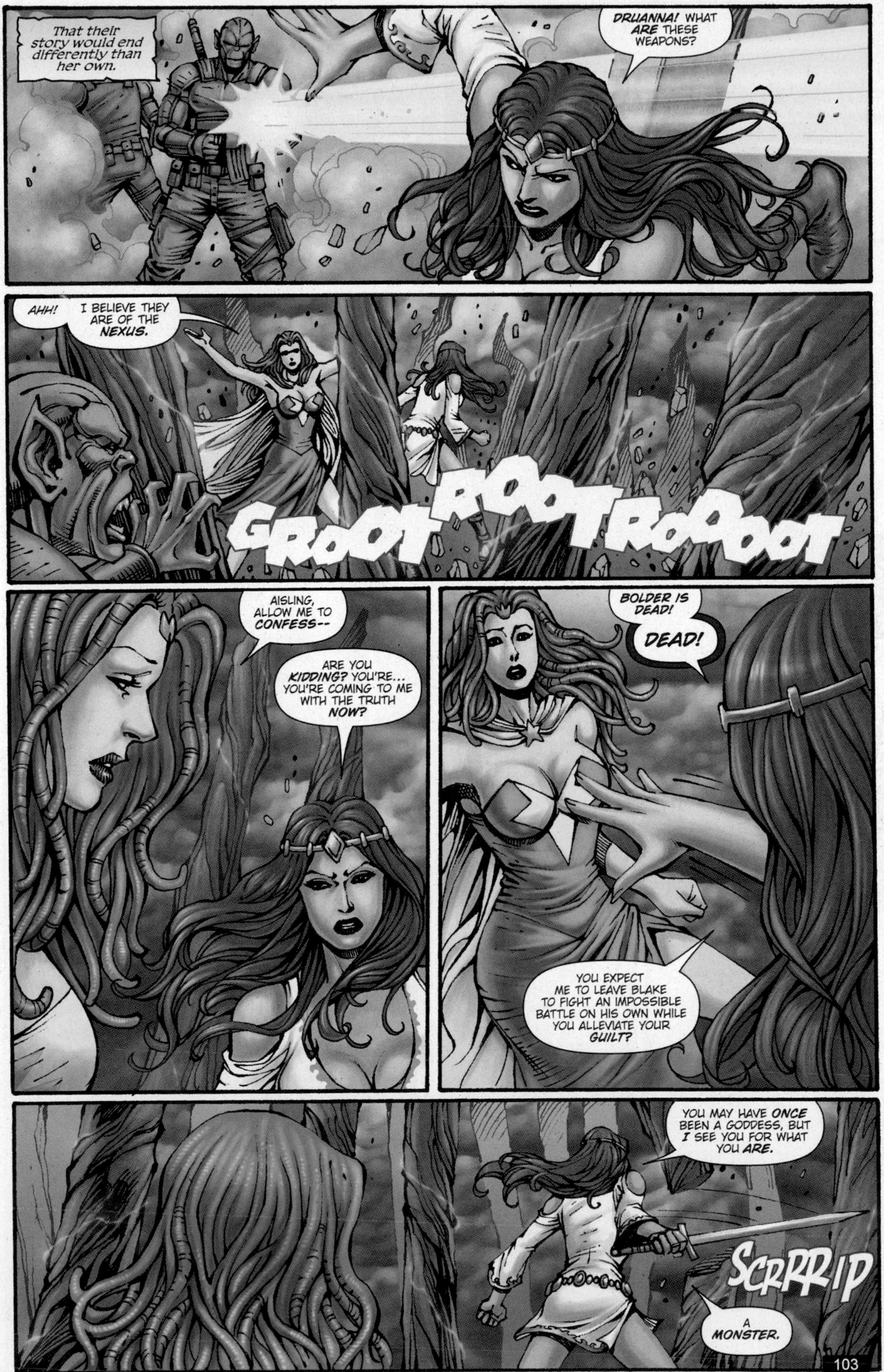
That their story would end differently than her own.
DRUANNA! WHAT ARE THESE WEAPONS?
AHH!
I BELIEVE THEY ARE OF THE NEXUS.
GROOT ROOT ROOT ROOOOT
AISLING, ALLOW ME TO CONFESS--
ARE YOU KIDDING? YOU'RE... YOU'RE COMING TO ME WITH THE TRUTH NOW?
BOLDER IS DEAD!
DEAD!
YOU EXPECT ME TO LEAVE BLAKE TO FIGHT AN IMPOSSIBLE BATTLE ON HIS OWN WHILE YOU ALLEVIATE YOUR GUILT?
YOU MAY HAVE ONCE BEEN A GODDESS, BUT I SEE YOU FOR WHAT YOU ARE.
SCRRRIP
A MONSTER.

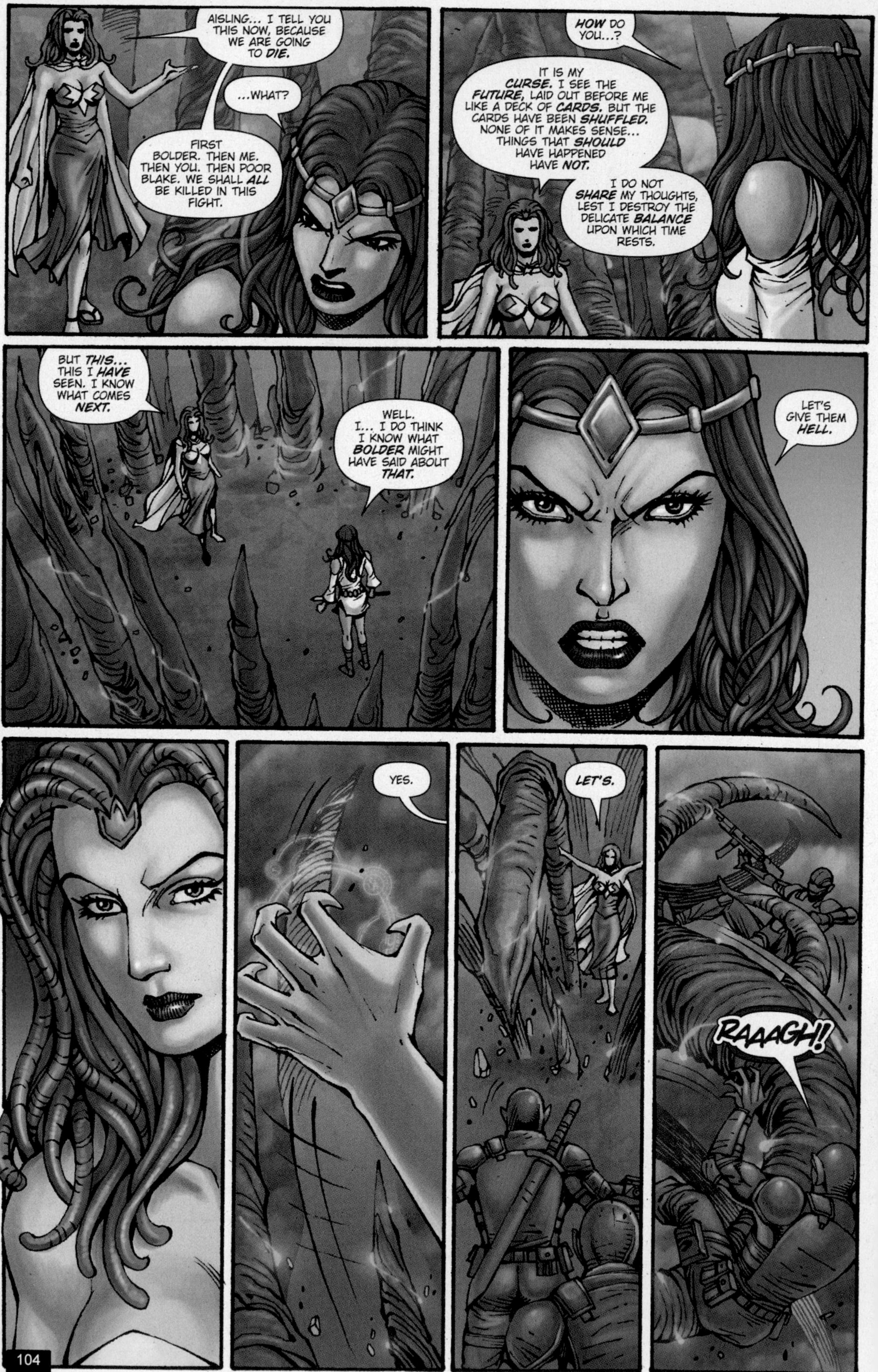
AISLING... I TELL YOU THIS NOW, BECAUSE WE ARE GOING TO DIE.
...WHAT?
FIRST BOLDER. THEN ME. THEN YOU. THEN POOR BLAKE. WE SHALL ALL BE KILLED IN THIS FIGHT.
HOW DO YOU...?
IT IS MY CURSE. I SEE THE FUTURE, LAID OUT BEFORE ME LIKE A DECK OF CARDS. BUT THE CARDS HAVE BEEN SHUFFLED. NONE OF IT MAKES SENSE... THINGS THAT SHOULD HAVE HAPPENED HAVE NOT.
I DO NOT SHARE MY THOUGHTS, LEST I DESTROY THE DELICATE BALANCE UPON WHICH TIME RESTS.
BUT THIS... THIS I HAVE SEEN. I KNOW WHAT COMES NEXT.
WELL. I... I DO THINK I KNOW WHAT BOLDER MIGHT HAVE SAID ABOUT THAT.
LET'S GIVE THEM HELL.
YES.
LET'S.
RAAAGH!!

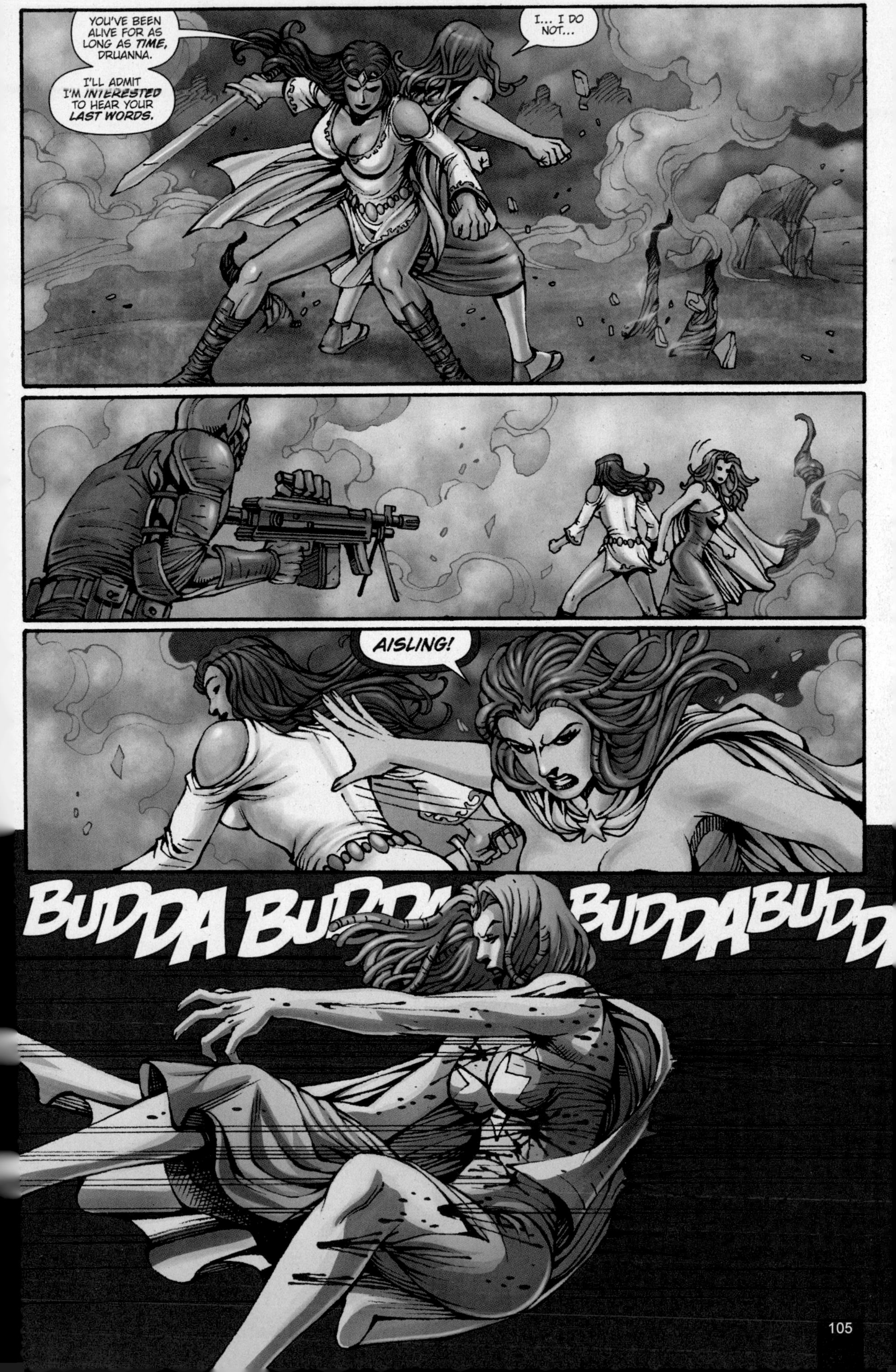
YOU'VE BEEN ALIVE FOR AS LONG AS TIME, DRUANNA.
I'LL ADMIT I'M INTERESTED TO HEAR YOUR LAST WORDS.
I... I DO NOT...
AISLING!
BUDDA BUDD
BUDDABUDD

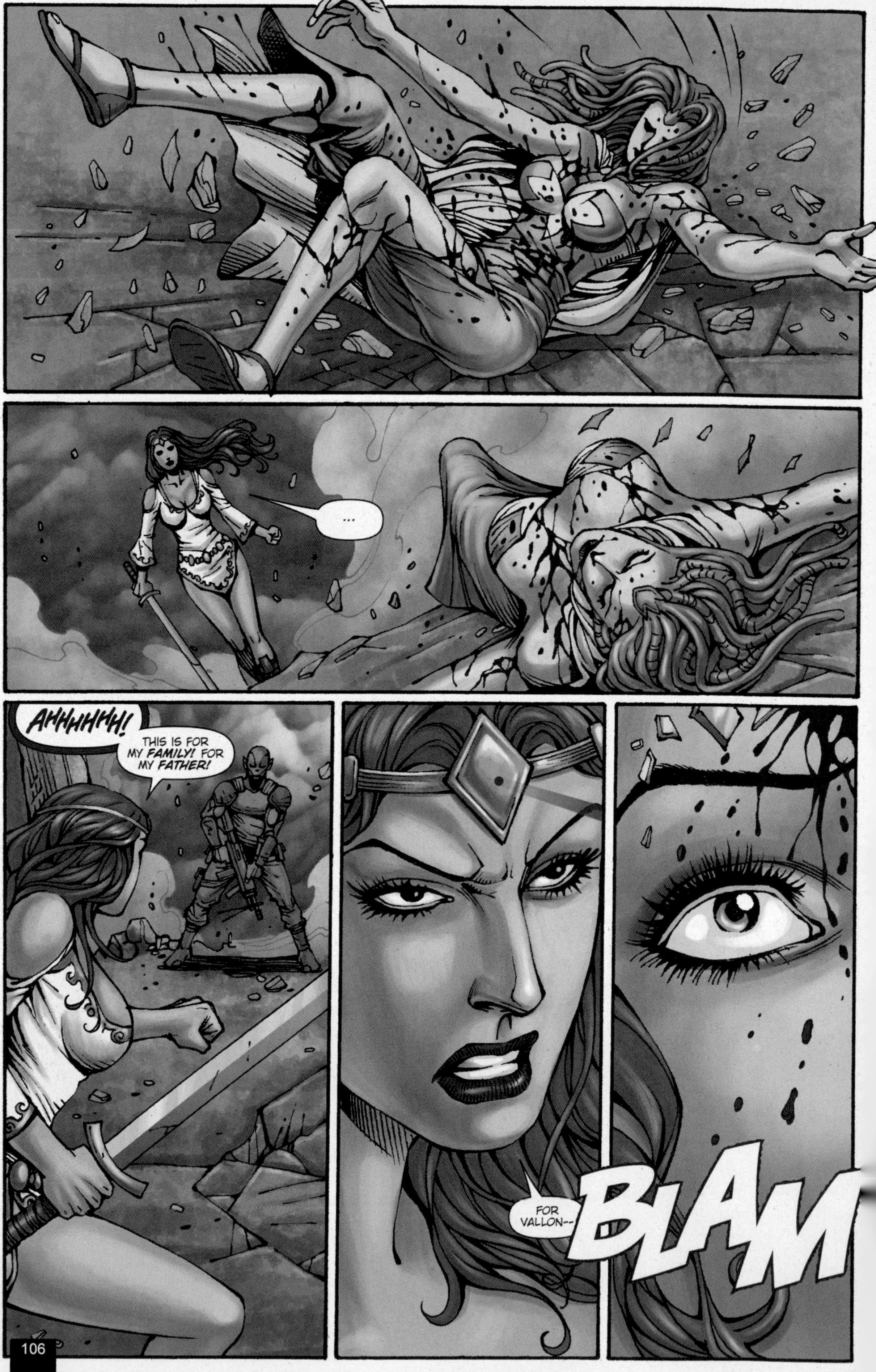
...
AHHHHHH!
THIS IS FOR MY FAMILY! FOR MY FATHER!
FOR VALLON--
BLAM

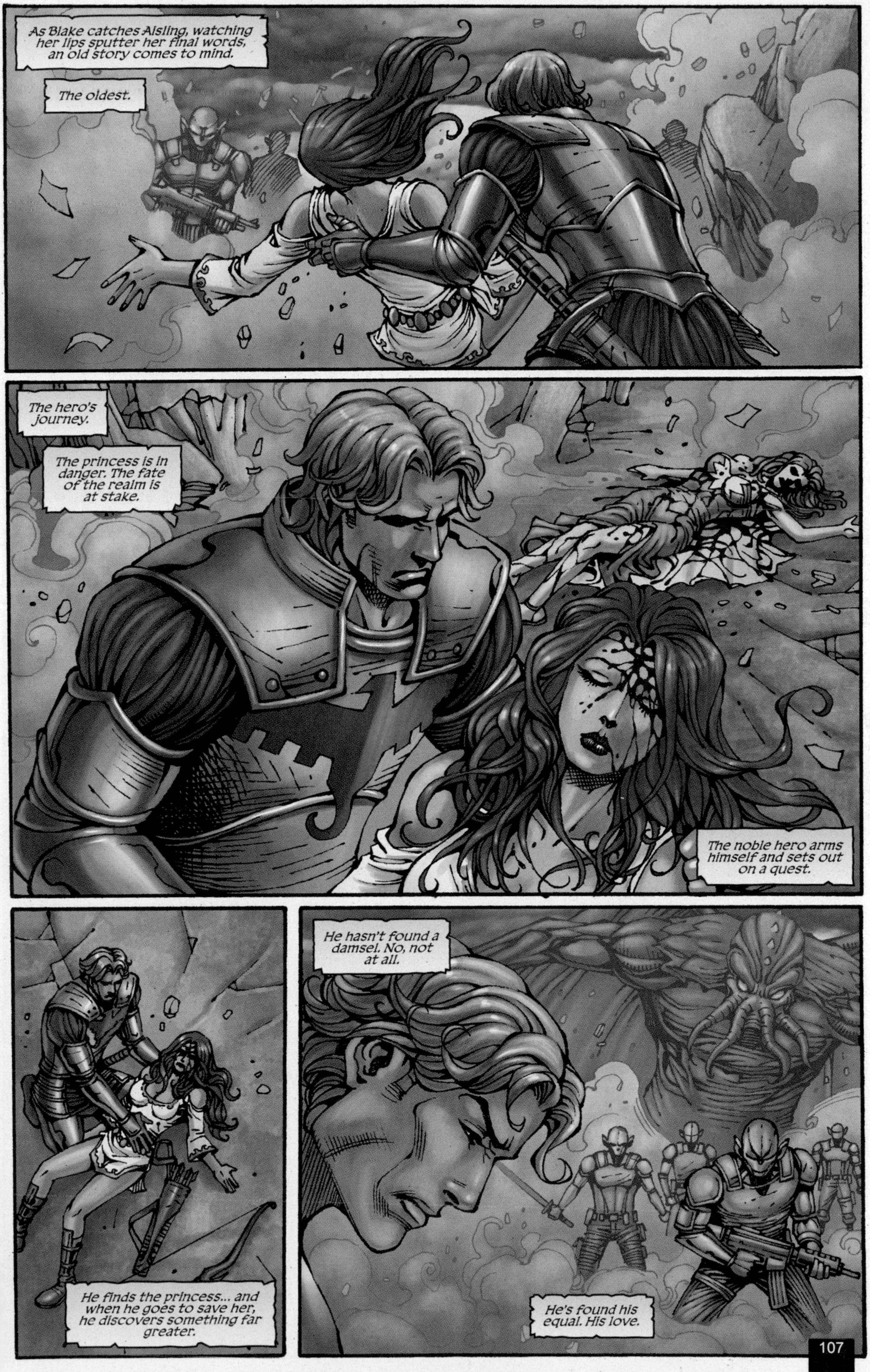
As Blake catches Aisling, watching her lips sputter her final words, an old story comes to mind.
The oldest.
The hero's journey.
The princess is in danger. The fate of the realm is at stake.
The noble hero arms himself and sets out on a quest.
He finds the princess... and when he goes to save her, he discovers something far greater.
He hasn't found a damsel. No, not at all.
He's found his equal. His love.

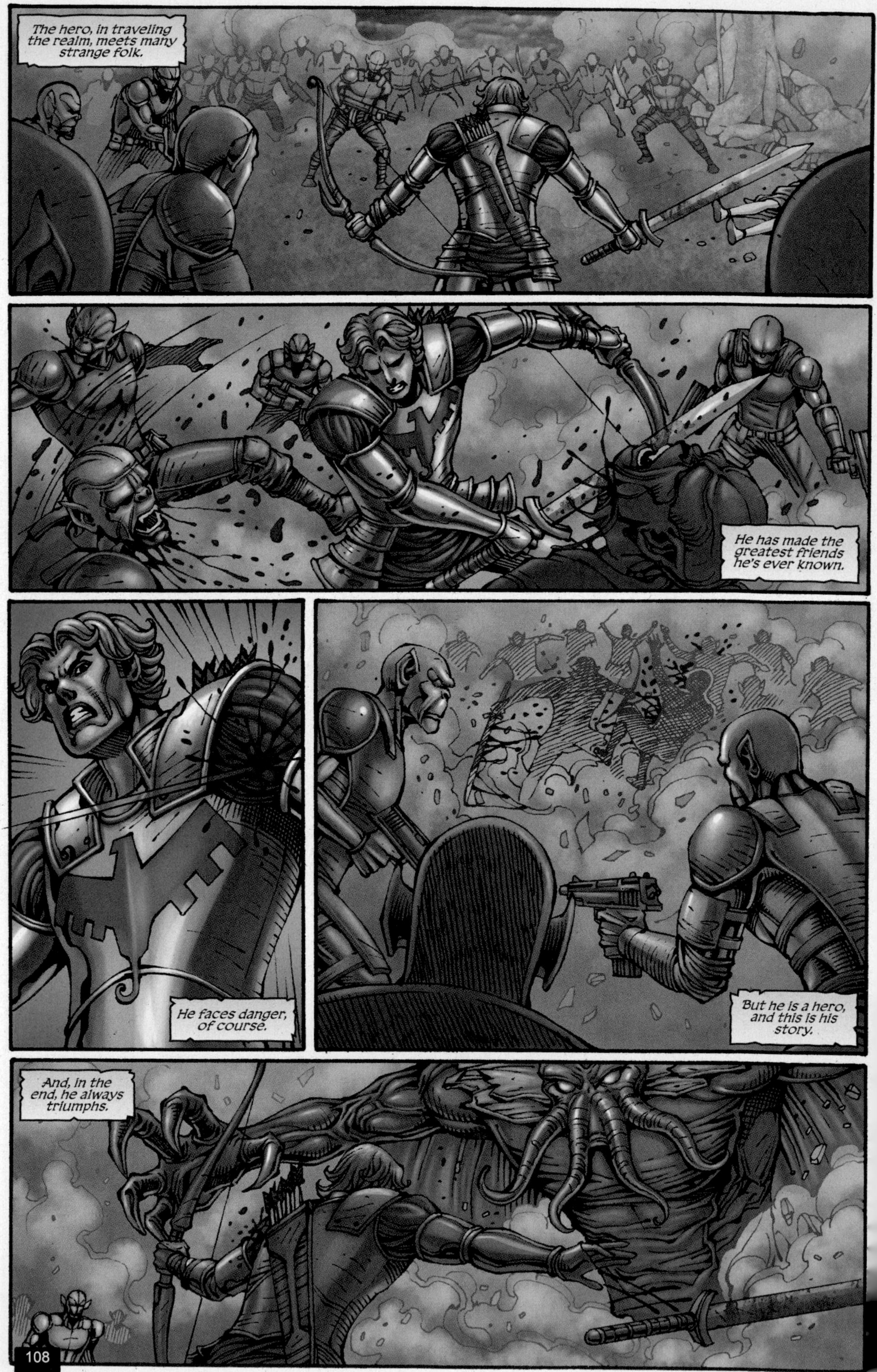
The hero, in traveling the realm, meets many strange folk.
He has made the greatest friends he's ever known.
He faces danger, of course.
But he is a hero, and this is his story.
And, in the end, he always triumphs.

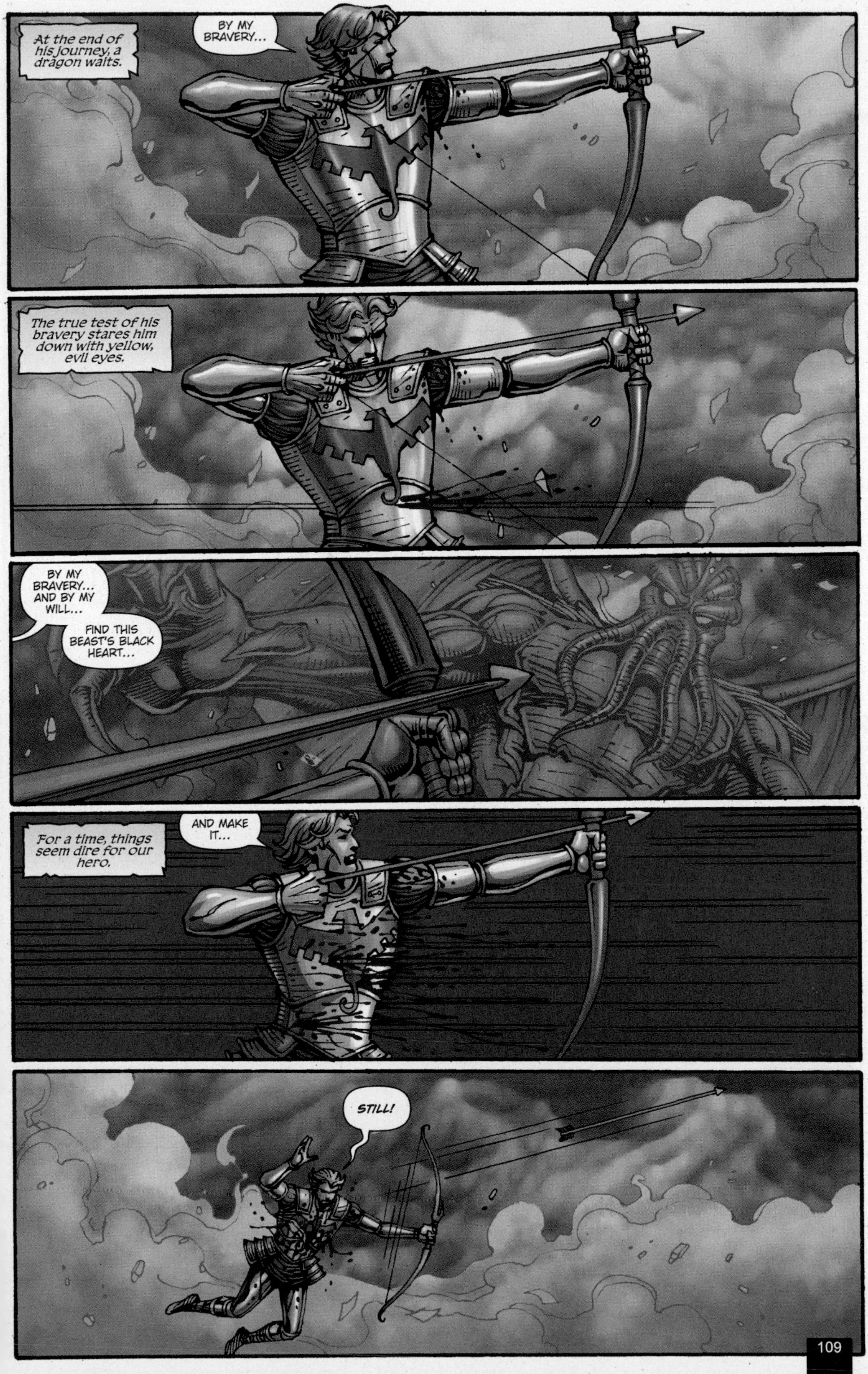
At the end of his journey, a dragon waits.
BY MY BRAVERY...
The true test of his bravery stares him down with yellow, evil eyes.
BY MY BRAVERY... AND BY MY WILL...
FIND THIS BEAST'S BLACK HEART...
For a time, things seem dire for our hero.
AND MAKE IT...
STILL!

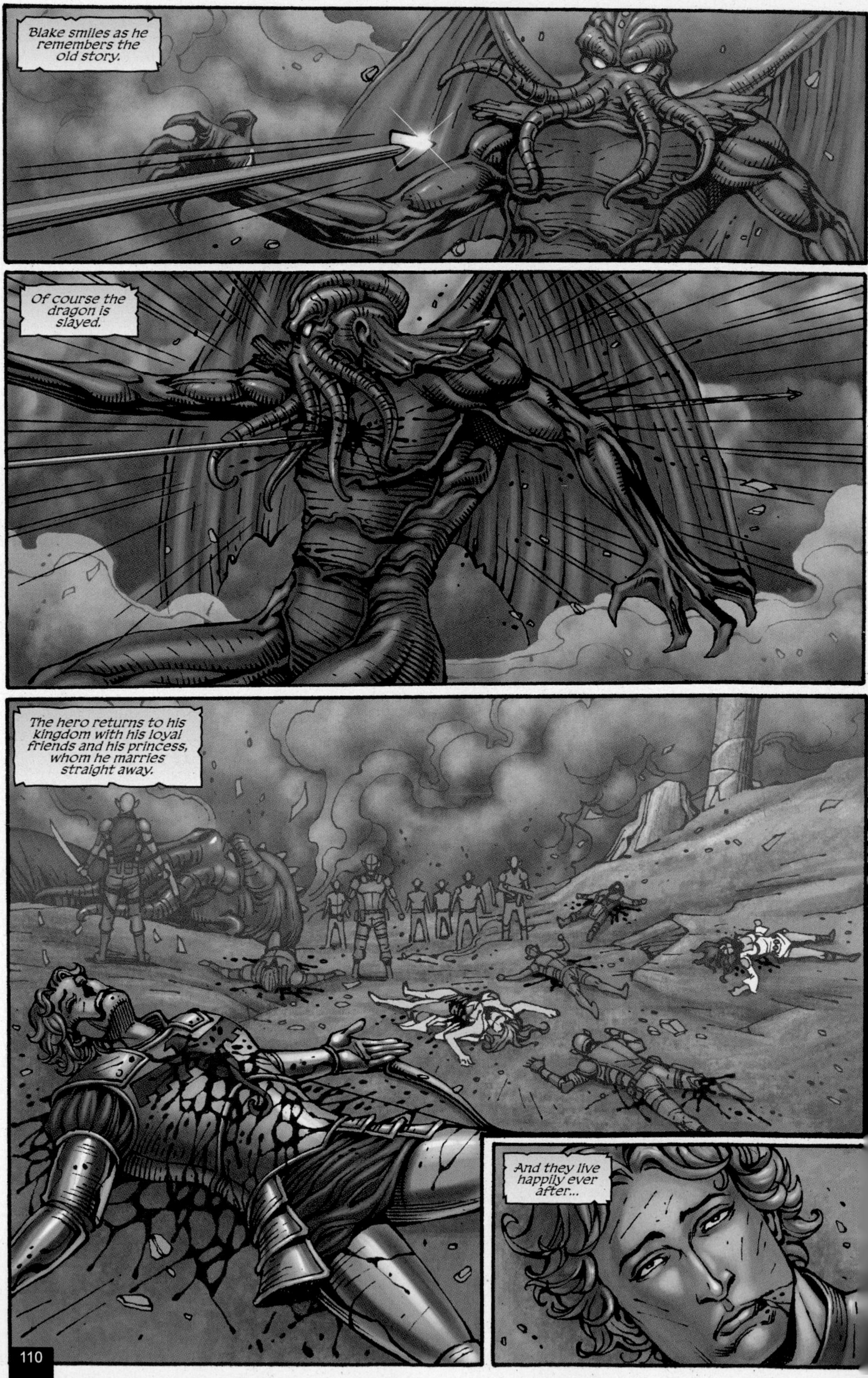
Blake smiles as he remembers the old story.
Of course the dragon is slayed.
The hero returns to his kingdom with his loyal friends and his princess, whom he marries straight away.
And they live happily ever after...

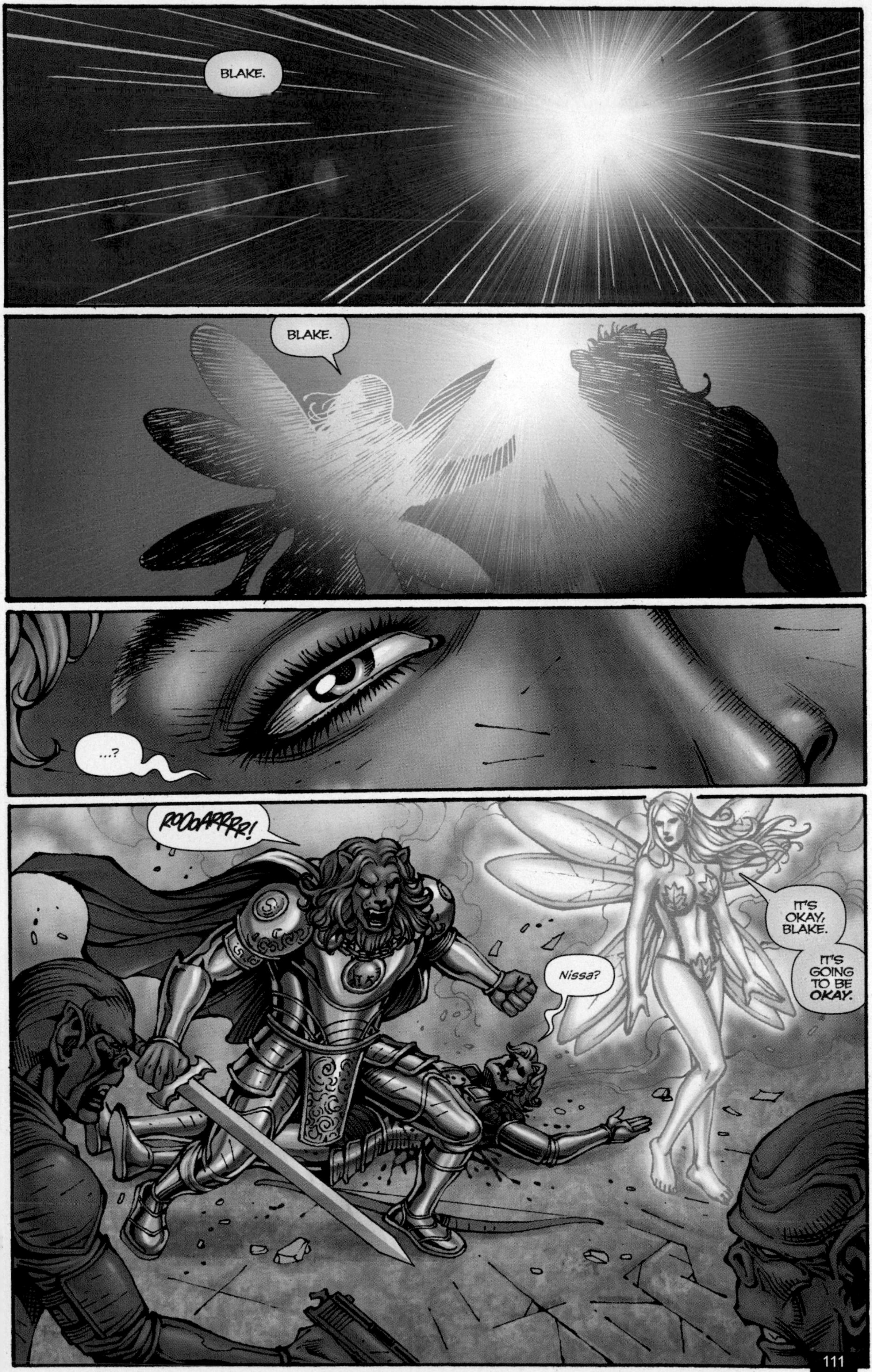
BLAKE.
BLAKE.
...?
ROOOARRRR!
IT'S OKAY, BLAKE.
IT'S GOING TO BE OKAY.
Nissa?

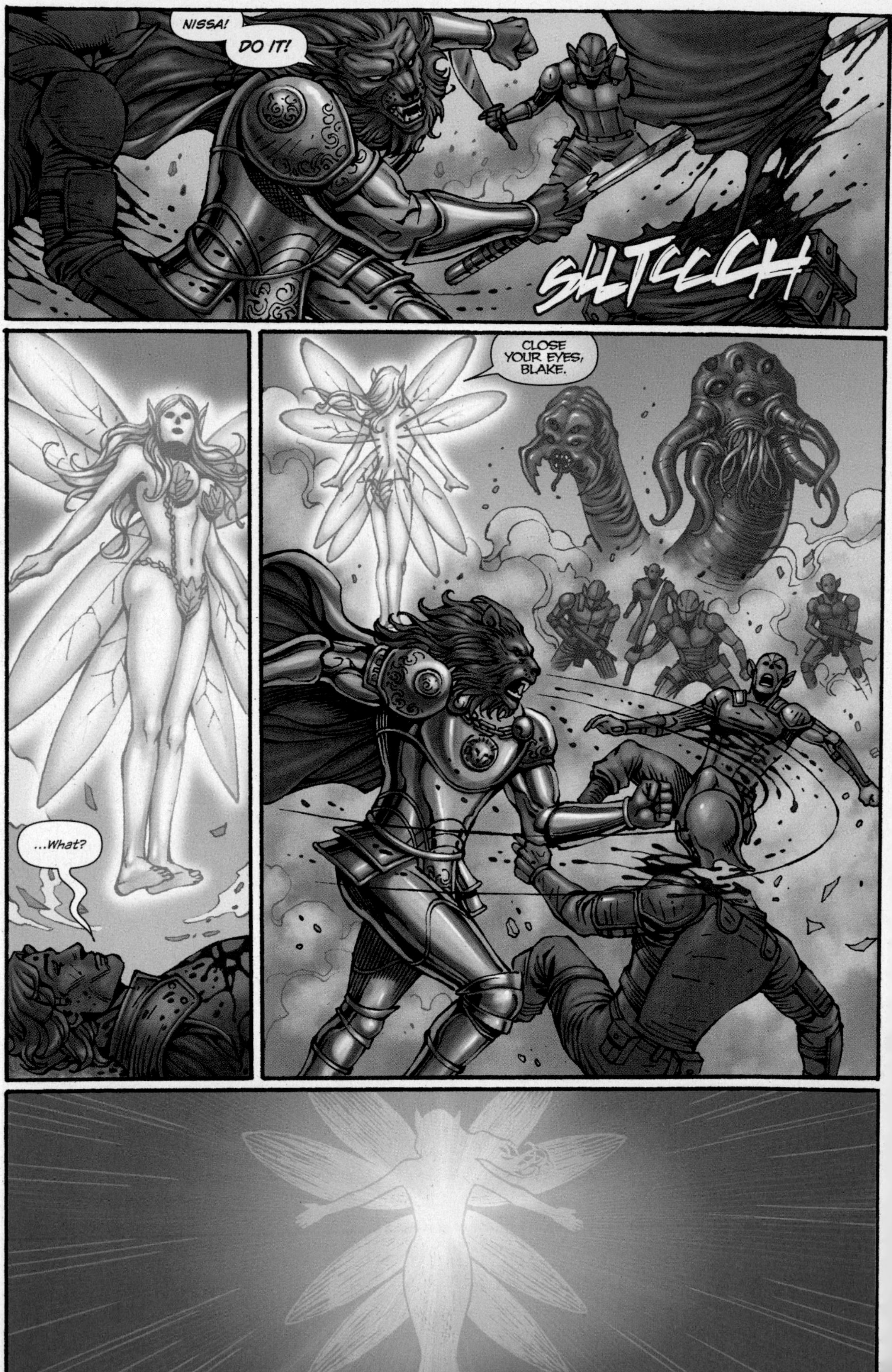
NISSA!
DO IT!
SHLTCCCH
...What?
CLOSE YOUR EYES, BLAKE.

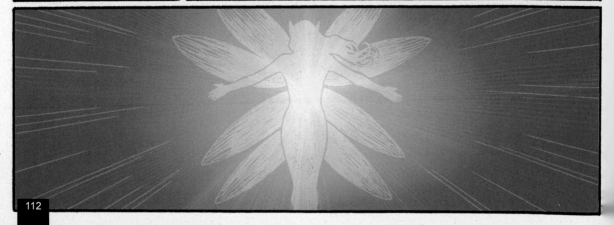

YOU FAILED AGAIN, BLAKE.
WOULD YOU HAVE LOVED ME?
SILK SKIN!
NO...
NO!

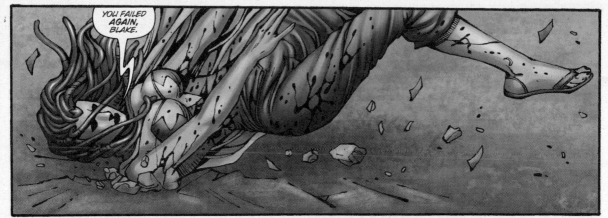

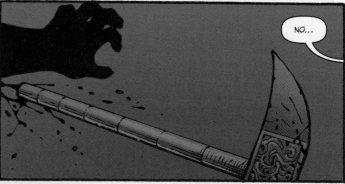

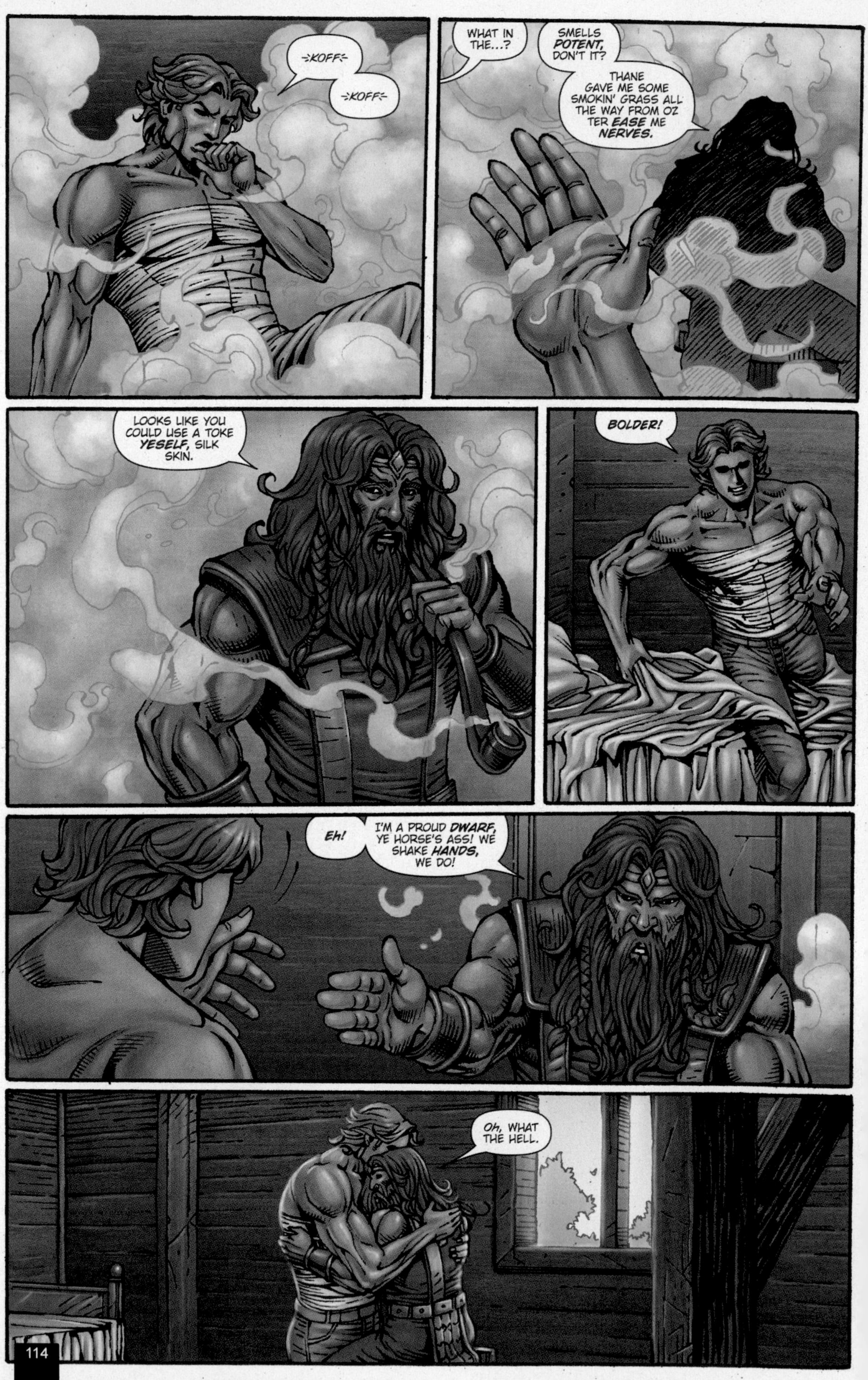

-KOFF-
-KOFF-
WHAT IN THE...?
SMELLS POTENT, DON'T IT?
THANE GAVE ME SOME SMOKIN' GRASS ALL THE WAY FROM OZ TER EASE ME NERVES.
LOOKS LIKE YOU COULD USE A TOKE YESELF, SILK SKIN.
BOLDER!
Eh!
I'M A PROUD DWARF, YE HORSE'S ASS! WE SHAKE HANDS, WE DO!
Oh, WHAT THE HELL.

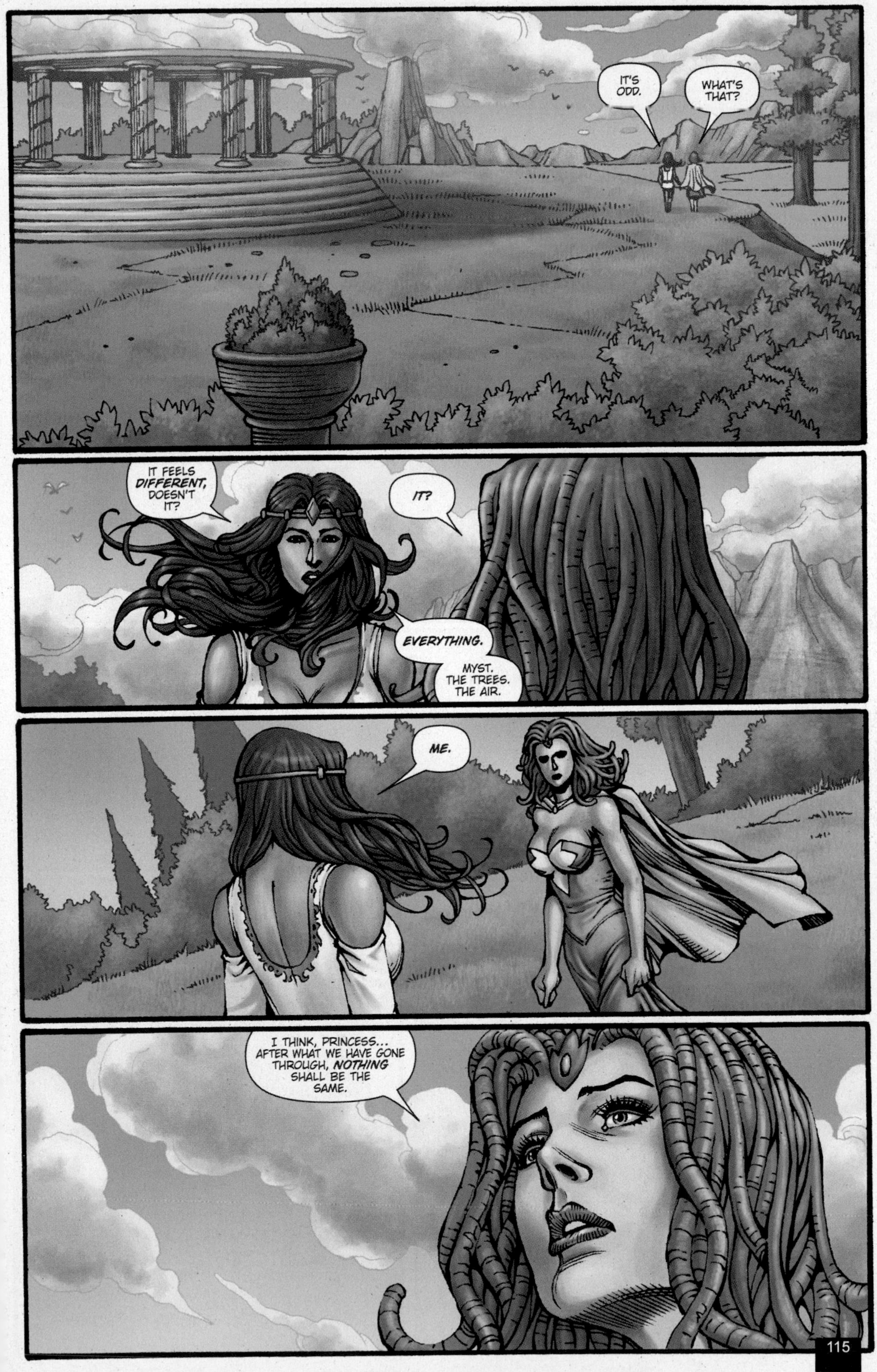
IT'S ODD.
WHAT'S THAT?
IT FEELS DIFFERENT, DOESN'T IT?
IT?
EVERYTHING.
MYST. THE TREES. THE AIR.
ME.
I THINK, PRINCESS... AFTER WHAT WE HAVE GONE THROUGH, NOTHING SHALL BE THE SAME.

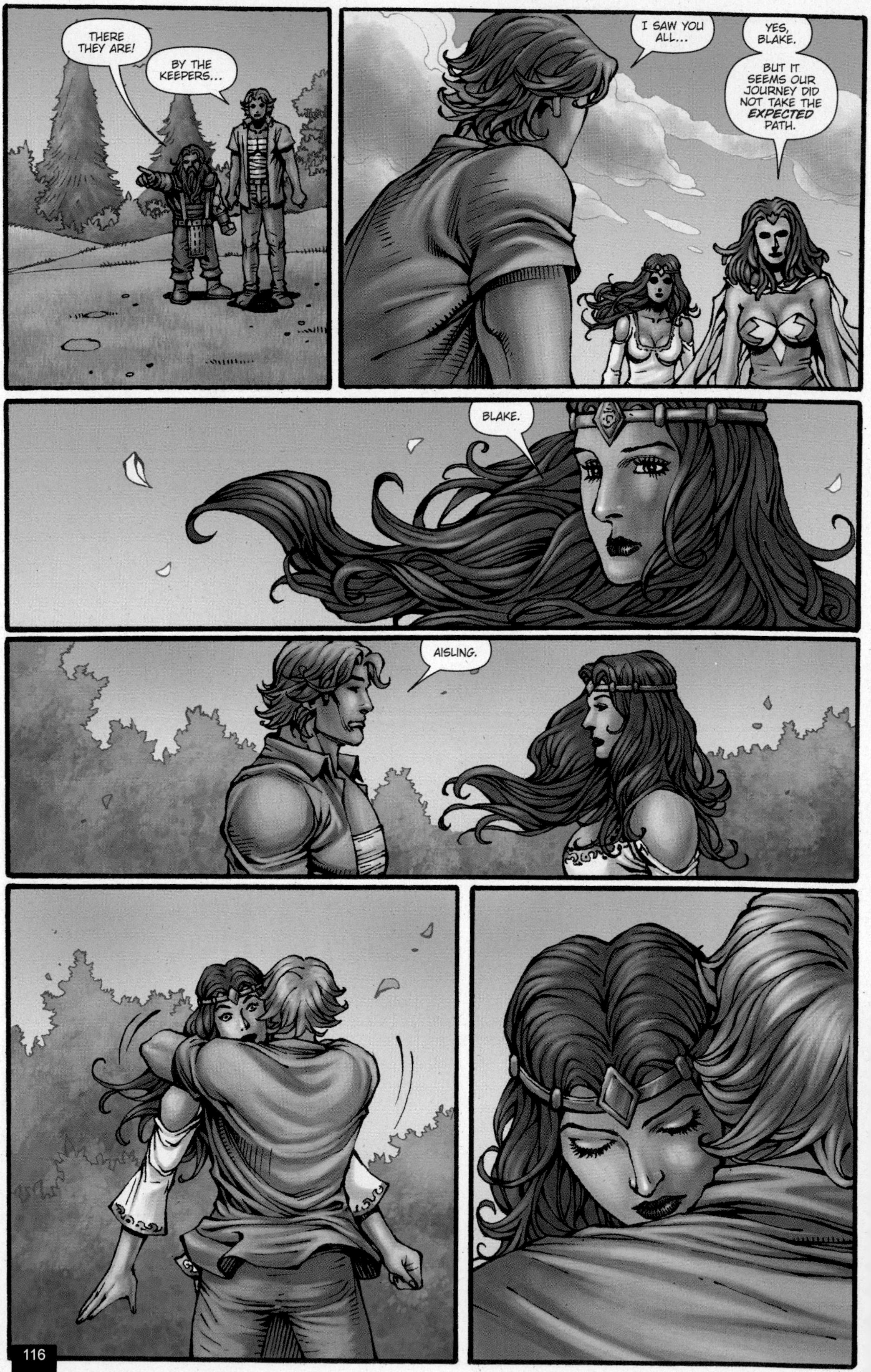

THERE THEY ARE!
BY THE KEEPERS...
I SAW YOU ALL...
YES, BLAKE.
BUT IT SEEMS OUR JOURNEY DID NOT TAKE THE EXPECTED PATH.
BLAKE.
AISLING.

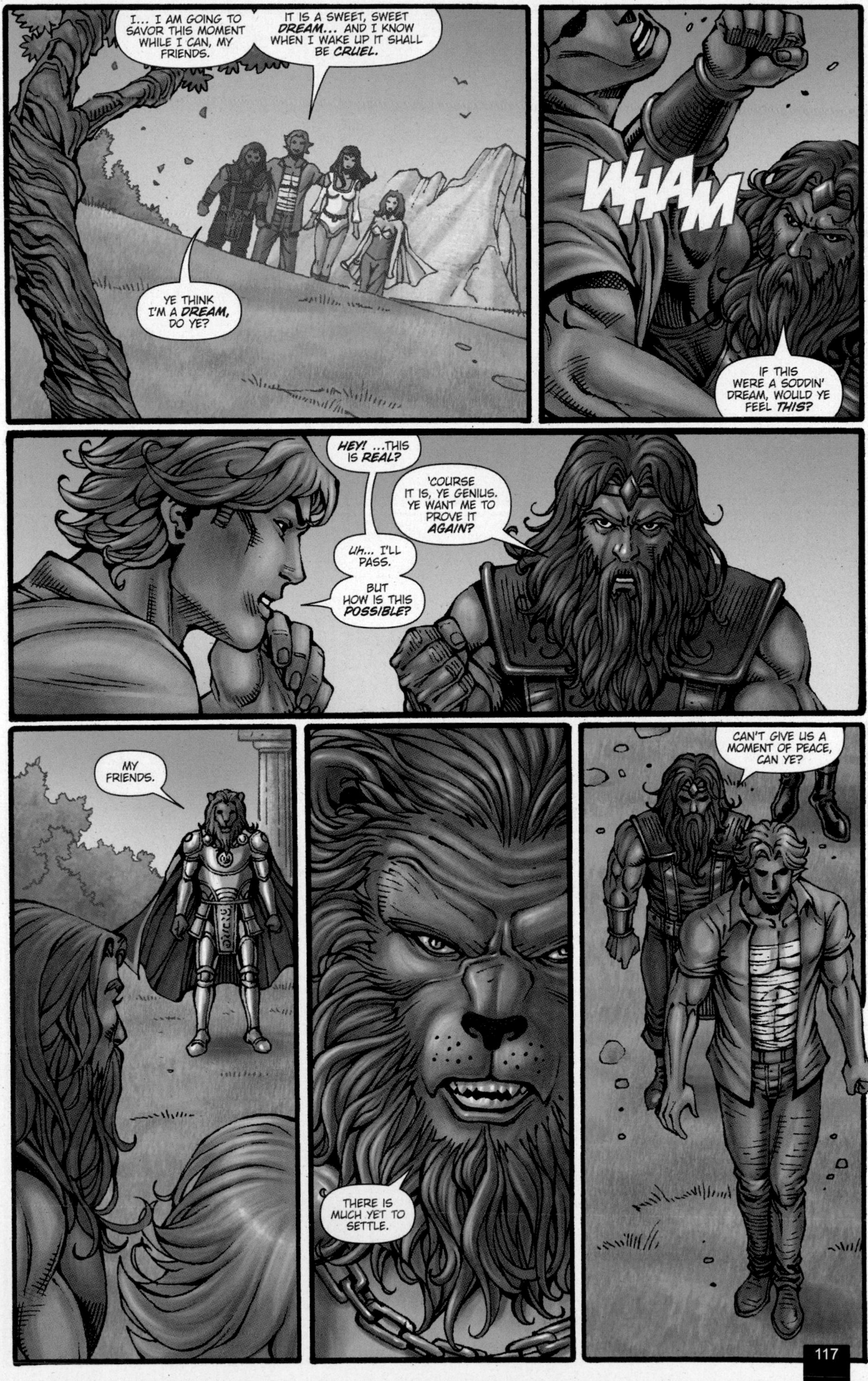
I... I AM GOING TO SAVOR THIS MOMENT WHILE I CAN, MY FRIENDS.
IT IS A SWEET, SWEET DREAM... AND I KNOW WHEN I WAKE UP IT SHALL BE CRUEL.
YE THINK I'M A DREAM, DO YE?
WHAM
IF THIS WERE A SODDIN' DREAM, WOULD YE FEEL THIS?
HEY! ...THIS IS REAL?
'COURSE IT IS, YE GENIUS. YE WANT ME TO PROVE IT AGAIN?
UH... I'LL PASS.
BUT HOW IS THIS POSSIBLE?
MY FRIENDS.
THERE IS MUCH YET TO SETTLE.
CAN'T GIVE US A MOMENT OF PEACE, CAN YE?

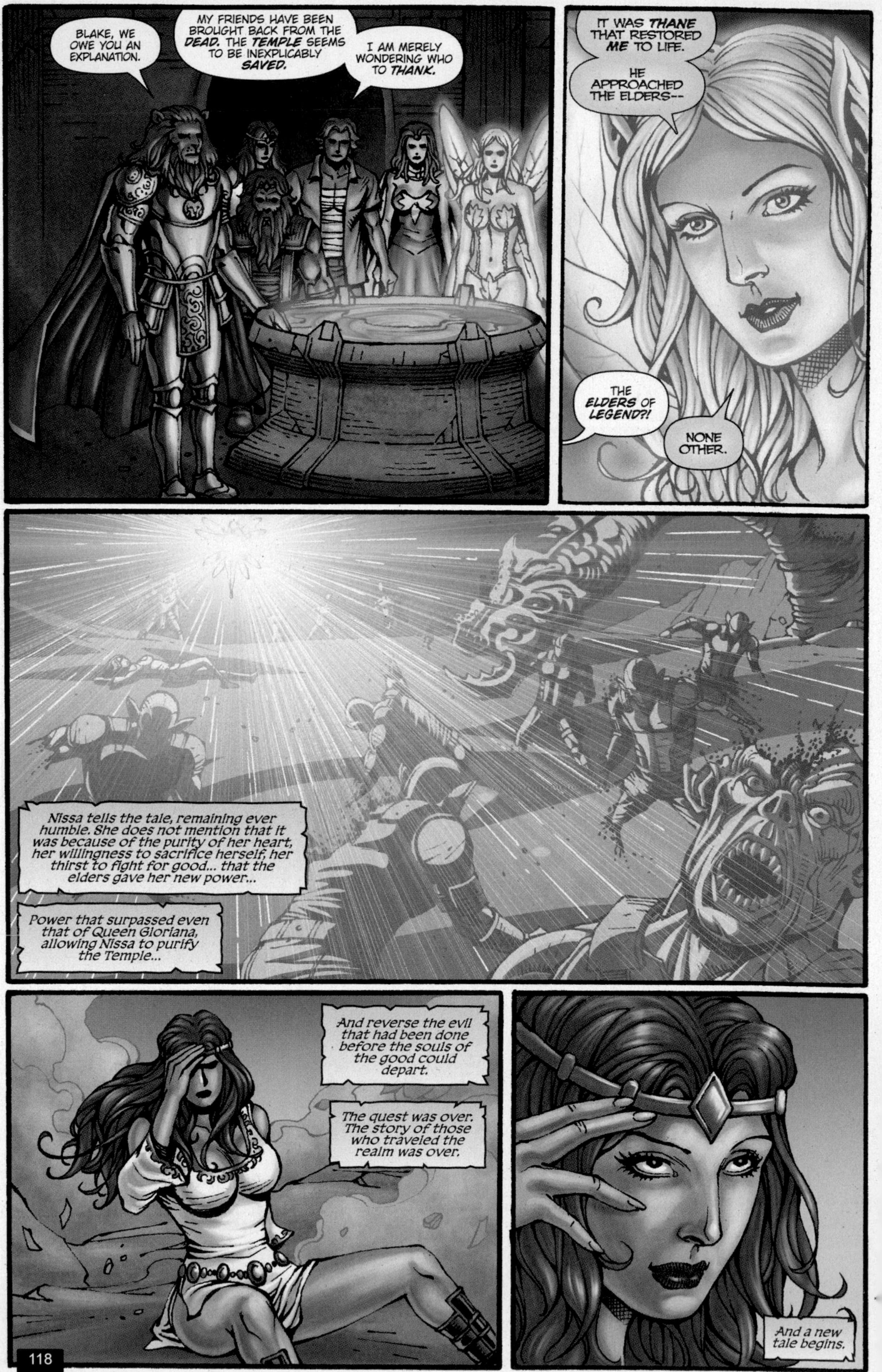
BLAKE, WE OWE YOU AN EXPLANATION.
MY FRIENDS HAVE BEEN BROUGHT BACK FROM THE DEAD. THE TEMPLE SEEMS TO BE INEXPLICABLY SAVED.
I AM MERELY WONDERING WHO TO THANK.
IT WAS THANE THAT RESTORED ME TO LIFE.
HE APPROACHED THE ELDERS--
THE ELDERS OF LEGEND?!
NONE OTHER.
Nissa tells the tale, remaining ever humble. She does not mention that it was because of the purity of her heart, her willingness to sacrifice herself, her thirst to fight for good... that the elders gave her new power...
Power that surpassed even that of Queen Gloriana, allowing Nissa to purify the Temple...
And reverse the evil that had been done before the souls of the good could depart.
The quest was over. The story of those who traveled the realm was over.
And a new tale begins.

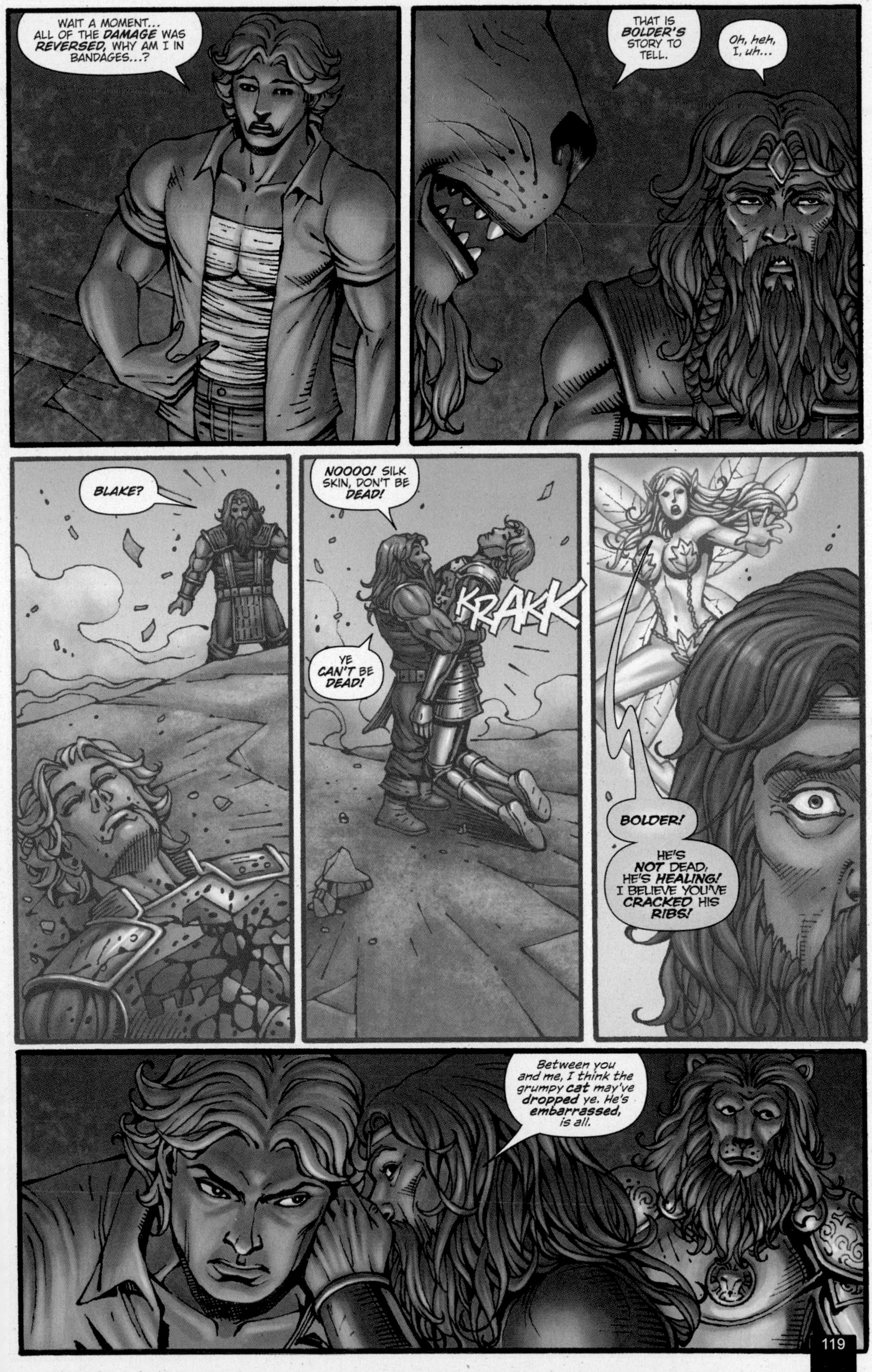
WAIT A MOMENT... ALL OF THE DAMAGE WAS REVERSED, WHY AM I IN BANDAGES...?
THAT IS BOLDER'S STORY TO TELL.
Oh, heh, I, uh...
BLAKE?
NOOOO! SILK SKIN, DON'T BE DEAD!
KRAKK
YE CAN'T BE DEAD!
BOLDER!
HE'S NOT DEAD, HE'S HEALING! I BELIEVE YOU'VE CRACKED HIS RIBS!
Between you and me, I think the grumpy cat may've dropped ye. He's embarrassed, is all.

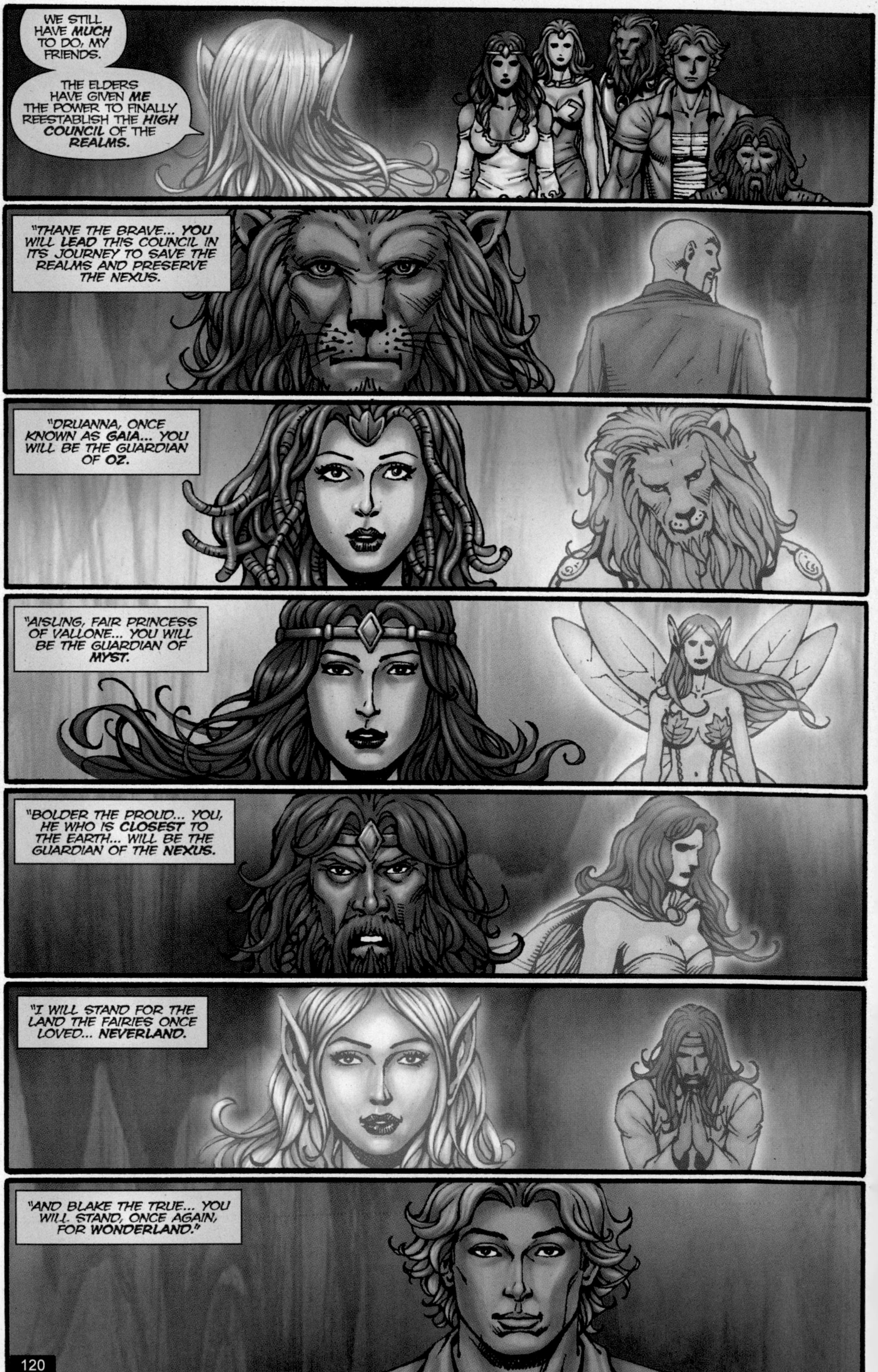
WE STILL HAVE MUCH TO DO, MY FRIENDS.
THE ELDERS HAVE GIVEN ME THE POWER TO FINALLY REESTABLISH THE HIGH COUNCIL OF THE REALMS.
"THANE THE BRAVE... YOU WILL LEAD THIS COUNCIL IN ITS JOURNEY TO SAVE THE REALMS AND PRESERVE THE NEXUS.
"DRUANNA, ONCE KNOWN AS GAIA... YOU WILL BE THE GUARDIAN OF OZ.
"AISLING, FAIR PRINCESS OF VALLONE... YOU WILL BE THE GUARDIAN OF MYST.
"BOLDER THE PROUD... YOU, HE WHO IS CLOSEST TO THE EARTH... WILL BE THE GUARDIAN OF THE NEXUS.
"I WILL STAND FOR THE LAND THE FAIRIES ONCE LOVED... NEVERLAND.
"AND BLAKE THE TRUE... YOU WILL STAND, ONCE AGAIN, FOR WONDERLAND."

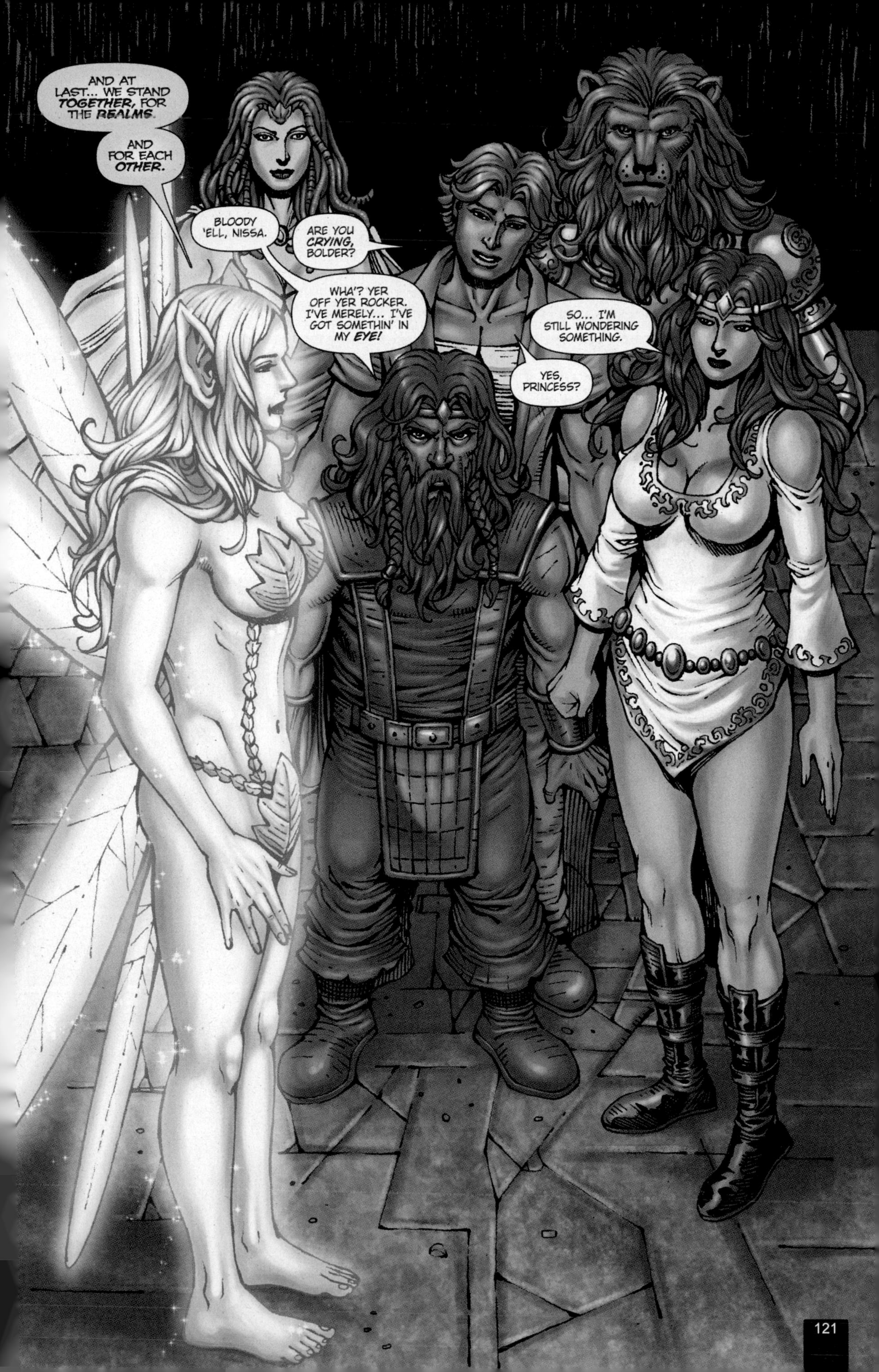
AND AT LAST... WE STAND TOGETHER, FOR THE REALMS.
AND FOR EACH OTHER.
BLOODY 'ELL, NISSA.
ARE YOU CRYING, BOLDER?
WHA'? YER OFF YER ROCKER. I'VE MERELY... I'VE GOT SOMETHIN' IN MY EYE!
SO... I'M STILL WONDERING SOMETHING.
YES, PRINCESS?

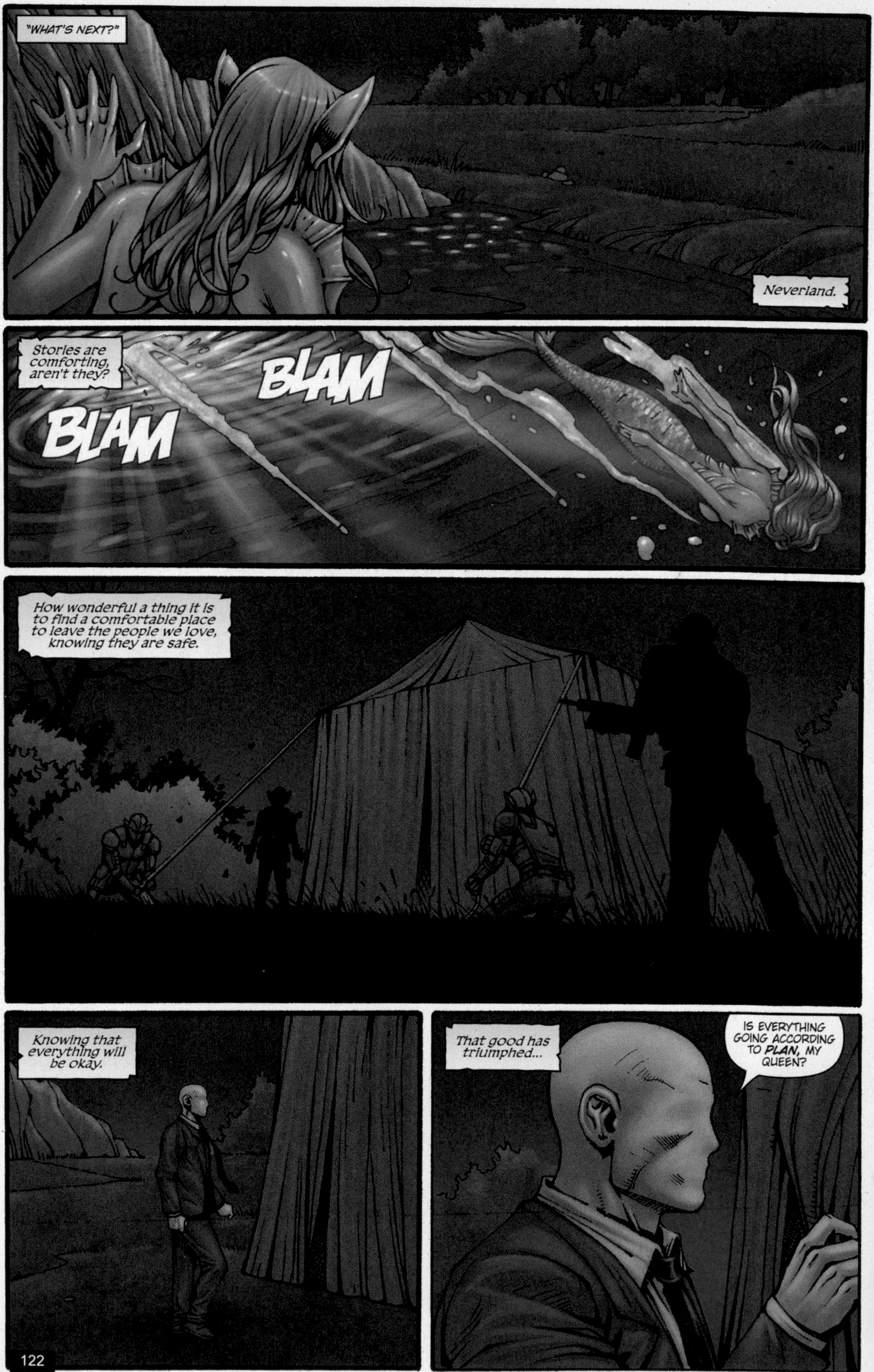
"WHAT'S NEXT?"
Neverland.
Stories are comforting, aren't they?
BLAM
BLAM
How wonderful a thing it is to find a comfortable place to leave the people we love, knowing they are safe.
Knowing that everything will be okay.
That good has triumphed...
IS EVERYTHING GOING ACCORDING TO PLAN, MY QUEEN?

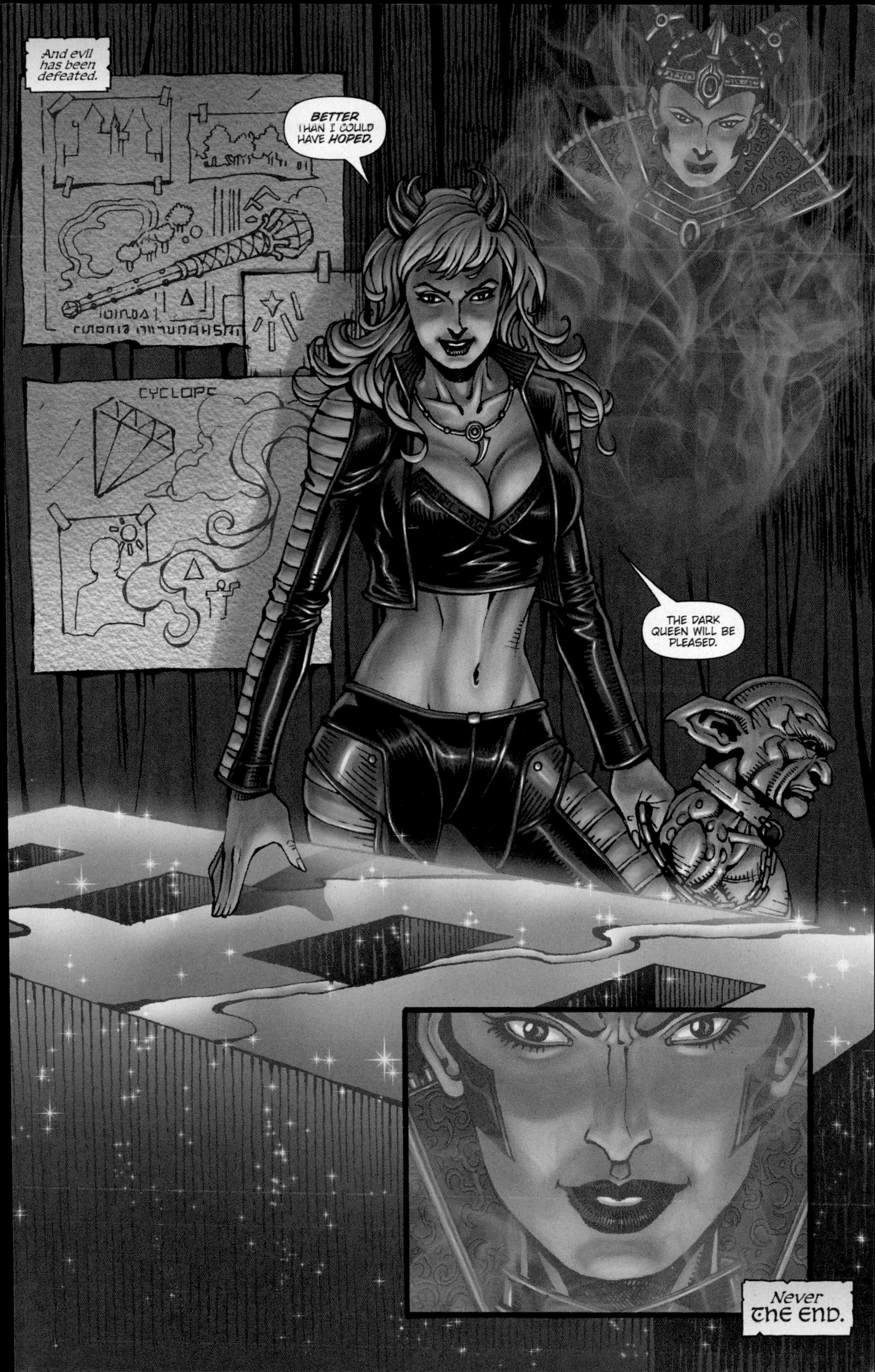
And evil has been defeated.
BETTER THAN I COULD HAVE HOPED.
THE DARK QUEEN WILL BE PLEASED.
Never THE END.

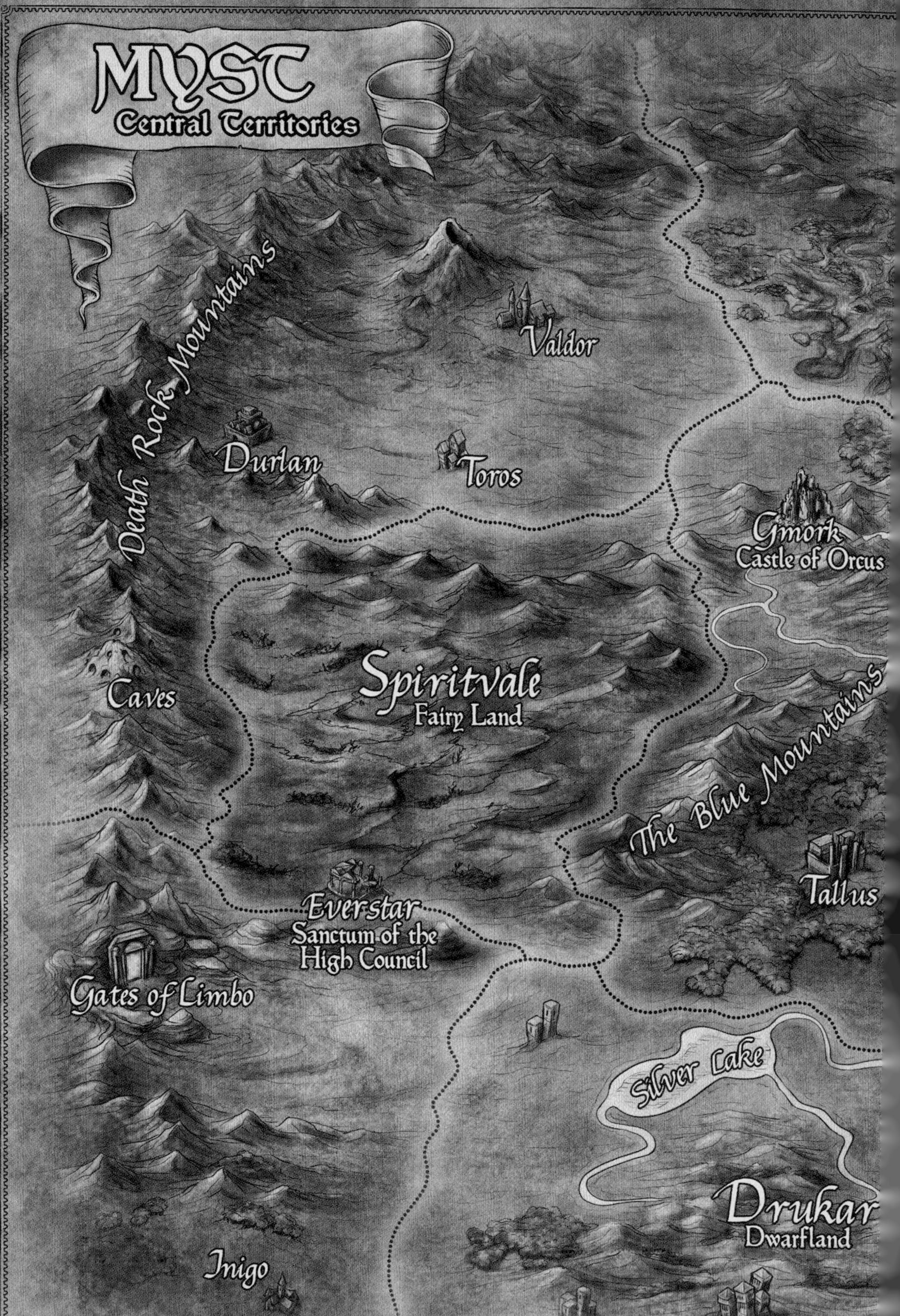
MYST
Central Territories
Death Rock Mountains
Valdor
Durlan
Toros
Gmork
Castle of Orcus
Spiritvale
Fairy Land
Caves
The Blue Mountains
Tallus
Everstar
Sanctum of the
High Council
Gates of Limbo
Silver Lake
Drukar
Dwarfland
Inigo

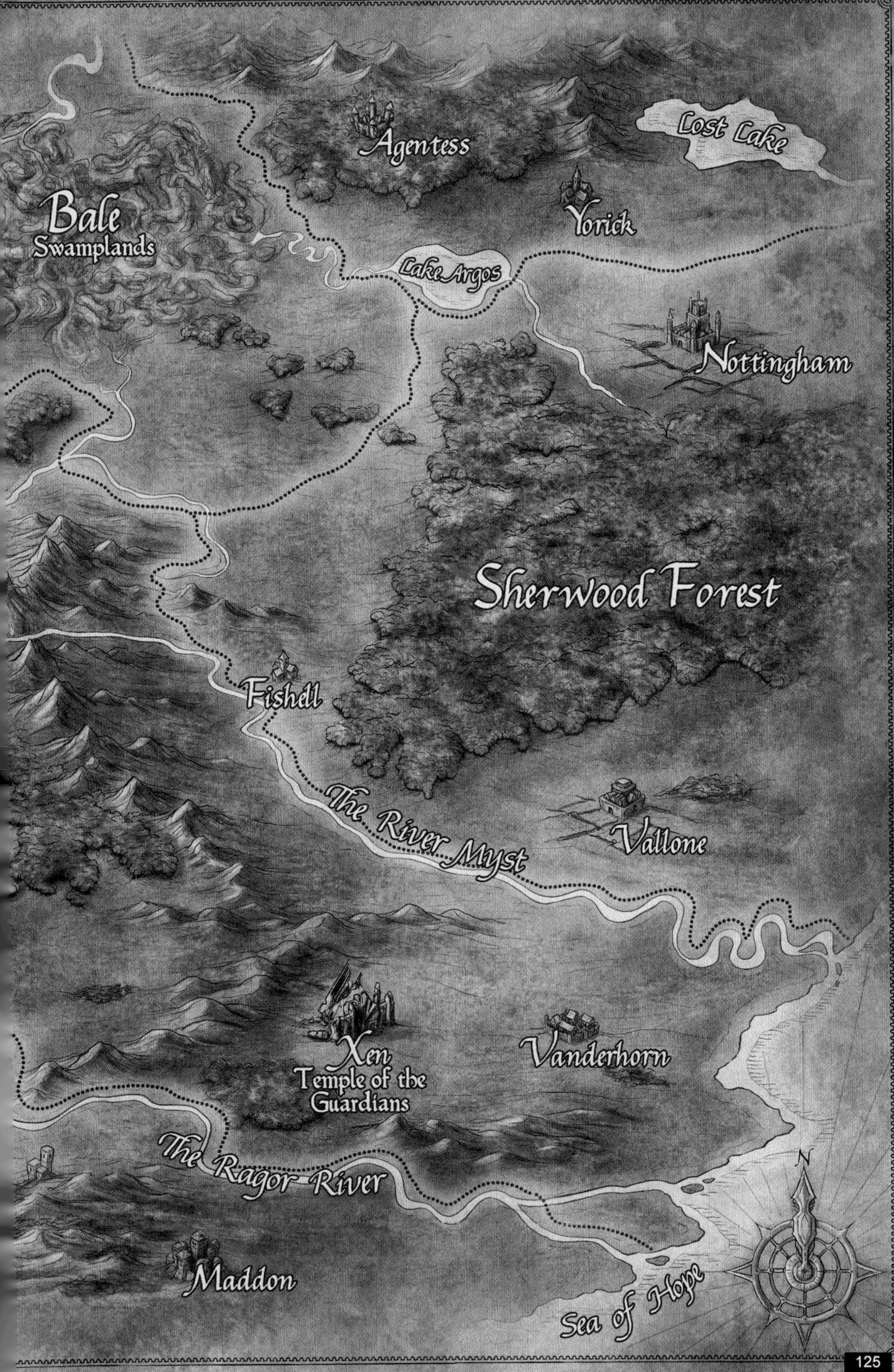
Agentess
Lost Lake
Yorick
Bale
Swamplands
Lake Argos
Nottingham
Sherwood Forest
Fishell
The River Myst
Vallone
Xen
Temple of the Guardians
Vanderhorn
The Ragor River
Maddon
Sea of Hope
N

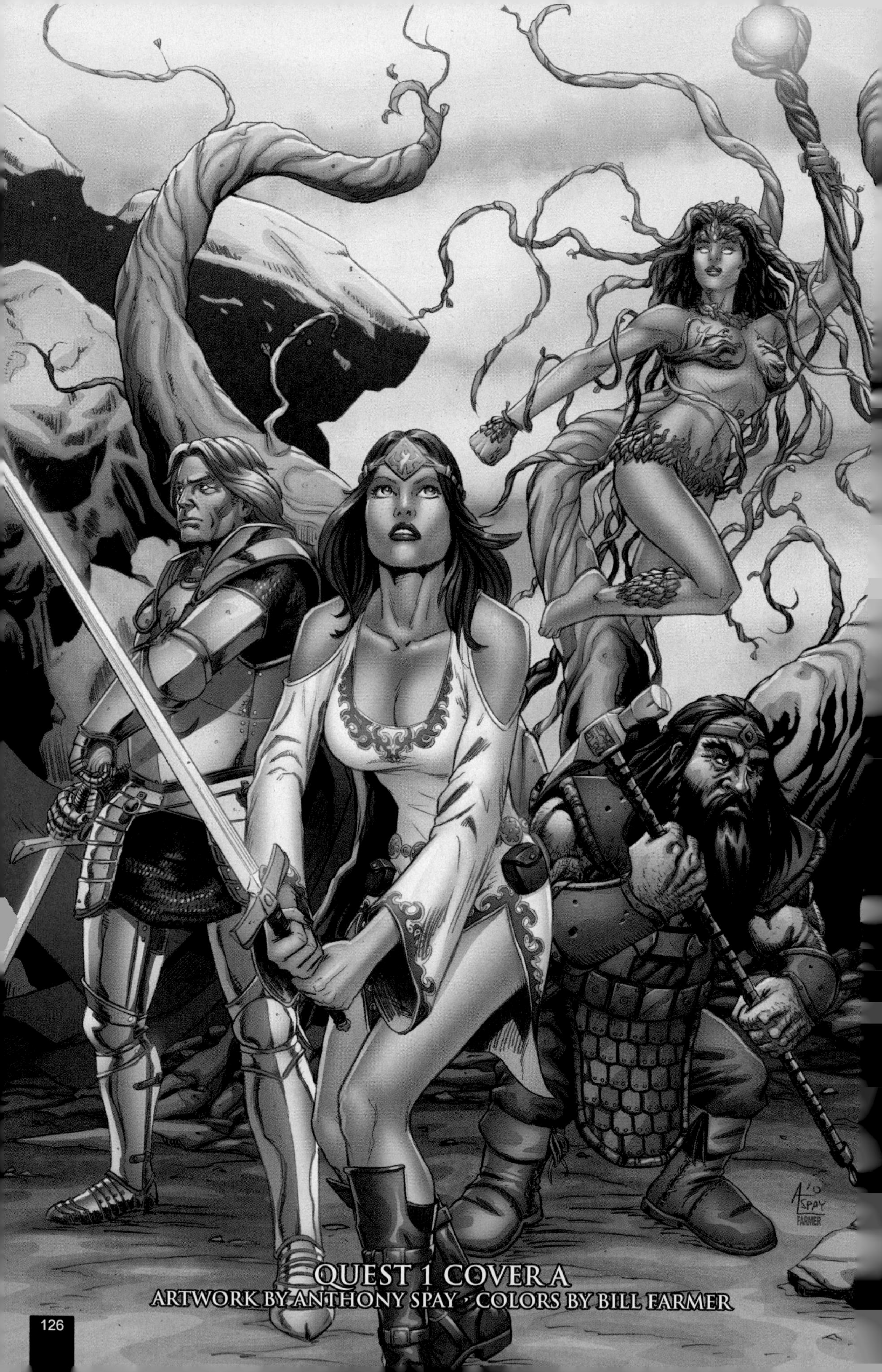

QUEST 1 COVER A
ARTWORK BY ANTHONY SPAY · COLORS BY BILL FARMER

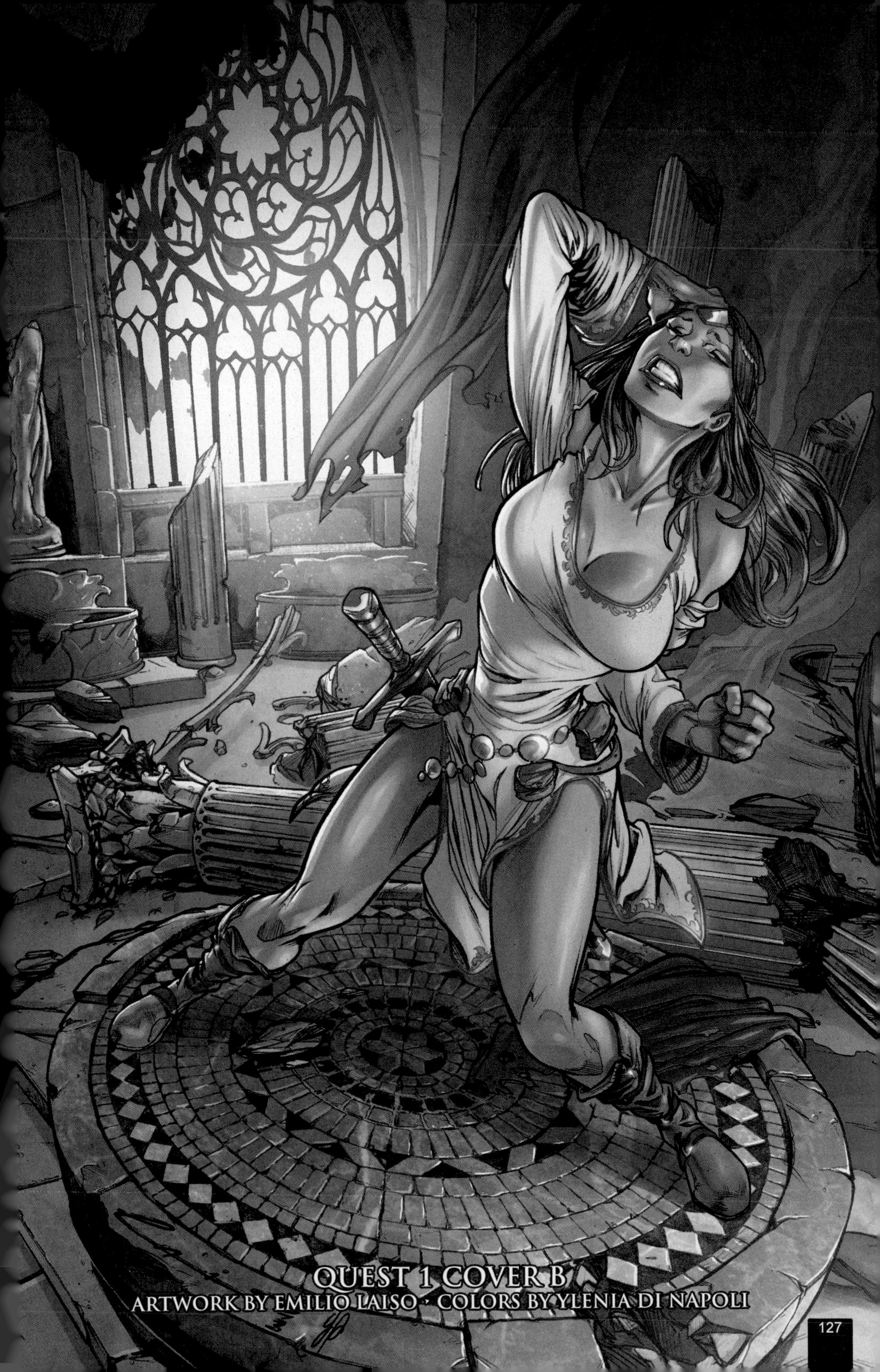

QUEST 1 COVER B
ARTWORK BY EMILIO LAISO · COLORS BY YLENIA DI NAPOLI

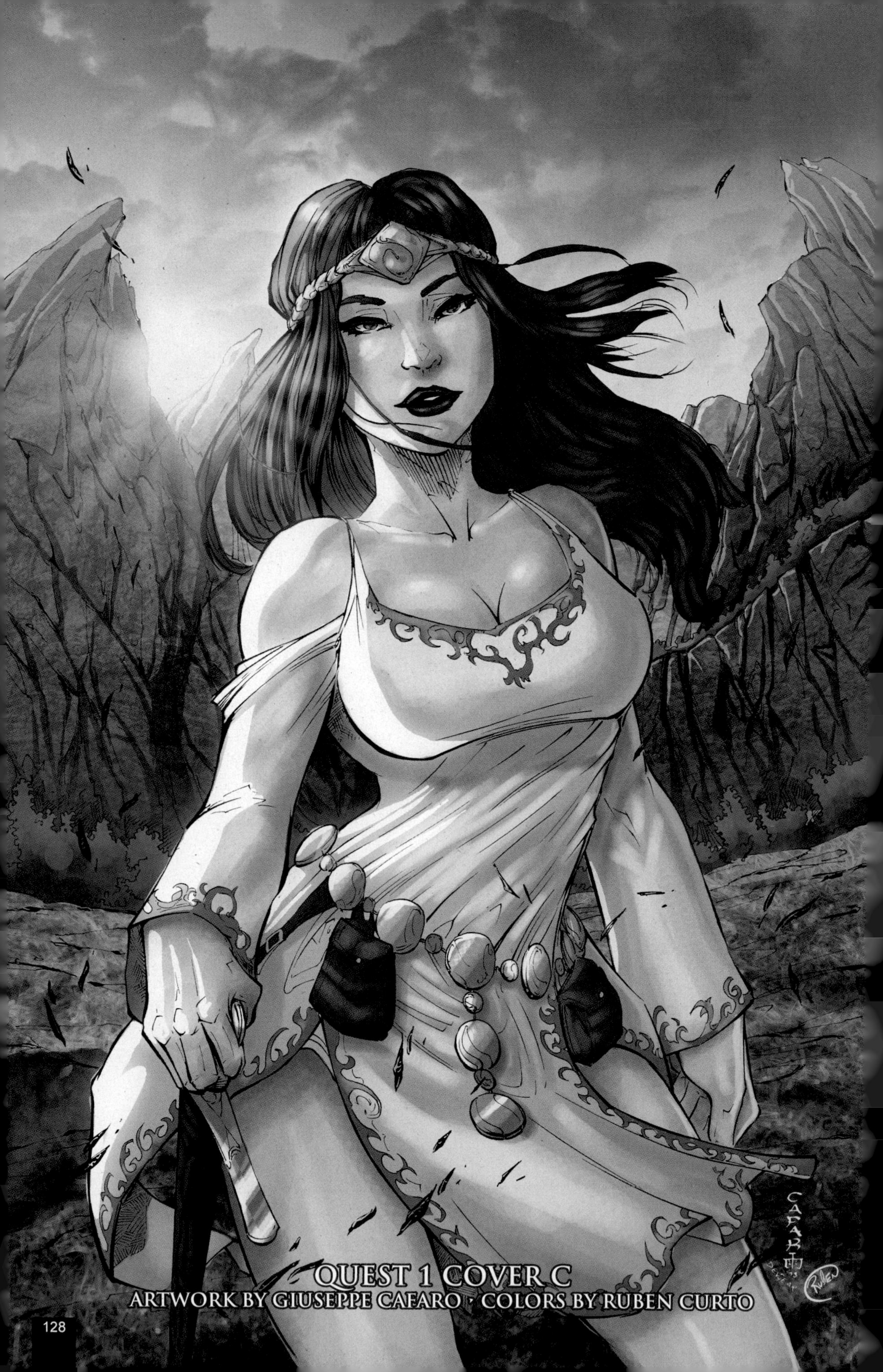
CAFARO
RUBEN

QUEST 1 COVER C

ARTWORK BY GIUSEPPE CAFARO · COLORS BY RUBEN CURTO

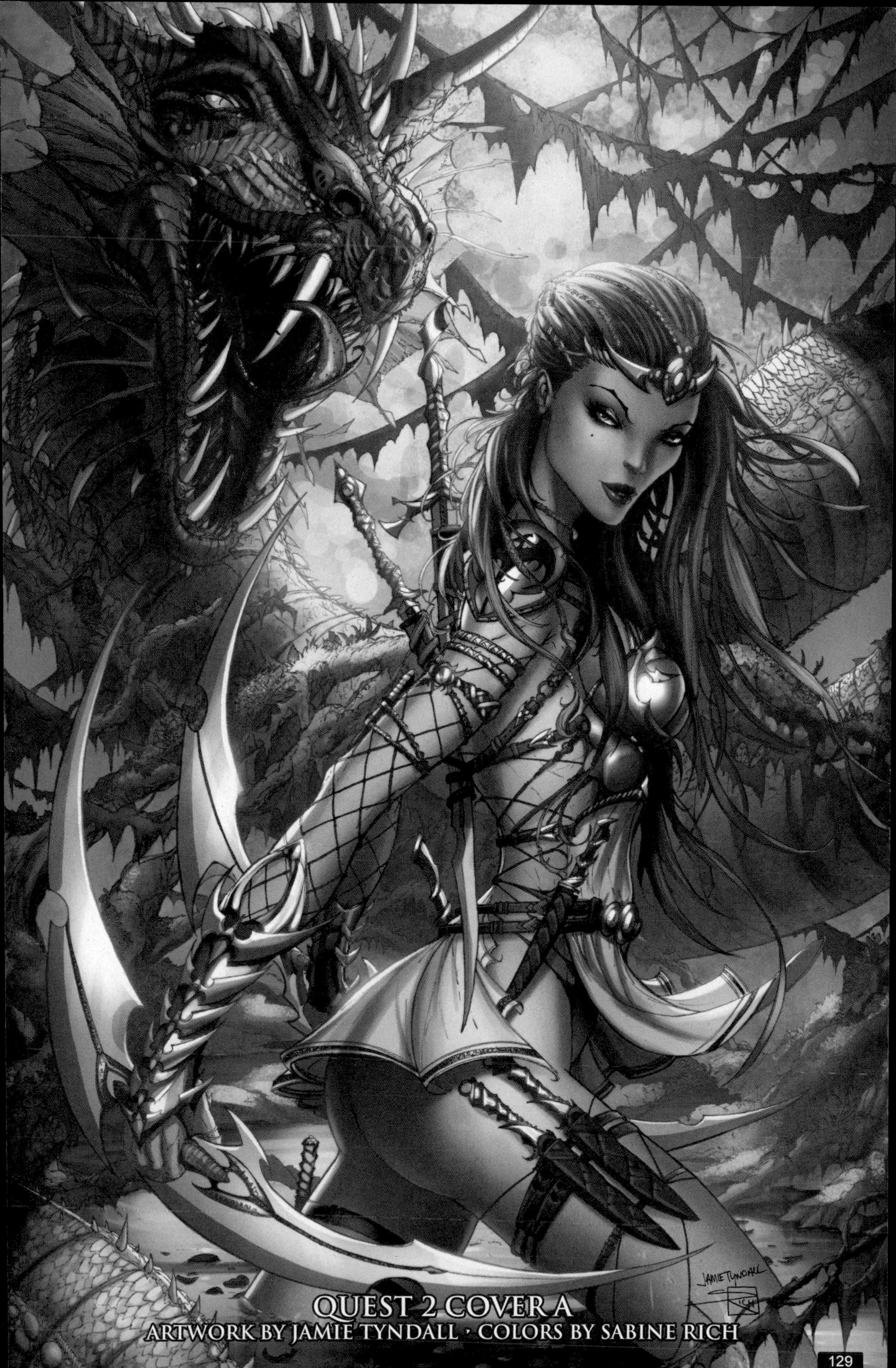
JAMIE TYNDALL

QUEST 2 COVER A
ARTWORK BY JAMIE TYNDALL · COLORS BY SABINE RICH

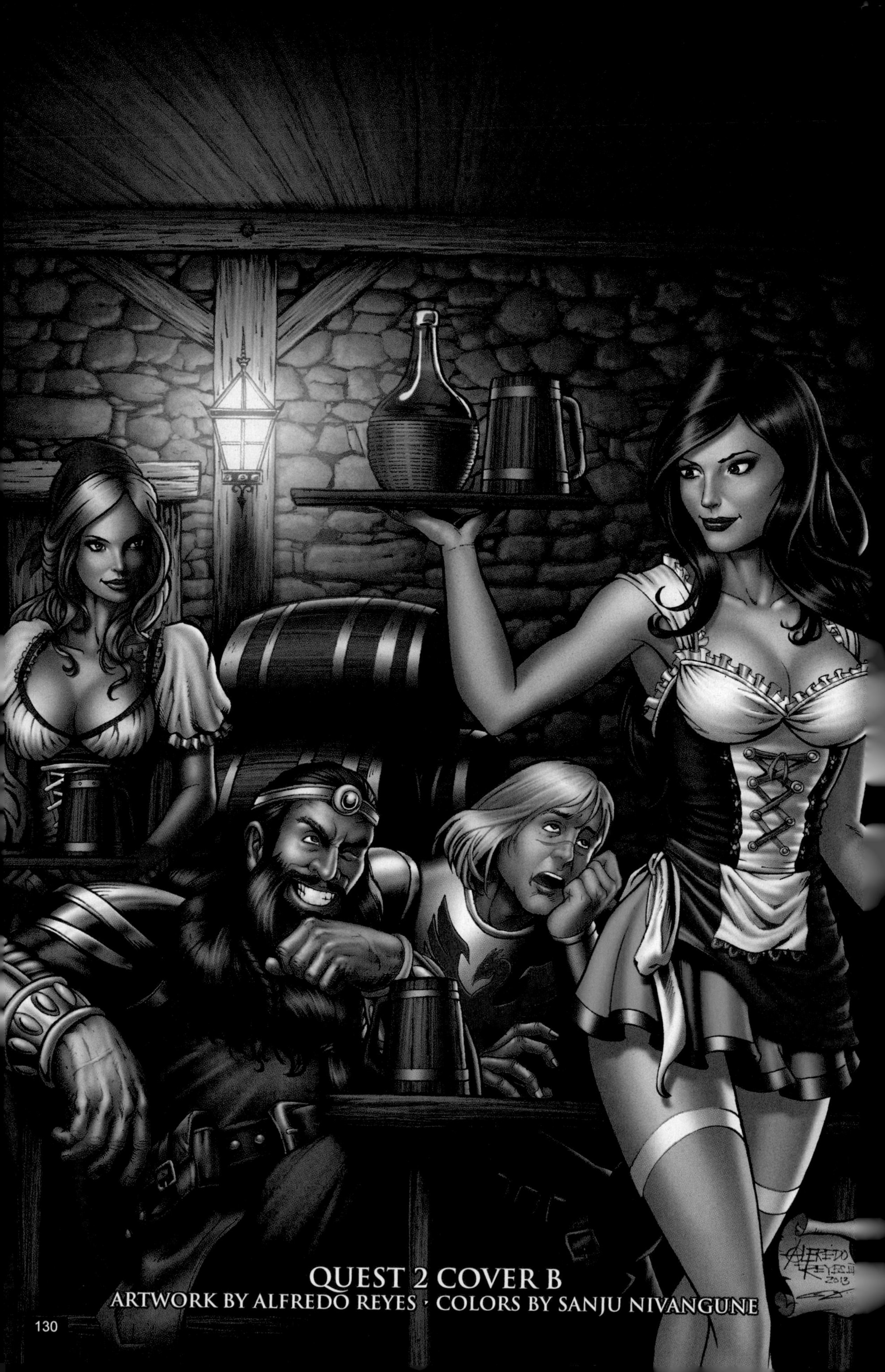
ALFREDO REYES III 2013

QUEST 2 COVER B
ARTWORK BY ALFREDO REYES · COLORS BY SANJU NIVANGUNE

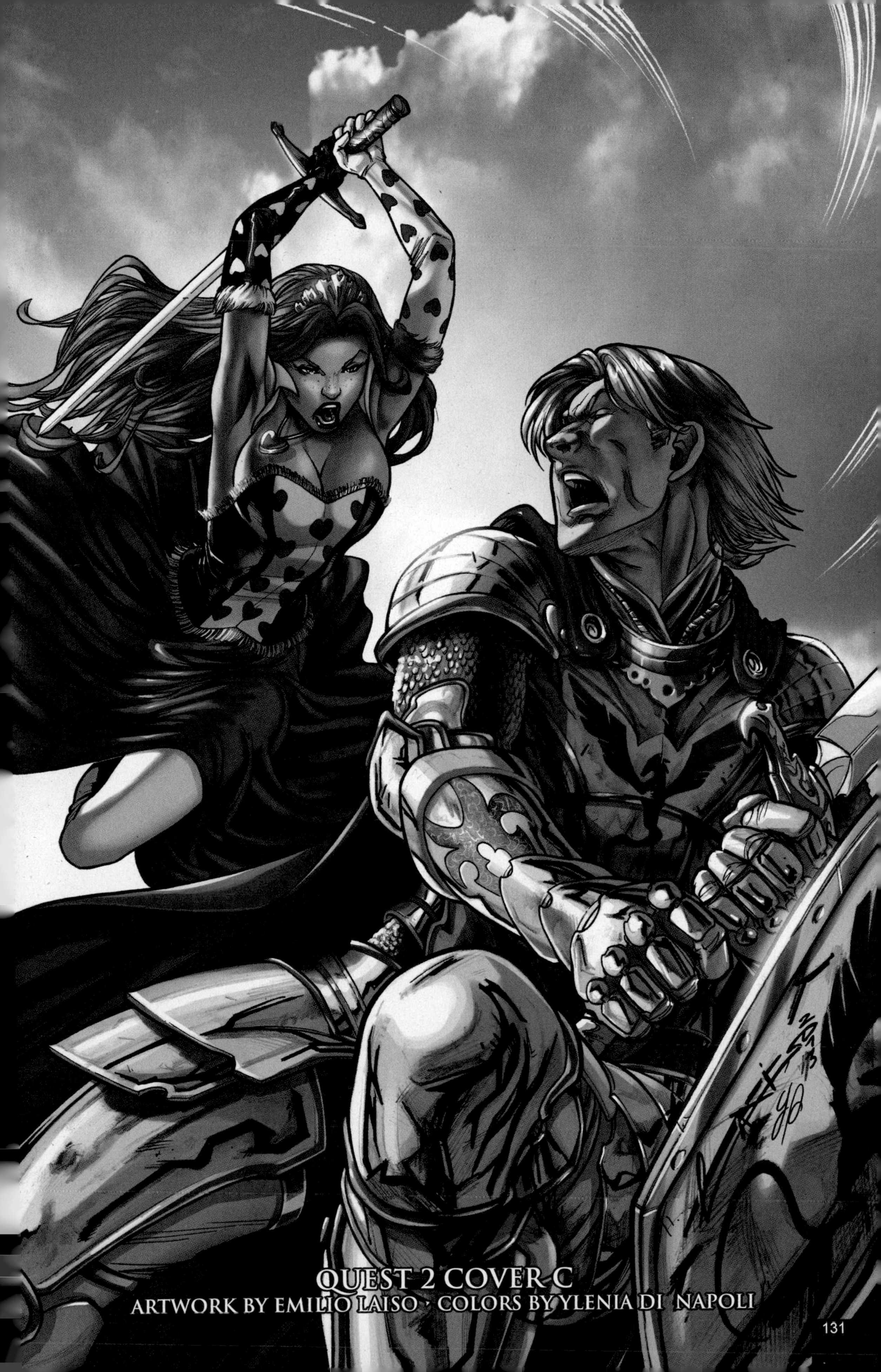

QUEST 2 COVER C
ARTWORK BY EMILIO LAISO · COLORS BY YLENIA DI NAPOLI

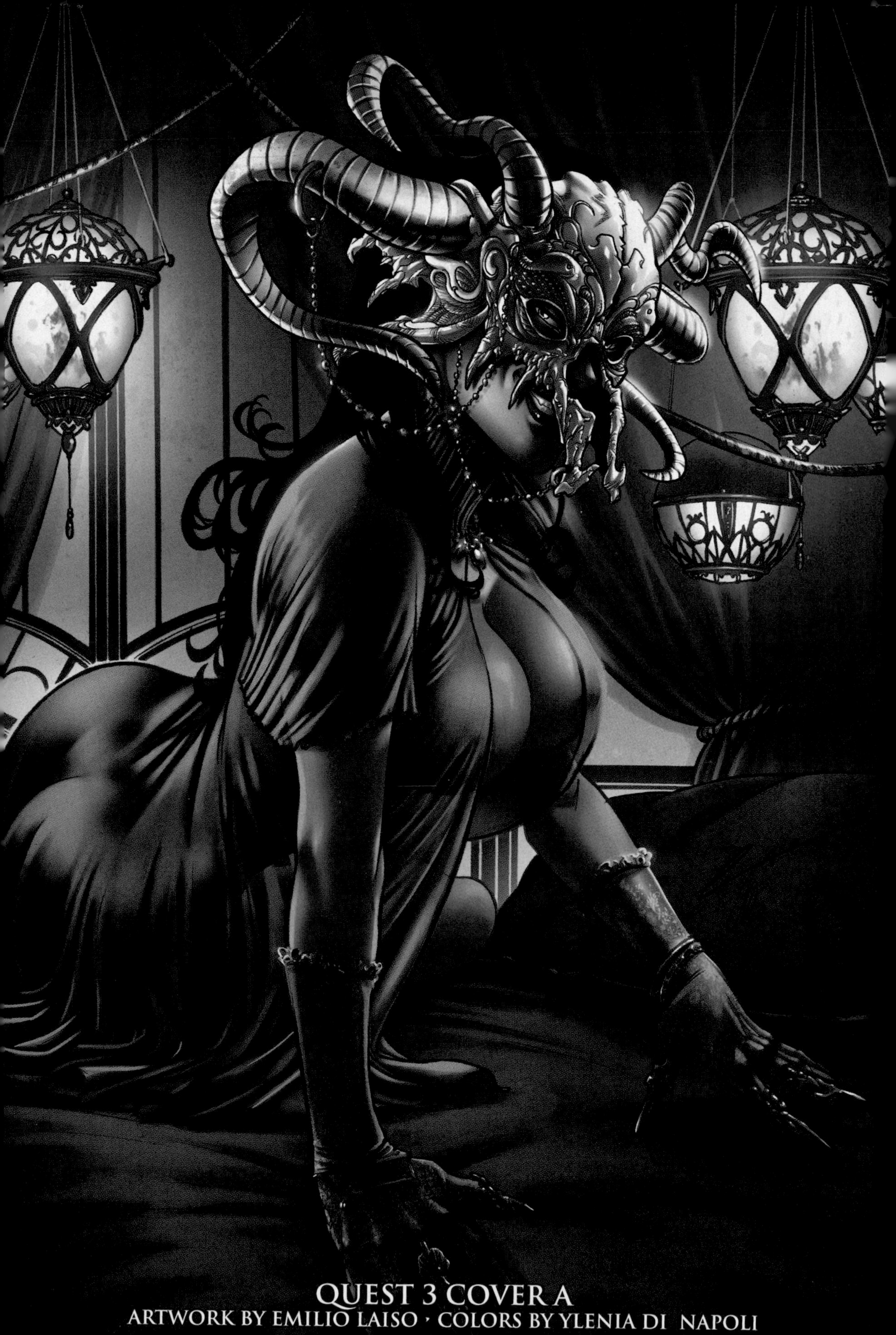

QUEST 3 COVER A
ARTWORK BY EMILIO LAISO · COLORS BY YLENIA DI NAPOLI

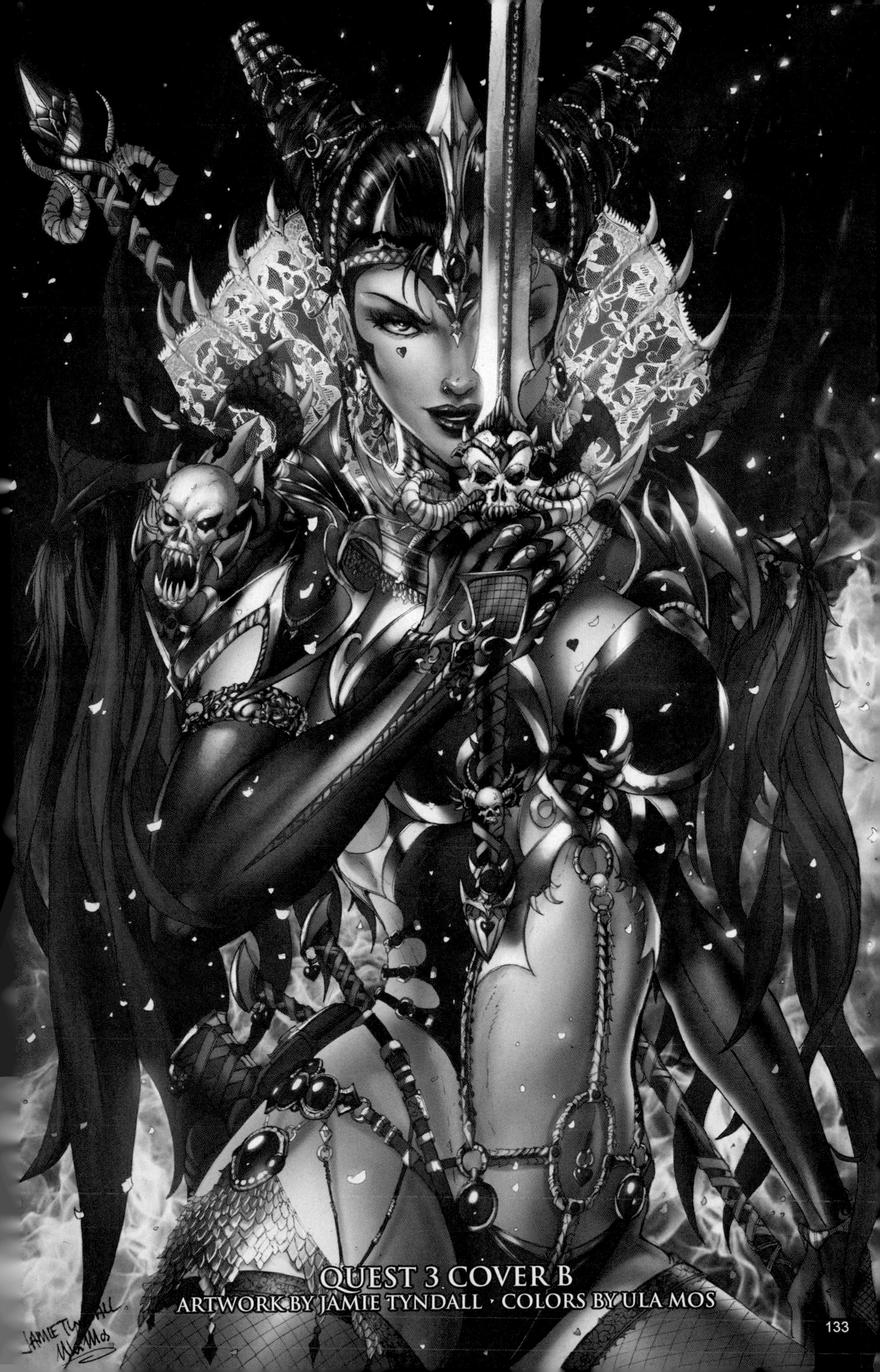

QUEST 3 COVER B
ARTWORK BY JAMIE TYNDALL · COLORS BY ULA MOS

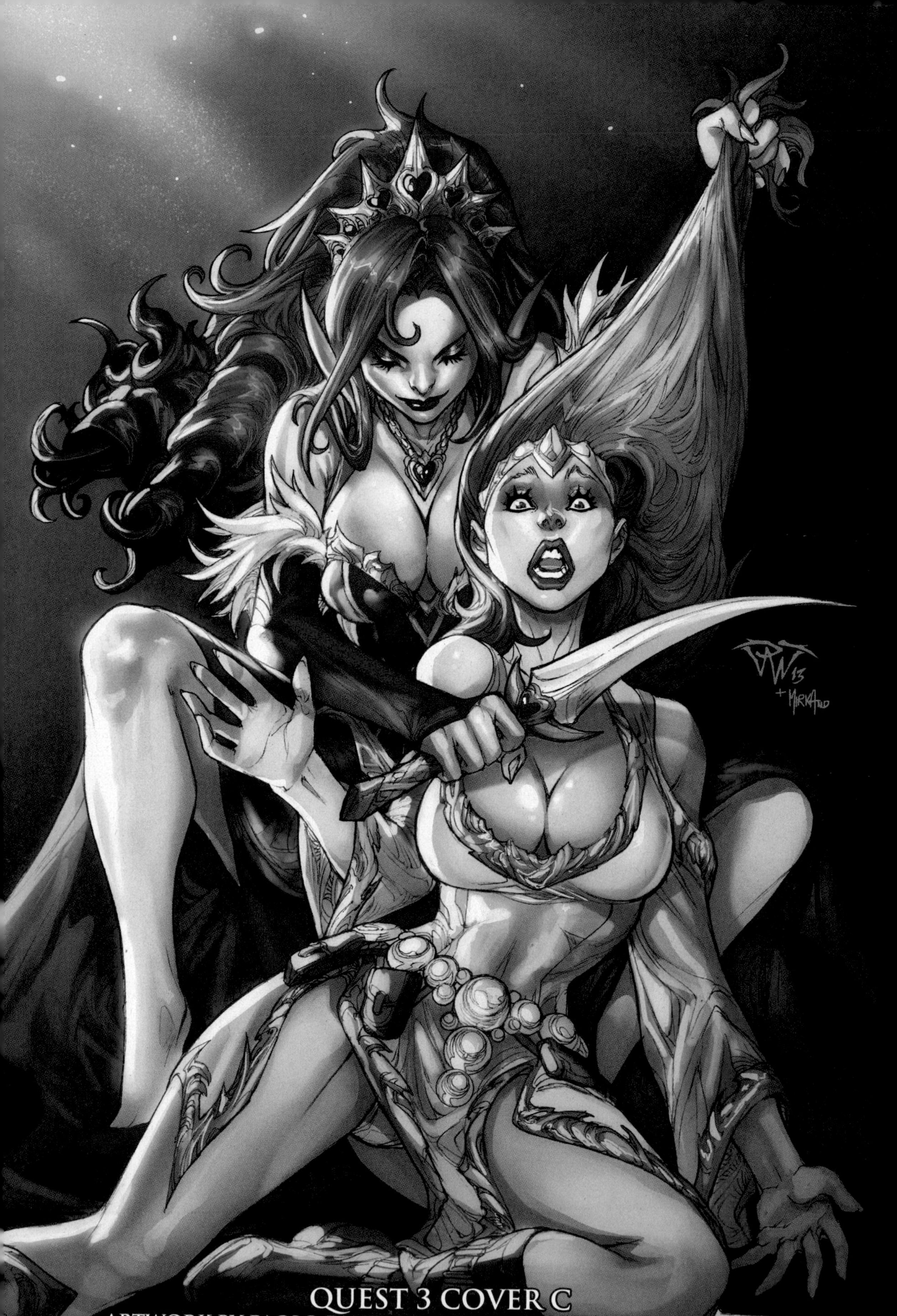

QUEST 3 COVER C

ARTWORK BY PAOLO PANTALENA · COLORS BY MIRKA ANDOLFO

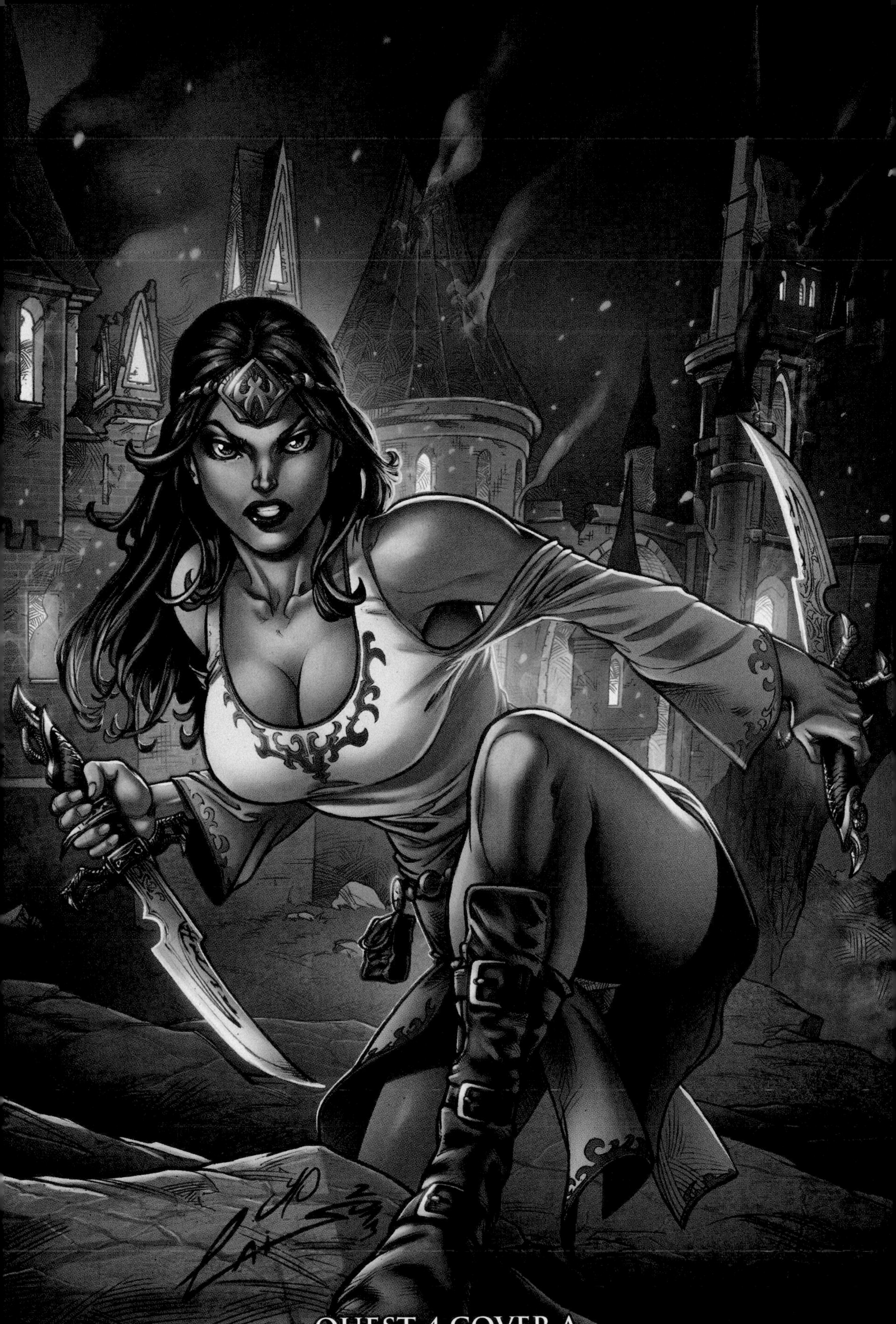

QUEST 4 COVER A

ARTWORK BY EMILIO LAISO · COLORS BY YLENIA DI NAPOLI

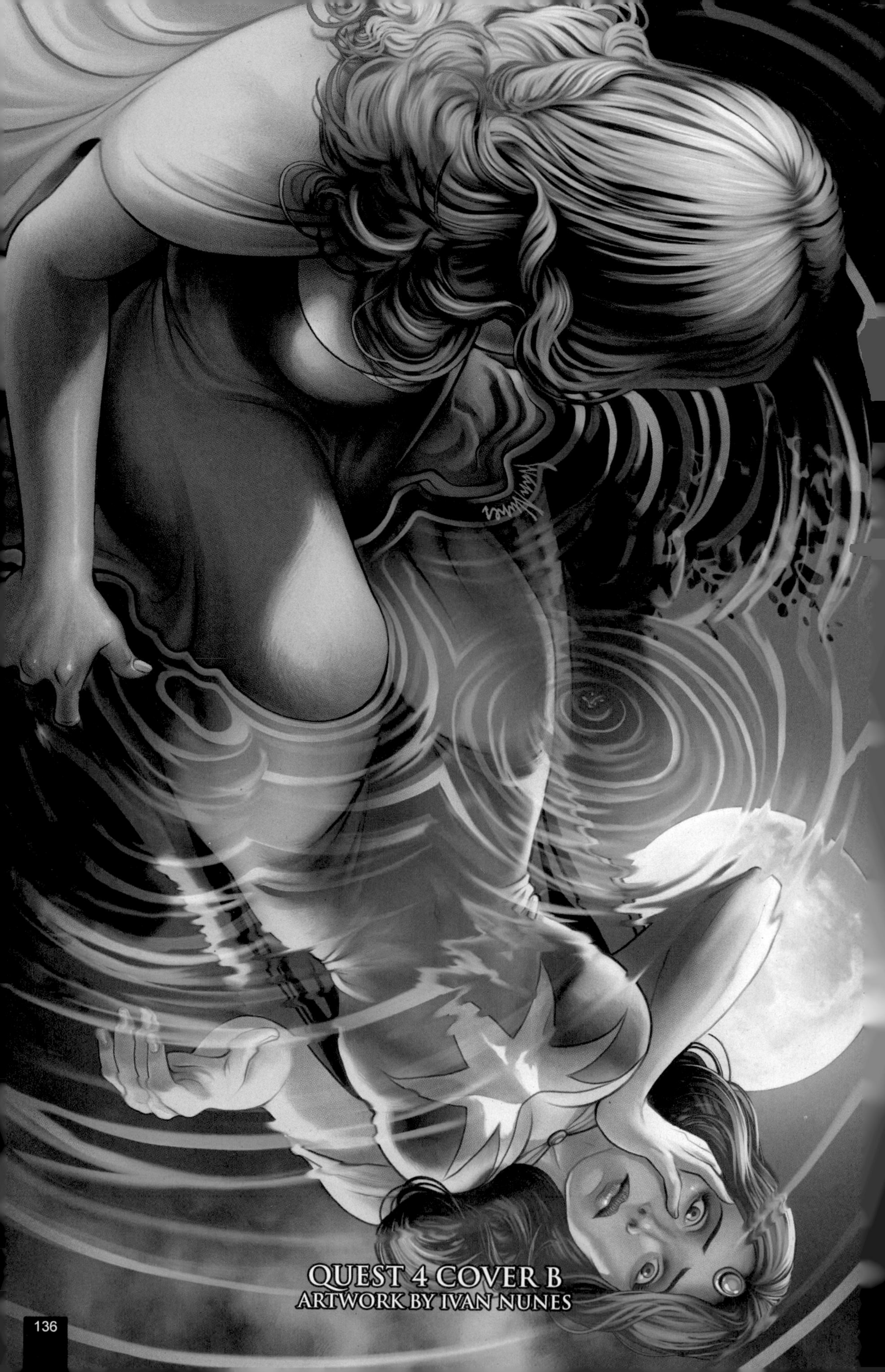

QUEST 4 COVER B
ARTWORK BY IVAN NUNES

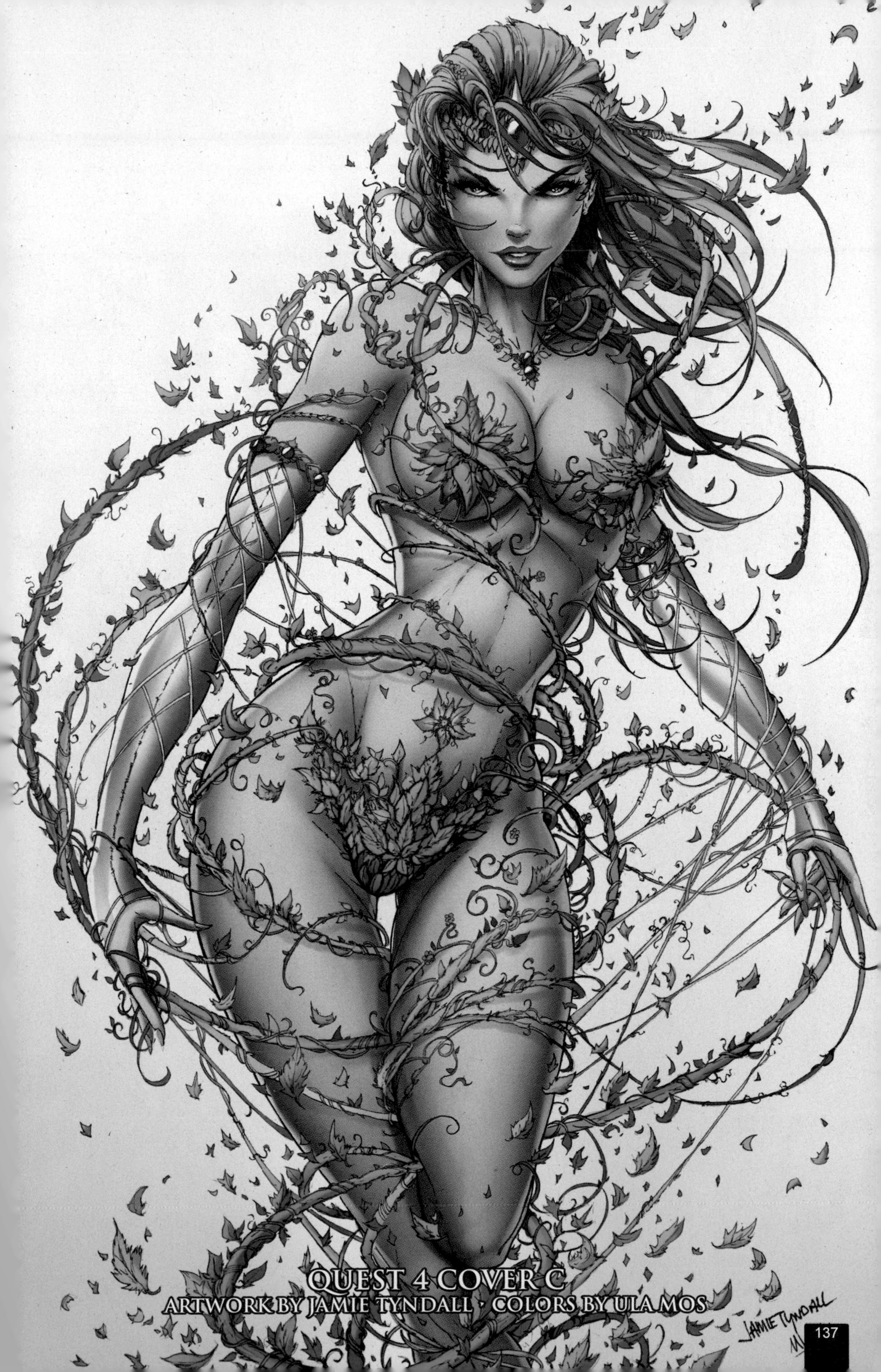
JAMIE TYNDALL

QUEST 4 COVER C
ARTWORK BY JAMIE TYNDALL · COLORS BY ULA MOS

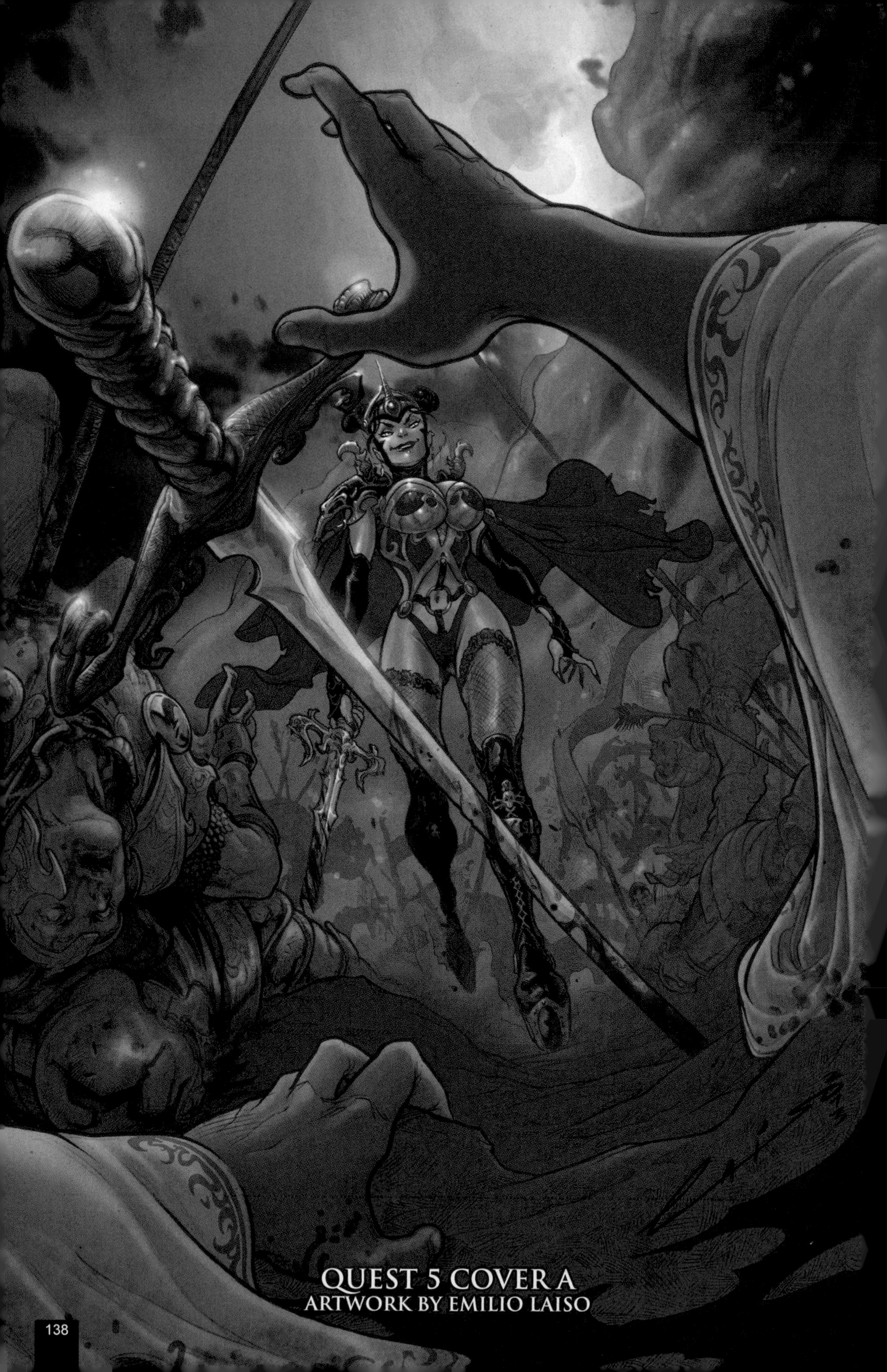

QUEST 5 COVER A
ARTWORK BY EMILIO LAISO

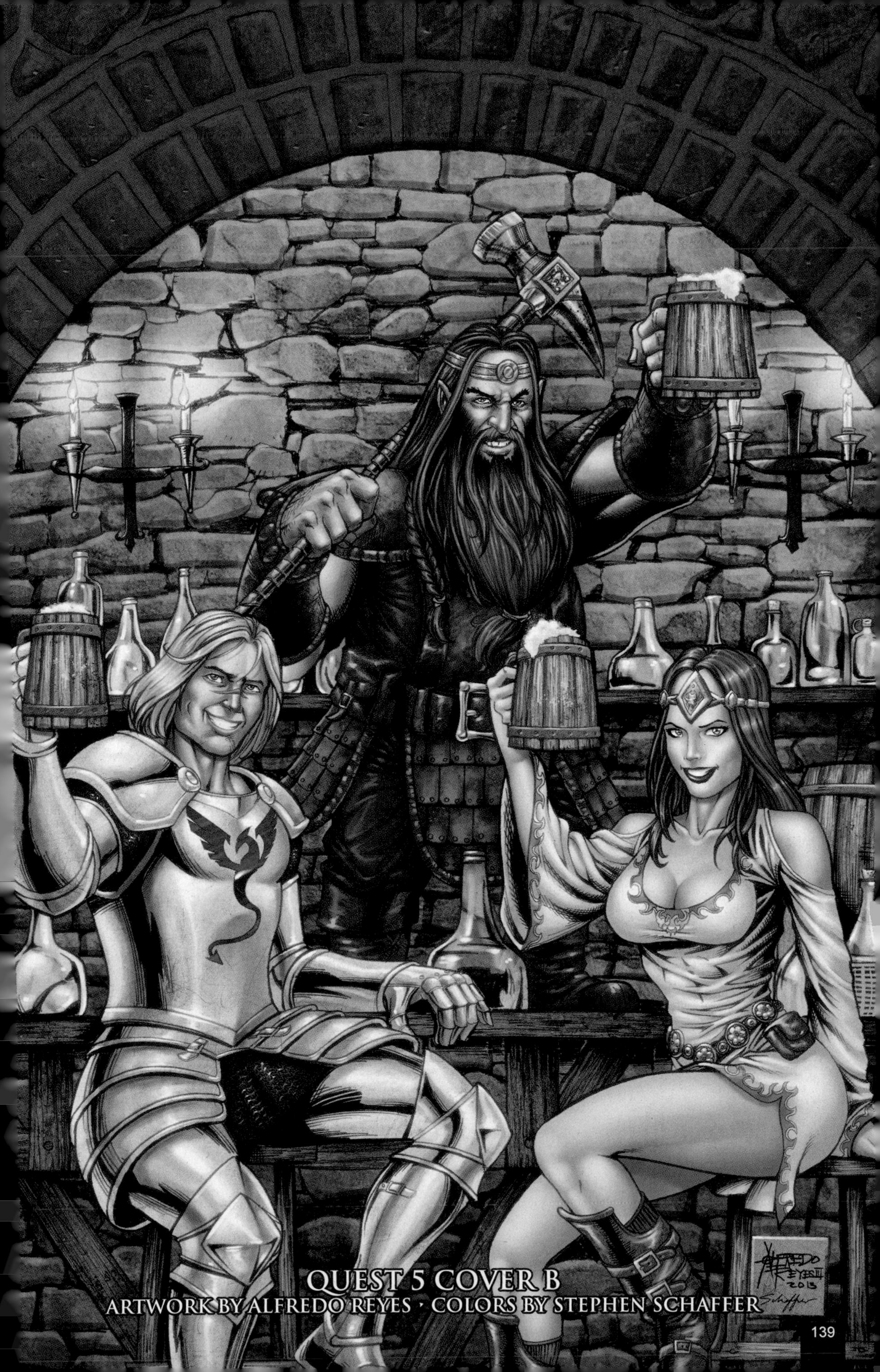

QUEST 5 COVER B
ARTWORK BY ALFREDO REYES · COLORS BY STEPHEN SCHAFFER

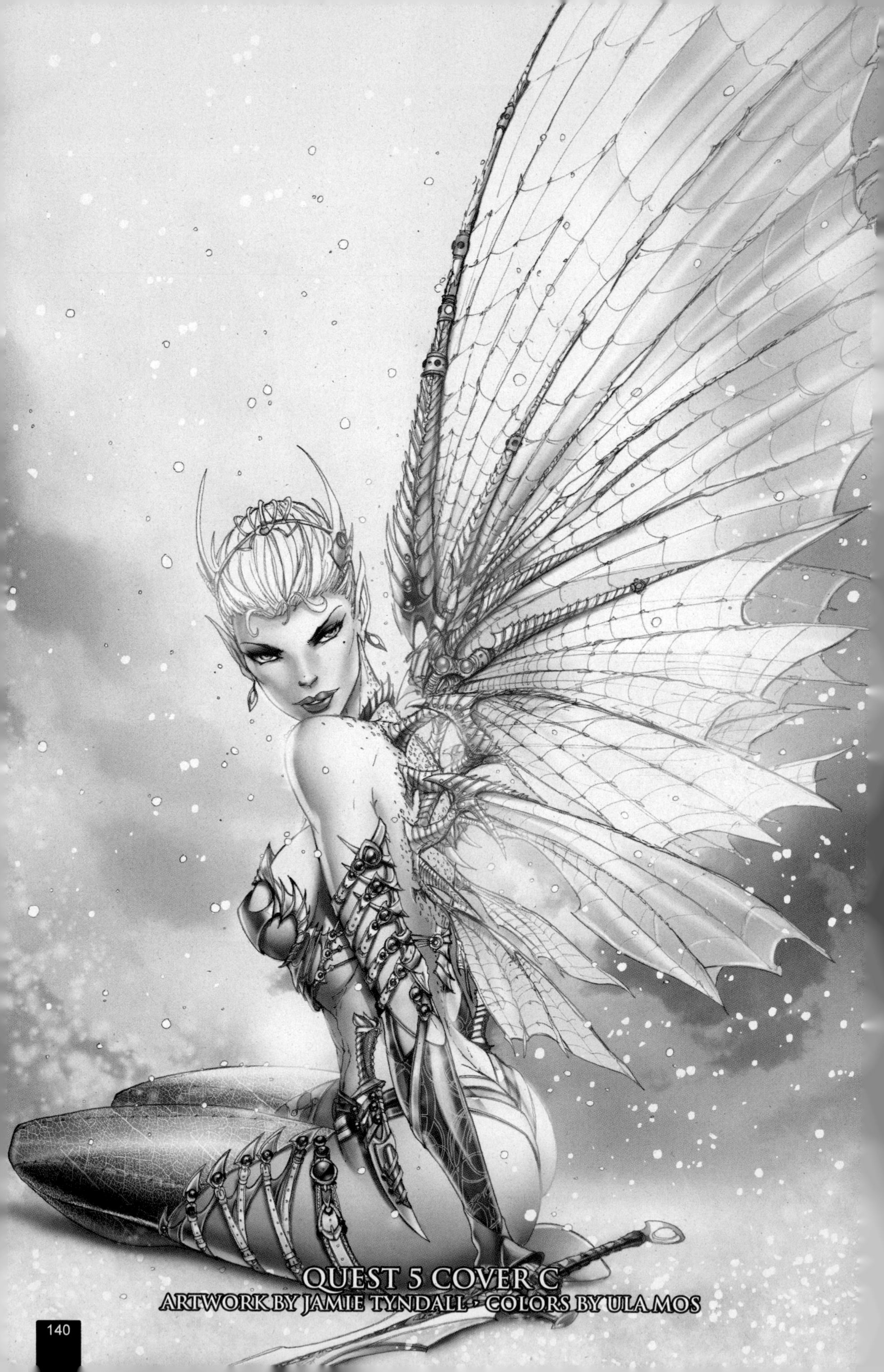

QUEST 5 COVER C
ARTWORK BY JAMIE TYNDALL · COLORS BY ULA MOS

Grimm Fairy Tales presents:

QUEST

AGE OF DARKNESS

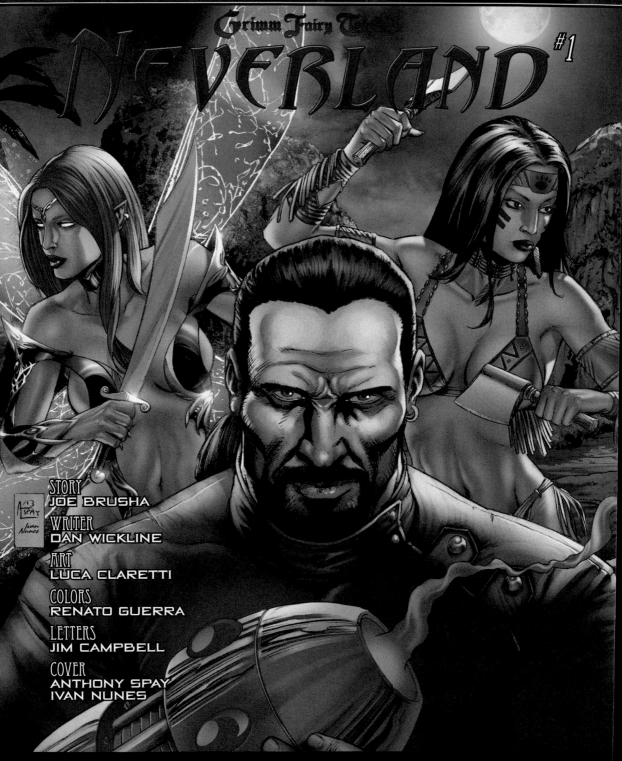

AGE OF DARKNESS

Grimm Fairy Tales

NEVERLAND #1

STORY
JOE BRUSHA

WRITER
DAN WICKLINE

ART
LUCA CLARETTI

COLORS
RENATO GUERRA

LETTERS
JIM CAMPBELL

COVER
ANTHONY SPAY
IVAN NUNES

AFTER SAVING HER NEPHEWS FROM THE EVIL PAN OF NEVERLAND, NATHAN CROSS MADE A LIFE WITH WENDY, THE WOMAN THAT HE LOVES. HOWEVER, WITH THE UNITED STATES GOVERNMENT RECRUITING FOR THEIR REALM KNIGHTS PROGRAM, IT WAS ONLY A MATTER OF TIME BEFORE THEY CALLED ON CROSS FOR HIS UNIQUE SKILLS.

FOR OVER A YEAR, CROSS HAS BEEN ACTING AS A REALM KNIGHT, SAVING THE WORLD FROM SUPERNATURAL THREATS ALONGSIDE A TEAM OF OTHERS LIKE HIM. BUT AS NATHAN'S PERSONAL LIFE AND HIS NEW DUTY COME INTO CONFLICT, WILL HE BE PREPARED WHEN A NEW EVIL RISES IN NEVERLAND?

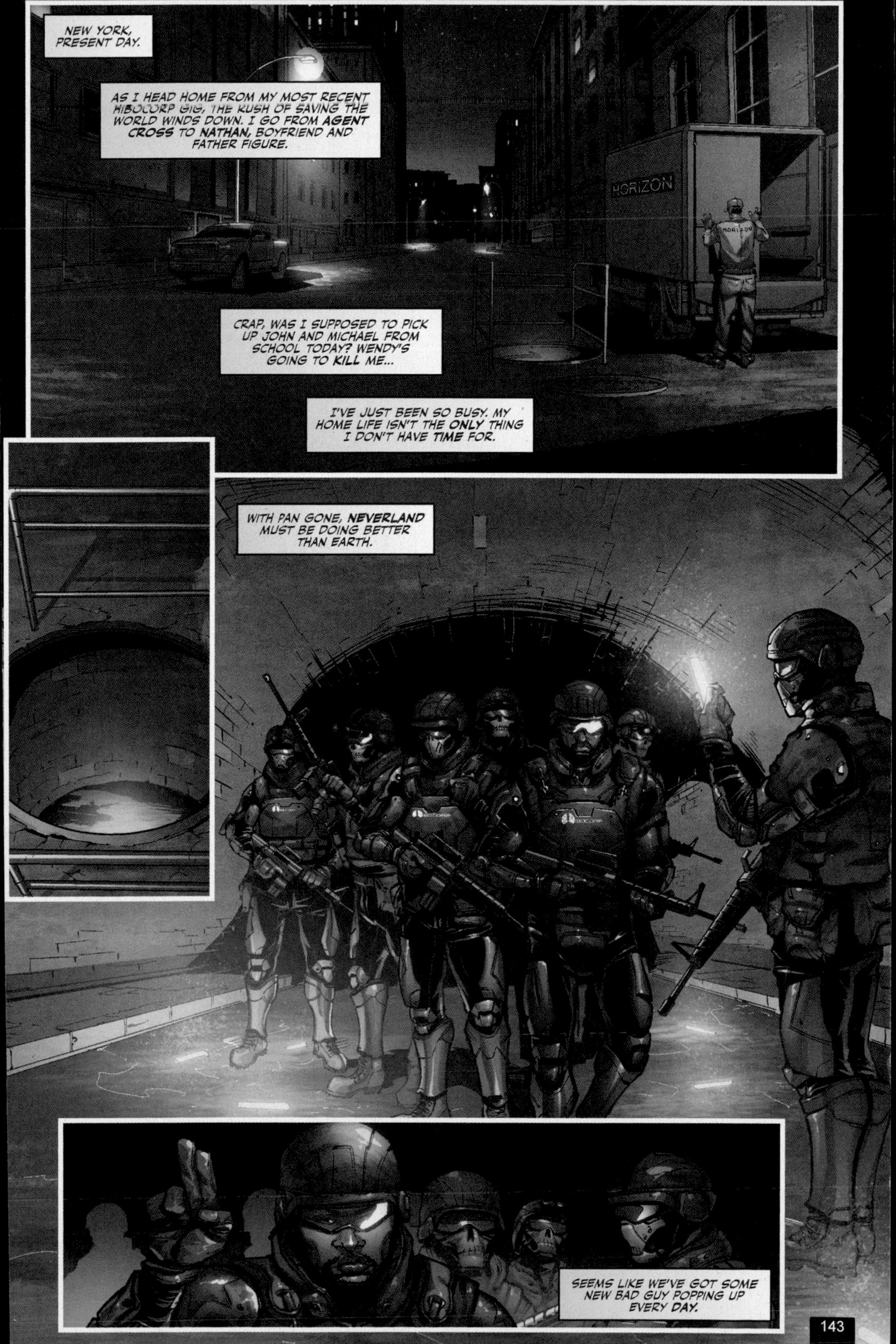
NEW YORK, PRESENT DAY.
AS I HEAD HOME FROM MY MOST RECENT HIBOCORP GIG, THE RUSH OF SAVING THE WORLD WINDS DOWN. I GO FROM AGENT CROSS TO NATHAN, BOYFRIEND AND FATHER FIGURE.
HORIZON
CRAP, WAS I SUPPOSED TO PICK UP JOHN AND MICHAEL FROM SCHOOL TODAY? WENDY'S GOING TO KILL ME...
I'VE JUST BEEN SO BUSY. MY HOME LIFE ISN'T THE ONLY THING I DON'T HAVE TIME FOR.
WITH PAN GONE, NEVERLAND MUST BE DOING BETTER THAN EARTH.
SEEMS LIKE WE'VE GOT SOME NEW BAD GUY POPPING UP EVERY DAY.

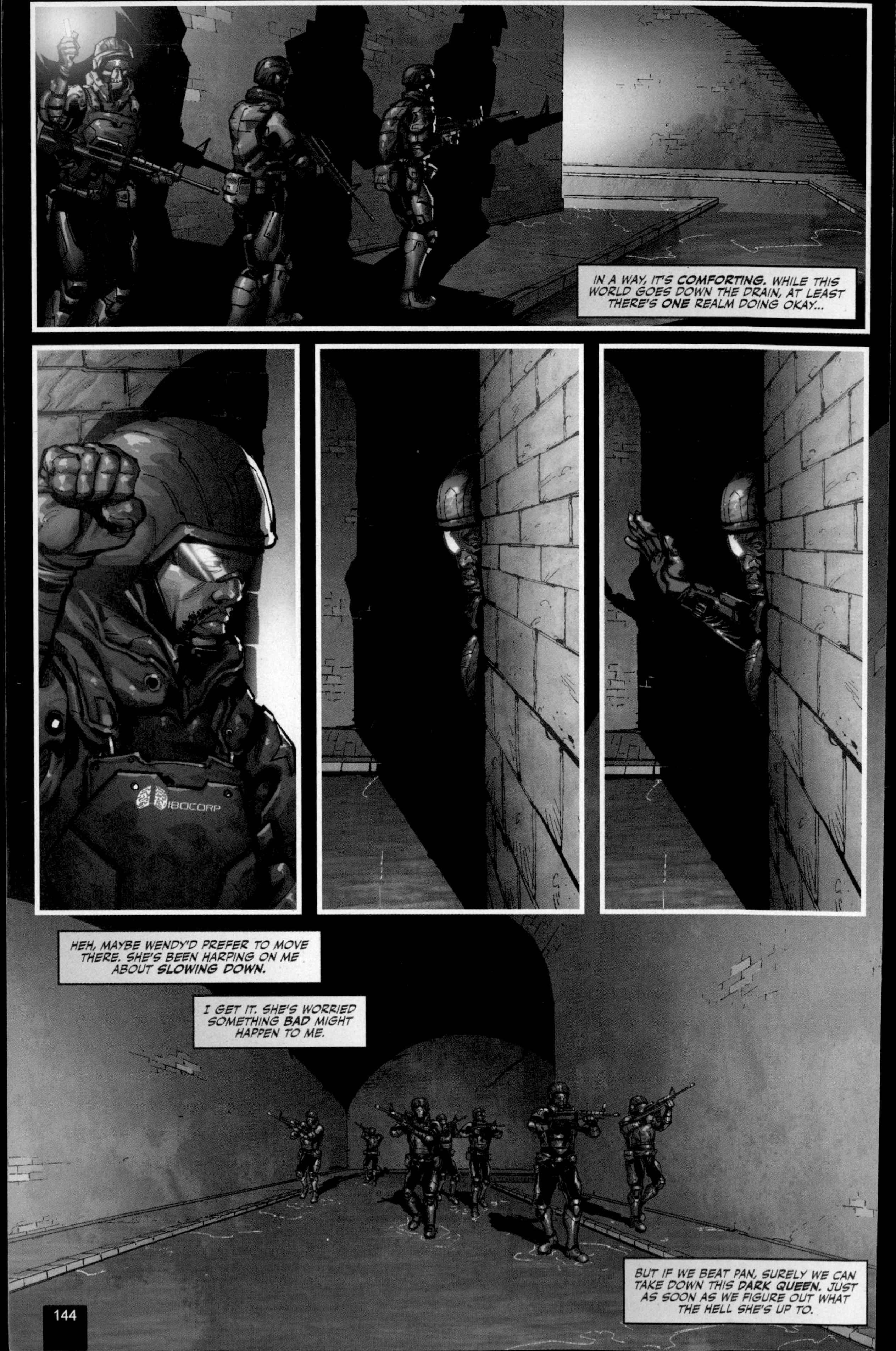
IN A WAY, IT'S COMFORTING. WHILE THIS WORLD GOES DOWN THE DRAIN, AT LEAST THERE'S ONE REALM DOING OKAY...
IBOCORP
HEH, MAYBE WENDY'D PREFER TO MOVE THERE. SHE'S BEEN HARPING ON ME ABOUT SLOWING DOWN.
I GET IT. SHE'S WORRIED SOMETHING BAD MIGHT HAPPEN TO ME.
BUT IF WE BEAT PAN, SURELY WE CAN TAKE DOWN THIS DARK QUEEN. JUST AS SOON AS WE FIGURE OUT WHAT THE HELL SHE'S UP TO.

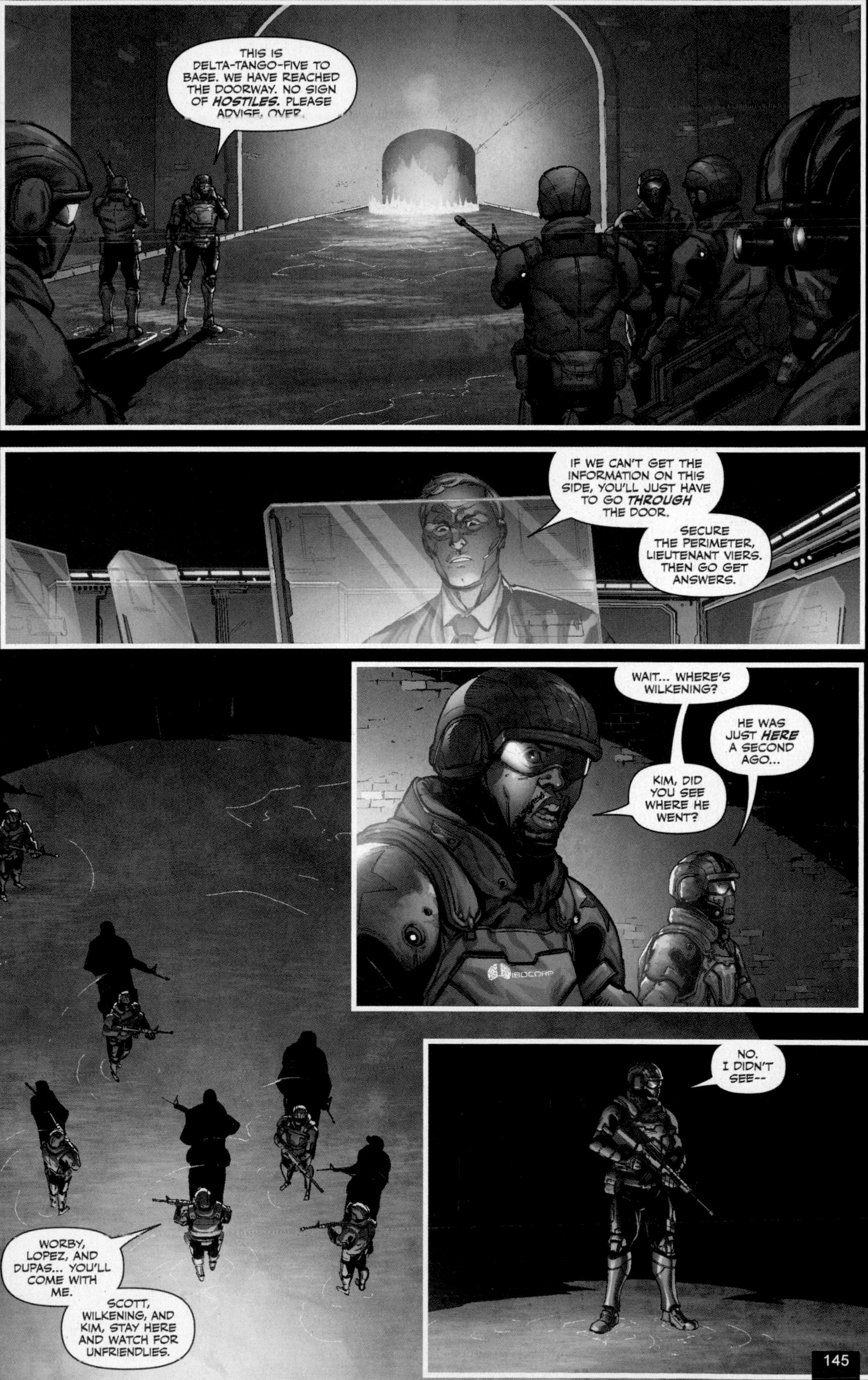
THIS IS DELTA-TANGO-FIVE TO BASE. WE HAVE REACHED THE DOORWAY. NO SIGN OF HOSTILES. PLEASE ADVISE, OVER.
IF WE CAN'T GET THE INFORMATION ON THIS SIDE, YOU'LL JUST HAVE TO GO THROUGH THE DOOR.
SECURE THE PERIMETER, LIEUTENANT VIERS. THEN GO GET ANSWERS.
WAIT... WHERE'S WILKENING?
HE WAS JUST HERE A SECOND AGO...
KIM, DID YOU SEE WHERE HE WENT?
WORBY, LOPEZ, AND DUPAS... YOU'LL COME WITH ME.
SCOTT, WILKENING, AND KIM, STAY HERE AND WATCH FOR UNFRIENDLIES.
NO. I DIDN'T SEE--

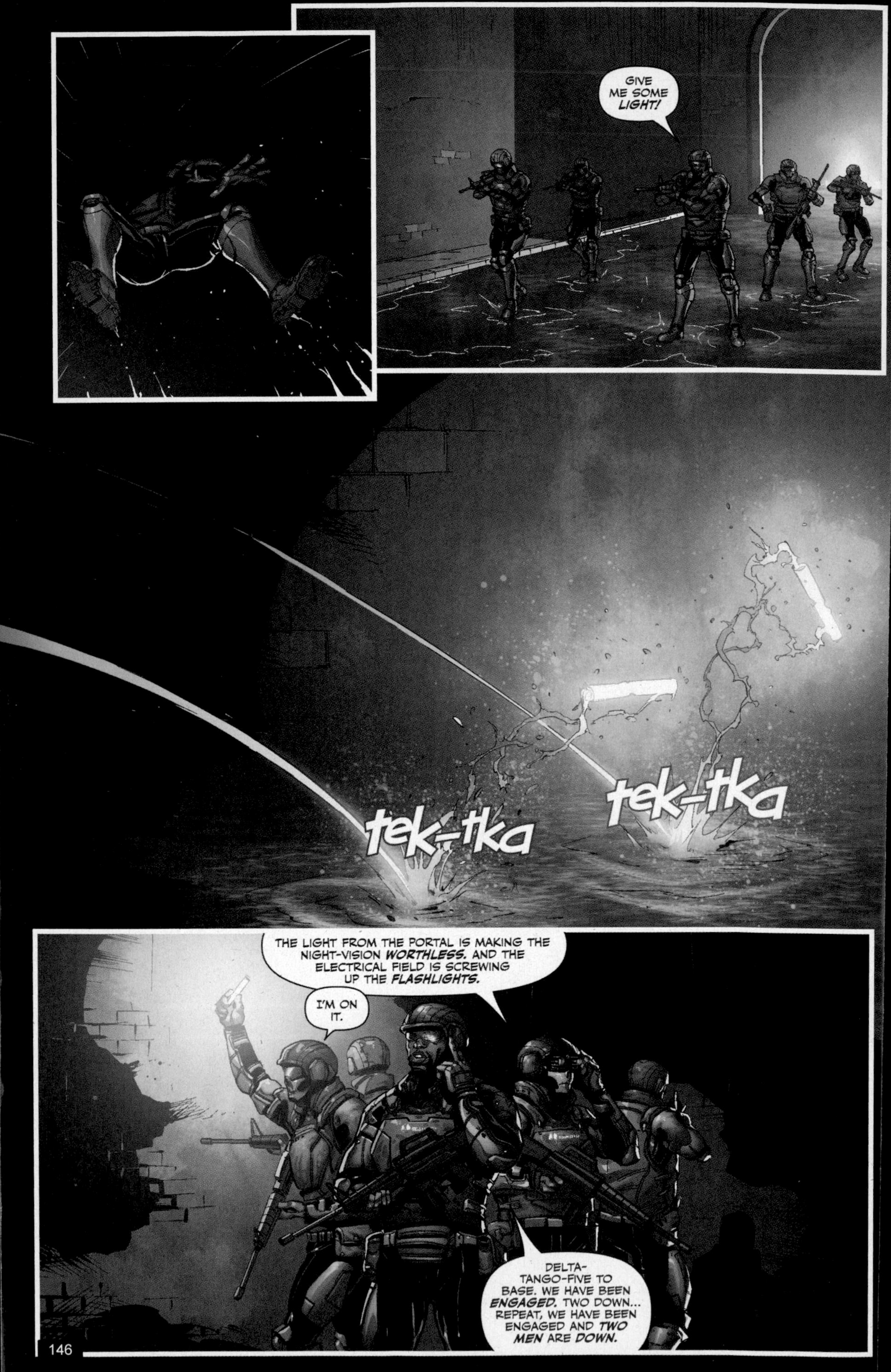
GIVE ME SOME LIGHT!
tek-tka
tek-tka
THE LIGHT FROM THE PORTAL IS MAKING THE NIGHT-VISION WORTHLESS. AND THE ELECTRICAL FIELD IS SCREWING UP THE FLASHLIGHTS.
I'M ON IT.
DELTA-TANGO-FIVE TO BASE. WE HAVE BEEN ENGAGED. TWO DOWN... REPEAT, WE HAVE BEEN ENGAGED AND TWO MEN ARE DOWN.

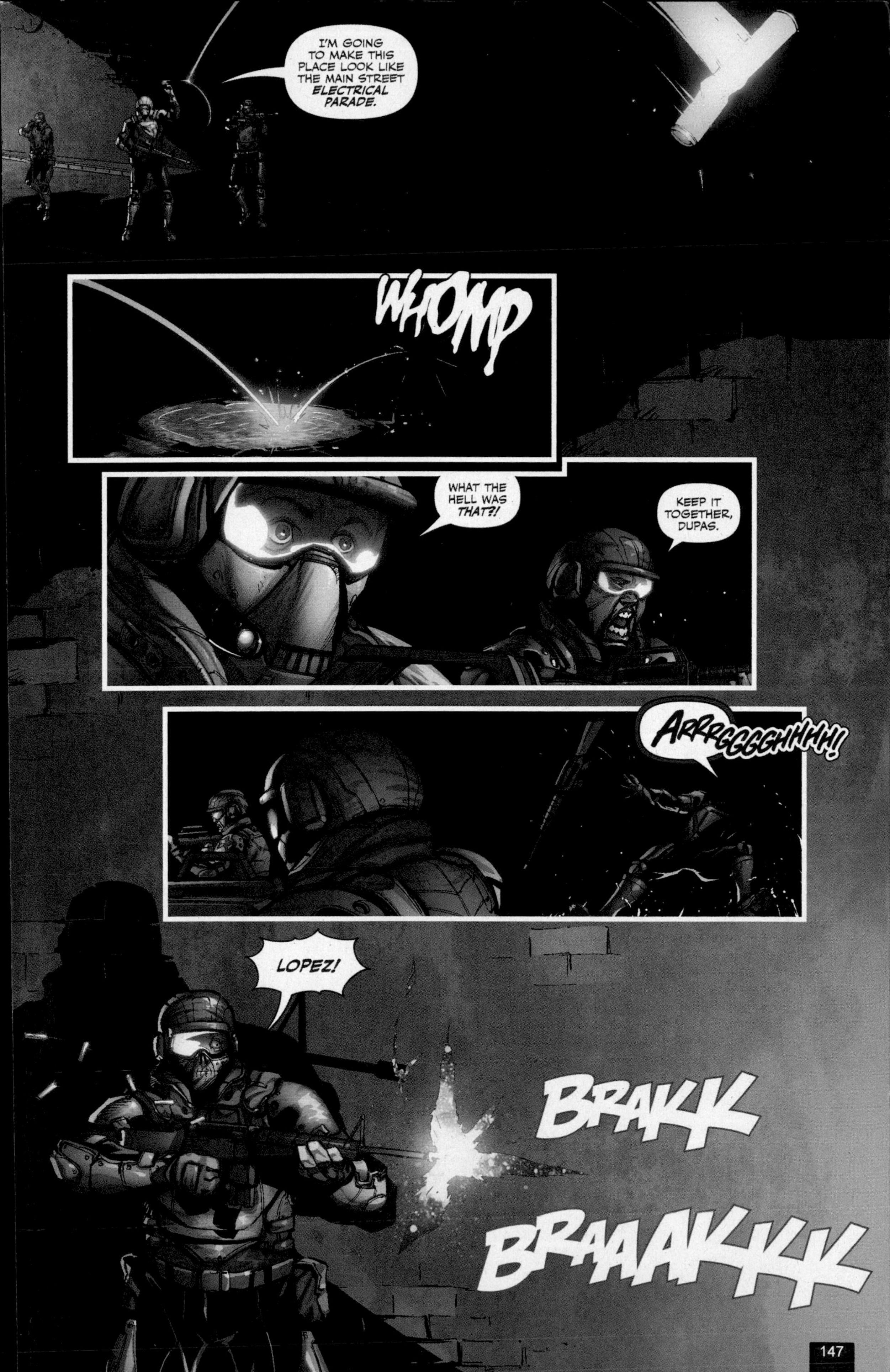
I'M GOING TO MAKE THIS PLACE LOOK LIKE THE MAIN STREET *ELECTRICAL PARADE.*
WHOMP
WHAT THE HELL WAS *THAT?!*
KEEP IT TOGETHER, DUPAS.
ARRRGGGGHHHH!
LOPEZ!
BRAKK
BRAAKKK

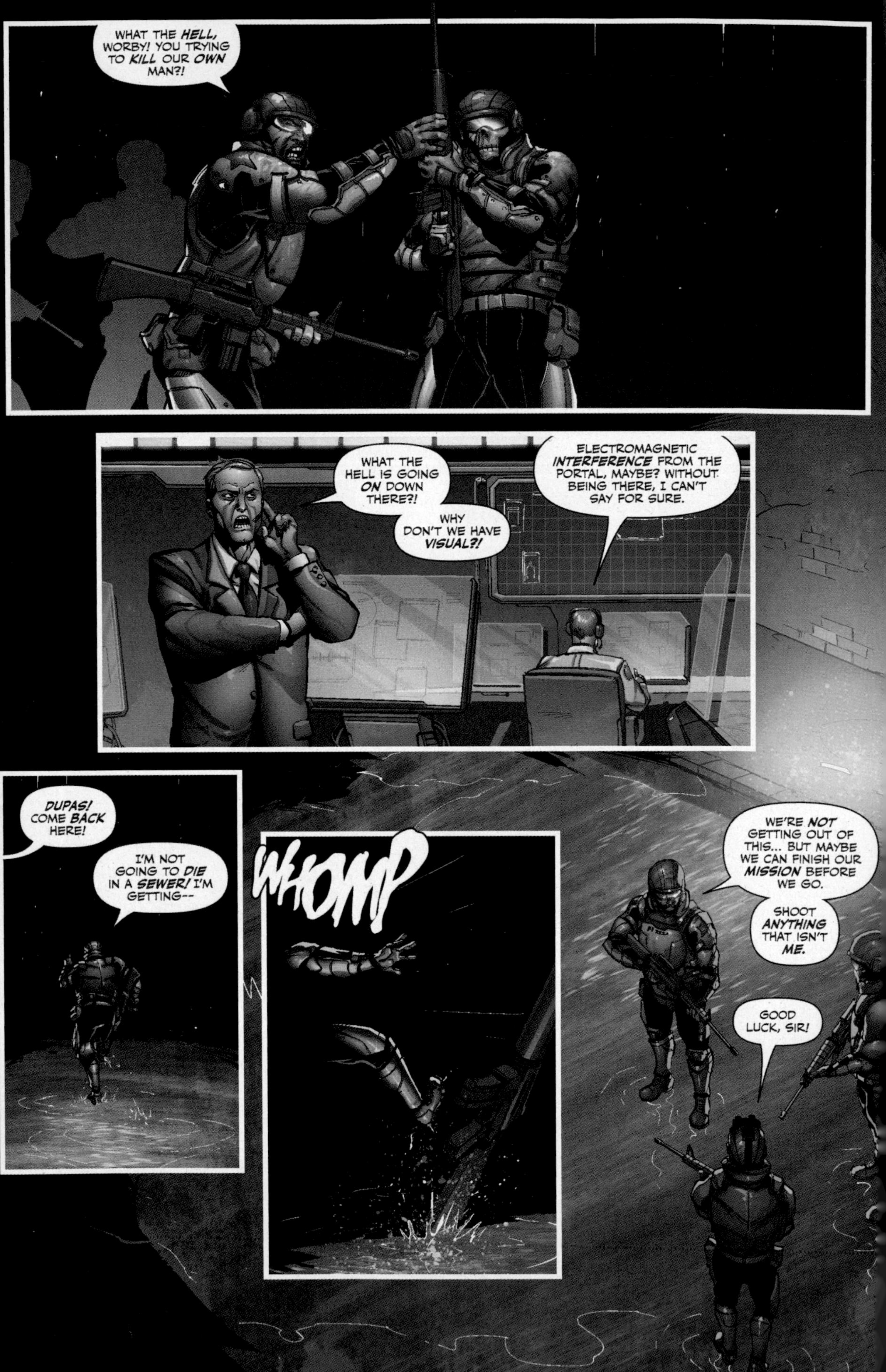
WHAT THE HELL, WORBY! YOU TRYING TO KILL OUR OWN MAN?!
WHAT THE HELL IS GOING ON DOWN THERE?!
WHY DON'T WE HAVE VISUAL?!
ELECTROMAGNETIC INTERFERENCE FROM THE PORTAL, MAYBE? WITHOUT BEING THERE, I CAN'T SAY FOR SURE.
DUPAS! COME BACK HERE!
I'M NOT GOING TO DIE IN A SEWER! I'M GETTING--
WHOMP
WE'RE NOT GETTING OUT OF THIS... BUT MAYBE WE CAN FINISH OUR MISSION BEFORE WE GO.
SHOOT ANYTHING THAT ISN'T ME.
GOOD LUCK, SIR!

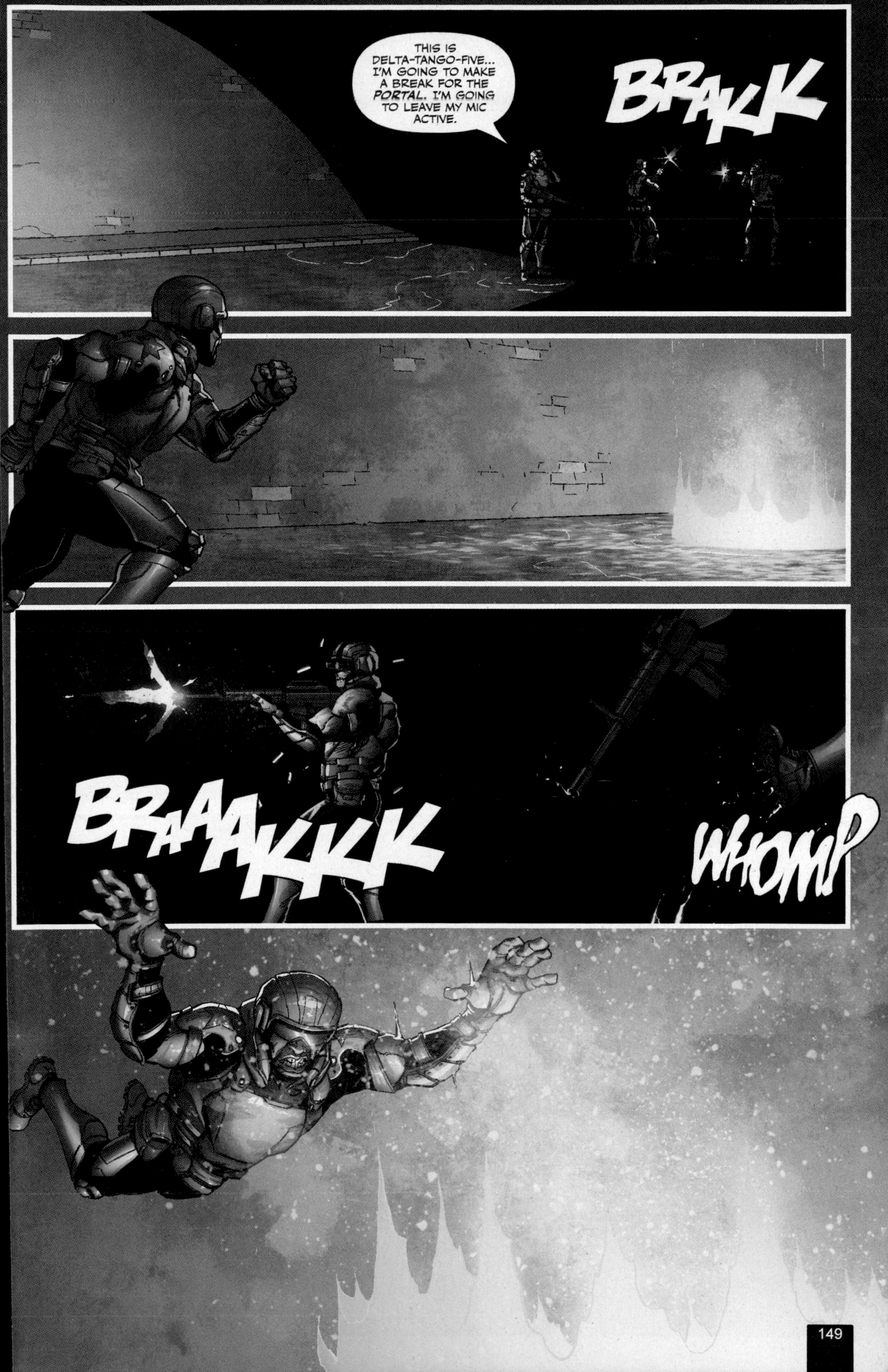
THIS IS DELTA-TANGO-FIVE... I'M GOING TO MAKE A BREAK FOR THE PORTAL. I'M GOING TO LEAVE MY MIC ACTIVE.
BRAKK
BRAAAKKK
WHOMP

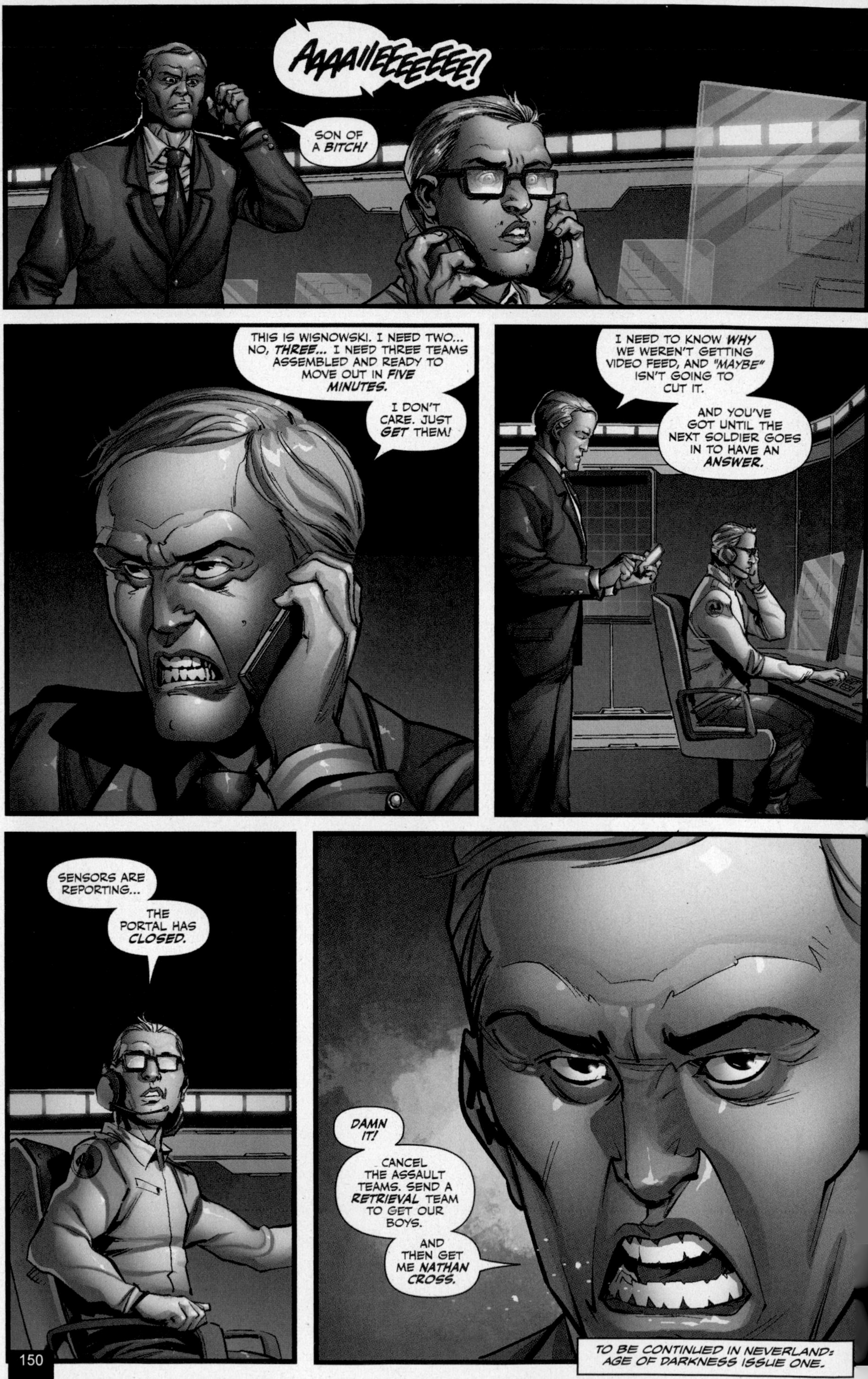
AAAAIIEEEEEEEE!
SON OF A BITCH!
THIS IS WISNOWSKI. I NEED TWO... NO, THREE... I NEED THREE TEAMS ASSEMBLED AND READY TO MOVE OUT IN FIVE MINUTES.
I DON'T CARE. JUST GET THEM!
I NEED TO KNOW WHY WE WEREN'T GETTING VIDEO FEED, AND "MAYBE" ISN'T GOING TO CUT IT.
AND YOU'VE GOT UNTIL THE NEXT SOLDIER GOES IN TO HAVE AN ANSWER.
SENSORS ARE REPORTING...
THE PORTAL HAS CLOSED.
DAMN IT!
CANCEL THE ASSAULT TEAMS. SEND A RETRIEVAL TEAM TO GET OUR BOYS.
AND THEN GET ME NATHAN CROSS.
TO BE CONTINUED IN NEVERLAND: AGE OF DARKNESS ISSUE ONE.

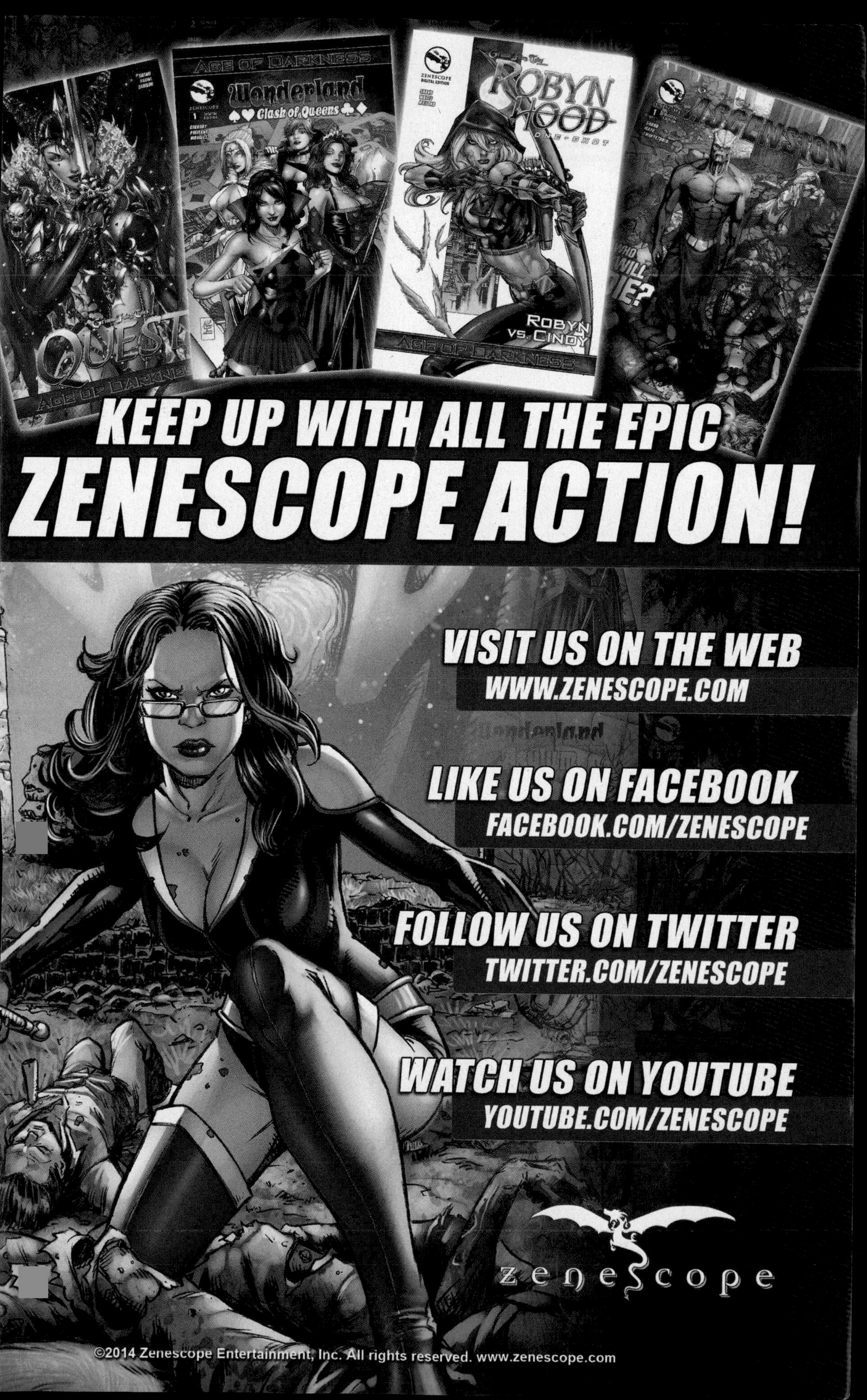

AGE OF DARKNESS
Wonderland
Clash of Queens
ROBYN HOOD
ONE-SHOT
ROBYN VS. CINDY
AGE OF DARKNESS
QUEST
AGE OF DARKNESS
KEEP UP WITH ALL THE EPIC
ZENESCOPE ACTION!
VISIT US ON THE WEB
WWW.ZENESCOPE.COM
LIKE US ON FACEBOOK
FACEBOOK.COM/ZENESCOPE
FOLLOW US ON TWITTER
TWITTER.COM/ZENESCOPE
WATCH US ON YOUTUBE
YOUTUBE.COM/ZENESCOPE
zenescope
©2014 Zenescope Entertainment, Inc. All rights reserved. www.zenescope.com

Grimm Fairy Tales presents:

QUEST

AGE OF DARKNESS